A POLITICAL DIARY, 1828-1830 (VOLUME 1)

A POLITICAL DIARY, 1828-1830 (VOLUME 1)

Ellenborough, Edward Law, Earl Of, 1790-1871 and colchester, Reginald Charles Edward Abbot, Baron, 1842-1919

General Books

www.General-Books.net

Publication Data:

Title: A Political Diary, 1828-1830
Volume: 1
Author: Ellenborough, Edward Law, Earl Of, 1790-1871 and colchester, Reginald Charles Edward Abbot, Baron, 1842-1919
Publisher: London : R. Bentley
Publication date: 1881
Subjects: Great Britain – Politics and government 1820-1830

1

A POLITICAL DIARY, 1828-1830 (VOLUME 1)

√

PBEEACE.

EDWAKD LAW, second Lord Ellenborough, 1 the author of this Diary, was born September 8, 1790. He was the eldest son of Edward Law, afterwards Attorney General and Chief Justice of England, who was raised to the peerage as Baron Ellenborough in 1802, son of Edmund Law, Bishop of Carlisle, author of ' Law's Theory of Eeligion." He was educated at Eton and St. John's College, Cambridge. Among his Eton contemporaries was the late Lord Stratford de Eedcliffe, who, though his senior, survived him nearly nine years, and with whom his personal friendship lasted throughout life, though just at the period included in the accompanying Diary he seems to have felt some dissatisfaction with his conduct as an ambassador serving under the Ministry of which he was a member. Lord Ellenborough throughout life felt a warm interest in Eton, but always spoke rather slightingly of his recollections of the University. Something of this appears in the remarks he makes on Academic voters at the time of Peel's defeat by Sir E. Inglis at Oxford. Probably the typical College Don of the days of Gibbon and Horace Walpole still lingered to a great extent in the earlier years of the present century. Lord Ellenborough used to say that the Fellows of St. John's only realised the evil of the Walcheren expedition when some one calculated the amount of its cost in bottles of port wine. His University career, however, was not

A Political Diary, 1828-1830 (Volume 1). Ellenborough, Edward Law, Earl Of, 1790-1871 and colchester, Reginald Charles Edward Abbot, Baron, 1842-1919

1

altogether undistinguished, as he was the author of the Prize Ode on the dethronement and exile of the House of Braganza, which figures in the 'Musas Cantabrigienses."

After leaving Cambridge, Lord Ellenborough made a tour in Sicily, then occupied and defended by the English, and the only part of the continent of Europe which the great struggle with Napoleon did not close to English travellers.

Growing up at the moment when England's great military triumphs were commencing in the Peninsula, Lord Ellenborough's first ambition was a military career. This, however, did not meet with his father's sanction.

On entering public life, his wish, he used to say, was to become a ' military statesman," an idea which naturally might suggest itself when the conduct of a great war was the most engrossing topic of Parliamentary discussion, and the military administration from home, perhaps somewhat unjustly, charged with grievous shortcomings. Throughout life Lord Ellen-borough retained an eager interest in all military questions; the progress of a campaign, the positions of contending armies, the geographical character of a theatre of war, were always favourite subjects of attention with him. From the commencement of his Parliamentary career he was strongly of opinion that the principal road to influence of any kind in English public life was through the power of speech. He set himself diligently to the cultivation of oratory as an art, and though undoubtedly possessed of great natural gifts of eloquence, he attributed mainly to such diligence and study the position he attained as a speaker of the first rank. He was convinced of the maxim ' orator fit,"

PREFACE. Vll and on this principle devoted his leisure to the assiduous study of what he thought the best models of ancient and modern eloquence. Not many years before the close of his career, he was occupying himself with a systematic perusal of Lucan, whom he considered ' as not perhaps a great poet, but to be looked upon as one of the first of orators

Lord Ellenborough (then the Hon. E. Law) entered Parliament in the year 1813. He was returned to the House of Commons, like so many who afterwards attained eminence, for a small close borough, the almost forgotten constituency of St. Michael's, in Cornwall. It was the second year of the Liverpool Cabinet, a Cabinet ' doomed to death' by the anticipations of lookers-on from the moment of its formation, yet destined to last from 1812 to 1827, when the one chief was withdrawn who could form an effective link between its discordant elements. His father, the Chief Justice Lord Ellen-borough, was a supporter of this Ministry. Introduced to office by Addington, he had followed him into the Talents Cabinet of 1806-7, had sided with him in its internal differences, and, after being engaged with him in partial opposition to the succeeding administration, had now seen him reunited to the old followers of Pitt as Home Secretary of the Cabinet formed after the death of Mr. Perceval. Of this Government Mr. Law was returned as a general supporter. He stipulated, however, for the right of independent action on the Catholic question; and, in spite of private ties soon afterwards formed, he, in some respects, after the close of the war, took a separate course on foreign policy.

In the latter part of this year he married Lady Octavia Stewart, sister of the then Foreign Minister, Lord Castlereagh, a union terminated by her death

VIll PREFACE.

within six years. He visited Vienna during the residence there of his distinguished brother-in-law as the representative of England in the Congress which in the year following met in that city to regulate the settlement of Europe. He thus naturally acquired a deeper interest in the foreign politics of England, and opportunities of a wider insight into European affairs, as well as a personal acquaintance with many of the principal personages of the political and diplomatic society of the Continent.

He never became, however, an indiscriminating adherent of the policy of his eminent relative. One of the acts of the Congress which excited much attention, and attracted much criticism, was the annexation of Genoa to the Sardinian kingdom. Genoa, which with Venice and Lucca was, down to the French revolution, one of the few solitary survivors of the Italian Eepublics of former ages, had, after a brief existence in a revolutionised form as the ' Ligurian Bepublic," been swallowed up in the French Empire. At the fall of Napoleon's power the English admiral on the coast had given without, it was said, full authority a sort of promise that the Genoese, if they took part against France, should be restored to their independence. The contrary decision of Lord Castlereagh has been vindicated in a great measure by events. At the time, too, it was difficult to show how an alternative could have been found. The oligarchical commonwealth which had lasted for nearly three centuries was precisely one of those governments which may endure for long, but can never be recalled to life. A revived democracy on the ' Ligurian ' pattern would at that time have been tolerated by none of the Continental Powers. Even if a petty principality was desired by the people, it was important not to leave so important a seaport in the hands of a State unable to

PREFACE.

defend it against an invader. Lord Ellenborough, however, with the view perhaps natural to his age, shared the sentiments of those who could not acquiesce in the transfer to an alien prince of the commonwealth of Andrea Doria, in contradiction, as was alleged, to the British promises on which the inhabitants had relied. He therefore declined the offer of Lord Castlereagh to appoint him one of the Commission for carrying this provision of the treaty into effect.

His desire at that time for the future of Italy a country which he frequently visited during the years immediately following if perhaps unattainable at that moment, at any rate anticipated much of what he lived to see realised. When in 1859-60 expressions of sympathy for Italy were put forward on every side, he remarked, ' I expressed my sympathy forty-five years ago." In a letter to Lord Brougham, published at the close of that year, he described the wish he had then entertained for the establishment of a large State in North Italy, which would have had every motive to join with Austria in closing the Alps against France, if assured of its own independence. It is curious that Lord Brougham, who at the outbreak of the war of 1859 was rather hostile to the Sardinian cause, vindicated his consistency as an old opponent of the treaties of 1815 by reminding the House of Lords that what he had most attacked was the handing over to Sardinia of Genoa. [1]In the year 1816 Mr. Law's name appears as speaking against some portions of the Treaties of Vienna,[1] Lord Ellenbo rough, however, was not blind to the objections to the method by which Italian unity was effected. Thus in 1860, while openly sympathising with what he thought the straightforward course of

Garibaldi, he thought the conduct of the Piedmontese Government to neighbours with whom it was nominally at peace ought to be called ' piratical."

especially as regarded the Netherland barrier, though, when the kingdom so created had been established for fifteen years, he considered, as his Diary will show, its downfall as an event to be regretted on European grounds. He took some part in the debates on the famous Six Acts, of which he was neither a supporter on all points, nor an unmitigated opponent, apparently considering them as not uncalled for, but as carried in some respects further than he could approve.

The death of his father at the close of 1818 elevated him to the Upper House, in which he was destined to sit for more than half a century. 1 Note

The accession of George IV. in 1820 was followed by the famous Bill of Pains and Penalties against Queen Caroline. Lord Ellenborough was one of those who opposed the Bill, though of opinion that if it were to be passed the Divorce Clause ought, in consistency, to form a part of it, as, if the evidence against the Queen was held sufficient to justify such a measure, it was, he thought, preposterous to consider that she ought to remain the King's wife.

The year 1821 was the commencement of a period of revolutions in several parts of Europe which awakened alarm or sympathy in almost every part of the Continent. The circular of Lord Castlereagh protesting against the theory of intervention put forward by the Courts of the Holy Alliance, while at the same time it censured the revolution at Naples by which the King 1 The death of Lord Ellenborough's father was shortly followed by that of his wife, a loss felt by him long and deeply. In the last years of his life he had restored an old chapel on his property in Gloucestershire. He here erected a memorial to her memory, with a Latin inscription attributing to her ' whatever good he had done or thought in his life." The letter on her death to Cardinal Consalvi, whom they had known intimately in Italy, will be found in Cretineau Joly's Memoires du Cardinal Consalvi.

had been forced to concede the democratic Constitution of Spain in 1812, was the subject of much criticism in and out of Parliament. While declining to accept the principles of the Congresses of Troppau and Laybach, the English Cabinet were disposed to acquiesce in the Austrian intervention agreed upon at the latter meeting for the purpose of opposing the ascendency of Carbo-narism. Lord Ellenborough vindicated in the House of Lords the language used by Lord Castlereagh, considering that a military revolt such as that which had occurred at Naples could never be regarded as a sure basis for liberty, but rather a precedent for setting up a dictatorship at the will of a despotic soldiery. At the same time he avowed strong sympathy with the Italians in their wish to reform the governments, whose evils he knew from having seen their operation. And as the question approached a violent solution, as those whom his Italian friends would have called ' barbari' moved southward to restore the absolute monarchy of the Two Sicilies, his feelings were still more warmly enlisted on the and-Austrian side, and he spoke strongly in favour of an English mediation between the contending parties.

By the tragical death of Lord Castlereagh (then become Marquis of Londonderry) on the eve of the Congress of Verona, the direction of British foreign policy was transferred to Mr. Canning. It may be enquired why there was not more sympathy between Lord Ellen-borough and Mr. Canning, introducing, as the latter Minister did, a bolder and, some might say, a more generous system of policy than that of his predecessor, with whose ideas, in spite of family ties and personal friendship, Lord Ellenborough had never been altogether agreed. But men do not always appear to their con-

Xll PREFACE.

temporaries as they do to the generation after them. To us Mr. Canning stands out as at once the foremost orator of the Parliament of England sixty years back, and as the fearless Foreign Minister who, perhaps at times with too much parade, asserted the right of England to an independent course among the Powers of Europe, and to a place in their councils worthy of its power and its history. To many of those among whom he moved his individual relations to colleagues and to rivals had as much to do with the estimate formed of him as the prominent acts of his official career which strike the attention of posterity. And as to these relations, he no doubt inspired very widespread distrust. Parts of his early career seemed to give plausibility to the view which regarded him as an interested intriguer. The grounds for such a charge, justly or unjustly, were drawn from his behaviour towards Castlereagh during the Portland Administration, and towards Addington after Pitt's retirement in 1801. No one was more likely to be influenced by such impressions as one who was both the brother-in-law of Castlereagh and the son of one of the closest friends of Addington.

Lord Ellenborough after this period inclined rather more than previously to the Opposition. He put himself in the forefront of the attack upon the Ministerial policy in reference to the French intervention in Spain in 1823. The nature and origin of the Constitution established by the Spanish Eevolutionists were open to the same objections as in the case of Naples. But Lord Ellenborough, in common with many others, felt it a discredit to England that French influence should be forcibly exerted once more in the country which a few years before had been so gloriously rescued from French dominion by British victories. It is probable that the

Foreign Minister's personal sentiments, and those of his chief, Lord Liverpool, were not so widely different from those of the speakers who were most impatient of their neutrality. Those who were outside the Government could hardly know, what the Cabinet seem to have had reason to believe, that the Powers of the Holy Alliance were ready, if necessary, actively to support France as their agent, and that in attempting to protect Spain we might, with no ally but those revolutionary forces which Canning compared to the winds in the bag of-ZEolus, have been involved in a struggle with the greater part of the Continent.

Lord Ellenborough was not reconciled to what he thought the abandonment of Spain by that recognition of the independence of South America by which Canning afterwards claimed to have called a New World into existence to redress the balance of the Old. Nor was he much influenced by the famous speech on sending troops to Portugal, which, according to Canning's biographer, was received with delighted applause from all parts of the House except from some of those behind him who leant to the doctrines of the Continental Alliance. He probably thought that its defiant tone incurred for a minor object the dangers that would have attended a similar course with regard to Spain. That treaty obligations required the despatch of troops to Portugal he admitted, but declined to see in it any great cause for enthusiasm.

In 1827 the illness of Lord Liverpool snapped the thread that held together the two portions of the Cabinet he had presided over so long. The most decidedly Tory section refused to follow Mr. Canning as his successor. Partly by promotions from offices of lower rank, partly by accessions from his old opponents, the new Prime Minister endeavoured to maintain a Coalition Cabinet which should defy the seceders, while steering clear of extreme principles on either side. ' The Whigs join us in a body," wrote Lord Palmerston, now for the first time a Cabinet Minister. This was true of Lord Lansdowne, and several of the leaders of that party. But Lord Grey, and those who were especially connected with him, stood aloof, distrusting the new Minister and the heterogeneous combination which he directed. Lord Grey[1] was the member 0f the Opposition whom Lord Ellenborough was most disposed to co-operate with. He took an early opportunity of expressing himself a determined opponent of the Ministry. In this he was probably actuated both by distrust of Canning and regard for the opinions of Lord Grey. But he was thus again brought into connection, in spite of difference on the Koman Catholic question and some other points, with the party which came to be led by the Duke of Wellington. He had hoped, as this volume will show, for an ultimate junction between the Duke and Lord Grey, a hope not so unreasonable at that time as subsequent events might make it appear. He succeeded, however, eventually in bringing Lord Eosslyn into the Duke's Ministry, and Lord Eosslyn, hitherto an ally of Lord Grey, brought, as will be seen, some additional support from outside.

In a few months from his attainment of the Premiership Mr. Canning died. It may be a question whether he could permanently have held together the hitherto discordant materials of his Administration. The task was too much for his successor, Lord Goderich, under whose leadership it fell to pieces without meeting Parliament.

[1 They were distantly related through the family of Lord Ellenborough's mother.]

Thus the ground was left open for the Duke of Wellington. It was attempted to form again a Government on the basis of that of Lord Liverpool, to bring together those who had taken opposite courses at the disruption consequent on his retirement. One or two of the most ultra of the High Tories, such as Lord Eldon and Lord Westmoreland, were left out to smoothe the way for those who returned from the Coalition camp. The Whig element of the Ministry of 1827 was left to fall back into Opposition.

Lord Grey's attitude to the new Ministry was understood not to be unfriendly. Lord Ellenborough, who had acted in Opposition with many of its members,[1] became a member of the Cabinet as Privy Seal. Then the attempted reunion of the friends of Mr. Canning with their old colleagues ere long led to a new separation. How the change of policy on the' Catholic Question 'by the Prime Minister created a still more bitter and more formidable split in the ranks hitherto most united in his support, and how the alienation of many of his friends, joined to the events on the Continent in 1830, led to the fall of his Government, and with it of the old Parliamentary system of England, these volumes will relate. As to Lord Ellenborough's own position, it may be observed that the office he at first held was one imposing no active duties and at the same time enjoying an official precedence which causes it to be usually reserved for some one belonging to the higher ranks of the peerage. He felt some dissatisfaction in holding a dignified sinecure with no duties except a general attention to the business of the Cabinet. He devoted himself, however, actively to" the foreign ques-[1 It seems that, had the Goderich Ministry met Parliament, he was to have moved the amendment to the Address in the House of Lords.]

VOL. i. a tions which came before it. It may appear as though in some respects his sympathies at this time as regards European affairs differed from those he expressed before or afterwards, as the early champion of Italy and Spain, or as, in later days, the advocate of Poland. But, in fact, Lord Ellenborough always was averse both to the principles of despotism and of democracy, though at particular times one of what he regarded as two opposite evils may have appeared the more to call for opposition. During most of the time embraced by this Diary Dom Miguel was apparently accepted by the Portuguese nation as king, and Lord Ellenborough agreed with his colleagues in deprecating either a European war or a general letting loose of the revolutionary party of Southern Europe in order to reverse their verdict. As regards Greece, there is nothing to show if he had ever regarded its cause more favourably. But the numerous instances, not merely of barbarous cruelty, but cruelty accompanied with gross breaches of faith, which alienated from the Greek cause many who saw much of the struggle on the spot, may reasonably have had the same effect on intelligent observers at a distance. Lord Ellen-borough had also a strong conviction, dating perhaps from what he remembered at the time of the Congress of Vienna, of the dangers of Eussian ambition and aggressiveness, which naturally led him to attach importance to the maintenance of the Turkish power.

Lord Ellenborough's desire, as he states in his remarks at the time, was to have attained to the Foreign Office on its falling vacant. Whether Lord Ellenborough or Lord Aberdeen would have been the more efficient Foreign Minister must be left to the judgment of the world. Lord Ellenborough might have incurred the charge of undue energy or rashness from opponents, but would scarcely, even by an antagonist, have been taxed with ' antiquated imbecility In the power of expounding and defending a policy in Parliament, which in England is scarcely less important than any other, there could be no comparison between them.

The Indian affairs with which Lord Ellenborough was concerned after his accession to the Board of Control are not of any very great contemporary interest. It will be seen that he was already at that time in favour of the abolition of the government by the Company, a change postponed at that time, but ultimately carried out in 1858.

Most of the domestic matters treated in these volumes matters of eager controversy in their day have been so decisively settled as to have only a historical interest. They belong to a past phase of English politics. The only phenomenon which forms, unhappily, an exception is the chronic difficulty of dealing with Irish disorder. It is otherwise with the foreign questions which fill a large part of them. The events of the last few years have given a fresh and living interest to the past conflicts and negotiations relative to every part of the Eastern Question. Bulgaria and Koumelia, Thessaly and Candia, the Armenian frontier, the possible approach of Eussia to the Euphrates, have again been topics of constant discussion in every political circle. The daily anticipations, reports, and eventual certainties as to the movements of Eussian and Turkish armies in 1828-29 might seem, as it were, to belong to 1877.

The perplexities which at the close of the war troubled the Cabinet of the Duke of Wellington are clearly analogous to the yet unsettled problems left behind by the war terminated by the Treaty of San Stefano. They may perhaps be worthy of perusal, not only as records of the recent past, but as having a still active bearing on the present and future of Eastern politics.

January 22, 1828.

WENT to the Eoyal Lodge in Windsor Park, with Lord Aberdeen, to receive the Privy Seal. The other new Ministers there were the Duke of Wellington, Lords Bathurst and Melville, Mr. Peel, Mr. Herries, and Mr. Goulburn. We were appointed to be there at three, but it was six before any one of us was admitted to the King. Lord Lansdowne, Lord Carlisle, and I suppose others of the old Ministers (but not the Duke of Portland, who is abroad, nor Lord Bexley), were there to deliver their seals. I saw the King first. The King was seated at the end of a long table prepared for the Council which was to have been held, for the purpose of my taking the oaths of office, if there are any, and the oath of a Privy Councillor, but by some oversight the Clerk of the Council had not been apprised of the intention to hold a Council, and was not there, so nothing could be done. The King looked extremely well. He said to me, ' Circumstances have not enabled me to become acquainted with you, but I knew your father well, and had the greatest respect and affection for him. I know you have very considerable talents,

VOL. I. B and I have no doubt you will exert them for the public service." These were nearly the King's words. I assured his Majesty of my gratitude to him for the favour conferred upon myself, and for his affection for my father, and assured him I would devote myself to his service. He then nearly repeated what he had said before, and concluded by expressing his confidence in me. I said, 'Your Majesty shall not be deceived." During the three or four hours we were waiting to be admitted we had a good deal of conversation on different political subjects. It was a quarter after six when Lord Aberdeen and I arrived at Apsley House to dinner. Mr. Herries had preceded us, and was desired to order dinner, but not liking, I suppose, after his quarrel with Huskisson, which was the proximate cause of the dissolution of the last Cabinet, to come alone into the room already occupied by Lord Lyndhurst, Huskisson, Dudley, Palmers ton, and Grant, he managed to come to dinner after Aberdeen, whom I left there. On finding they had only been at dinner five minutes, I went home to change my dress, and deposit the Privy Seal, and on returning found the party I have mentioned sitting round half a round table; the Chancellor opposite the chair left for the Duke, then Dudley, Huskisson, Palmerston, Grant, and Aberdeen. I placed myself by Aberdeen; on the other side of the Chancellor was Herries. Huskisson, whom I knew only by sight, made a slight cold bow to me. Dudley looked as black as thunder, and the others rather out of humour. After about half an hour Lords Melville, Bathurst, Peel, and Goulburn came in. We then had more conversation, but there was no appearance of cordiality or gaiety. The Duke came twenty minutes later.

We had some conversation, begun by Huskisson, on the topic of the King's Speech. Huskisson wished that the speech should communicate the withdrawing of the troops from Portugal, declare that they were sent as a measure of policy, as well as on account of the casus fcederis having arisen, and that our conduct had been guided by the principle of preserving peace and the settlement made in 1815. Dudley said: 'In fa, ct the expedition to Portugal had completely succeeded.' ⚡I see their object is to procure an approbation of Mr. Canning's policy.

Herries, whom I saw for the first time, is a plain, ordinary-looking, clerk-like man, full of in formation. Neither he nor Goulburn look as if they belonged to a Cabinet. They are of the class of under-secretaries.[1]

The difference was great between our way of talking at the Lodge and at the Duke's. At the Duke's the courtesy was that of men who had just fought a duel.

Aberdeen brought me home, and he had observed, as well as myself, the extreme coldness of our new allies. He does not like our position at all. The Treaty bothers him. [2][1]This record of Lord Ellenborough's first impressions of these statesmen, on being brought into official relations with them, must not be taken as reflecting his matured judgment of colleagues with whom he acted for many years in office and Opposition.

[2] The Treaty of London, often referred to in this Diary, was signed on July G, 1827, by Lord Dudley, Prince Lieven, and Prince Poligaac, on behalf of England, Russia, and France. It embodied the provisions of the Protocol agreed to by the Duke of Wellington during his mission to Russia relative to the terms of mediation between Greece and Turkey. But a I wish the junction with Huskisson had never been ' made. Wallace's name was as good for the commercial interest. We get few votes, and abandon our strong ground with the country. Besides I doubt the fidelity of these men.

January 23.

The ' Times," Brougham's newspaper, attacks Huskisson for joining Canning's enemies. Lady Canning has written to him and calls his conduct base, mean, dirty, and dishonourable. The violent attacks upon Huskisson and his men for joining us may have made them feel so awkward, and have made their looks so black yesterday.

The ' Times ' has the report of the Ordnance having been offered to Lord Eosslyn. As the Duke had not received any answer yesterday from Lord E., this secret must have been betrayed, too, by one of the Cabinet.

Went to the Privy Seal Office. The clerk said the Seal could not be used till I had been sworn in before the Privy Council. It seems the new peers are in a great hurry to have their patents sealed. The Seal is always to accompany me, even if I leave town for a night. The clerk seals in my presence.

Went to the Cabinet room at the Foreign Office and read there from two to six. Then saw Dudley.

Dudley's dispatches are very well written, correctly and clearly, and at no unnecessary length.

The Greek question remains in this state. Three secret article, suggested by Baron Damas, bound the three Powers, in case the mediation "was not accepted by the Porte, to compel the cessation of the armed struggle, though without taking part in the hostilities between the two belligerents. This ultimately resulted in the forcible expulsion of Ibrahim Pacha's troops from the Morea by the French under Maison.]

continues note 2 from p. 3

propositions have been made 1. To give aid in money to the Greeks; 2. to blockade Constantinople; 3. to occupy Moldavia and Wallachia.

To all these Dudley has stated some objections, and the decision stands over.

Metternich declares Austria would go to war to prevent the permanent occupation of Moldavia and Wallachia.

Austria declines affording her intervention.

Metternich says Prussia is with her. Dudley says Prussia wants Austria to join the Treaty.

I read Codrington's further explanation. It is miserably done and unsatisfactory.

France will, under the new Ministry, adopt the same line of policy as to Greece.

La Ferronais, who was long in Eussia, says the Emperor did not desire the Protocol; but that, having once become committed, he must persevere and do all by himself, if the others will not do it with him. This is inconsistent with the account of the Emperor Nicholas's feelings given, soon after his accession, in Lord Strang-ford's letter to Canning.

The Emperor, according to La Ferronais, says he must maintain the high ground he attained at Aker-mann.

It is reported that the Eussians will, by the cessions to be made by Persia, acquire the passes of Mount Ararat, the complete command of Armenia, and a road to Constantinople. Georgia occupied before the war 75,000 men.

January 24.

Went to the Cabinet for the first time. The Duke read the Speech, which, with no substantial alteration, was approved. He afterwards communicated Lord Eoss-lyn's declining the office of Master-General, which was done in a very handsome manner, expressing that he should not go into systematic opposition, but that he did not feel that confidence that he should generally agree in the measures adopted, which would alone justify his acceptance.

I received this morning a letter from Lord Grey in which he said that my accepting office when I had determined on giving personal support to the Government, was the part of an honourable mind, resolved to do so in the most effectual manner. His line will be as far removed from systematic opposition as it is from connection with the Government. So far from feeling any hostility to the Duke's Government, it will give him great pleasure if he should be enabled to support it. I showed the letter to the Duke.

After deciding on the Speech we considered what was to be done about the Corn Bill. Huskisson thought there must be one; that it should be the measure of the Cabinet, and he was so pledged to the principle of that of last year, that he must resign if it was not preserved.

He represented his peculiar situation, which I understand. There are two great parties in the State represented by two parts of the Government. The comparison is not only between the parts of the Government, but between those of the State. A breaking-up of the Administration on this point would produce a quarrel between the Houses, and great irritation between the manufacturing and agricultural interests.

The Duke then addressed us on the subject of the separation of the army from the Treasury. His feelings were strongly excited, and he evidently would have been desirous of retaining the army. This we are to decide to-morrow, in his absence. There was some discussion relative to the production of papers. I said they should not produce a paper without considering to what the production of it might lead, and that if they once began to give papers about the battle of Navarino, they might be obliged to give all, which might most materially embarrass the negotiation with Turkey.

While we were sitting came a dispatch with accounts from Paris, that in the French King's Speech his intentions with regard to the evacuation of the Spanish fortresses would be declared in a satisfactory manner.

On the whole I should say our first meeting passed off well. If we can get through the Corn Laws we shall do very well. If we cannot agree upon that we shall break up.

January 25.

Cabinet at 2. Decided unanimously that the Duke should resign the army, and that there should be a Corn Bill, supported by the Government, on the principle of that of last year, by which is meant, on the principle of a graduated scale of duty.

The Speech was finally settled. It having been originally that his Majesty's object was to maintain the repose of Europe on the basis on which it was founded by the last general treaty of peace, it was objected by Aberdeen that that treaty of peace did not comprehend Turkey, upon which, after much discussion, the words, it has rested since, were adopted on my suggestion. The Duke wishing to introduce the words actual possession, to which Peel and others objected.

It was decided that no papers should be given, besides the treaty itself, on the ground that the transaction was not terminated, and that the treaty being acted upon by three Powers, the papers could not properly be published without the consent of the others.

It would be an act of gross injustice towards Cod-rington to bring his conduct under examination in his absence, and to try him or his letters. The questions put to Codrington were properly put, the answers have been received, and the Administration does not think itself called upon, under all the circumstances, to proceed to any ulterior measures. In fact, if the investigation led to the conclusion that he had acted against his instructions, he would have acted against the law of nations, and compensation would be required; but, if we gave compensation, the other Powers would not, and this would separate us.

Besides, the Turks have ceased to lay any stress upon the battle of Navarino, and to revive the question would revive their claims, and throw new obstacles in the way of the successful termination of the negotiation.

January 26.

Went to the Cottage to be sworn in as a Privy Councillor and Lord Privy Seal. In the Park I passed

Lord Beresford and asked him to come with me, which he did. He was going down to kiss hands on being made Master-General of the Ordnance.

There were present at the Council the Duke of Wellington, Lord Bathurst (President), Lord Aberdeen, Peel, Herries, and Goulburn. Lord Conyngham (Lord Steward) came in to talk to us.

The King sent for the Duke of Wellington and objected to the term untoward, as applied to Navarino, and to the epithet material, where he was made to express his hope that the untoward event would not be a material obstacle to an amicable adjustment, c. As Huskisson and the others had approved of the word untoward we retained it. We changed the form of the sentence, and made the King express his hope that the battle would not impede, c. He wished to have the word unloosed for, instead of untoward. Peel thought the word untoward would bring us into a scrape.

As I was not a Privy Councillor I only went as far as the door of the Council Chamber with the rest, and when they were seated I was sent for, and bowing to the King walked to his right side, where a stool was placed, upon which I knelt on both knees and made my oath as Privy Councillor. I then took the oath as Privy Seal. After each oath I kissed the King's hand. As a new Privy Councillor I had to walk round the table and shake hands with all the Privy Councillors. By the time I had got back to the chair next to the King, which the Duke of Wellington had left for me as Privy Seal, and which the Clerk of the Council had told me I was to take, Peel was already on his knees taking his oath as Secretary of State. I, by gesture, asked the Duke of Wellington if I was to take the vacant chair, on which the King pointed to it for the Duke, and to the back chair for me; there thus remained a vacant chair between the Duke and Herries, next to whom I sat. Whether the King did this to show his respect for the Duke or his dislike to me I know not. [1]

My Lord President read the titles of the orders in Council. The King said, ' Approved, and ordered to be published in the " Gazette," ' which words the Clerk repeated. The Secretary for the Home Department then read the King's Speech.

Lord Beresford having taken my carriage that he might be in time to dine with the Duchess of Kent, I went with the Duke of Wellington. We had a great deal of conversation on various subjects, till we got to Hounslow, where I found my carriage.

Lieven has sent the Duke a long statement of the case of Russia, which he read on his way, but had not finished. I am to see it. Russia, in this paper, claims the right of settling her affairs with Turkey, without intervention of any other Power, and attributes it to her own extreme goodness that she has acted with her allies in this case.

I find I agree with the Duke in all my views of foreign policy.

[1 Lord Ellenborough had incurred the dislike of George IV. by a Speech on the third reading of the ' King's Property Bill in 1823, in which he questioned the expediency of giving the King, especially when he had no children to provide for, the power of leaving away from his successor property enjoyed by him before his accession.]

I do not think, from what the Duke said, that there will be any difficulty in coming to a mezzo termine as to the Corn Law. I told him I thought if we exacted too much there would be a greater difficulty in carrying the Bill through the Commons than there would be, if we exacted too little, in carrying it through the Lords.

January 27.

Hardinge called while I was at breakfast. He gave me an account of a conversation between Lambton and Lord Londonderry, in which Lambton endeavoured to persuade Lord Londonderry to go into Opposition. It seems copies of my amendment [1] are about, and that they want some one to move it to embarrass me. If I am well, I care not for all their attacks.

Lord Lowther is very angry he wanted the Woods and Forests.

January 28.

Decided as to Codrington, that it should be said that the honours were given for valour and conduct as an officer. That the circumstances under which the battle took place were not such as to induce the Government to withdraw from his command an

Admiral who had acted in the most perfect concert with the Admiral of the Allied Powers, and whose conduct had [1 Lord Ellenborougfts Amendment. Lord Ellenborough appears to have intended moving an amendment to tlie Address in answer to the King's Speech if the Goderich Ministry had remained in office. As it probably would have been hostile to the foreign policy of the Ministry, it would have been embarrassing to himself and his colleagues after the formation of the new Ministry to have attention called to it, especially as the Foreign Office was still in the hands of Lord Dudley.]

received the approbation of the States with which we were allied, in the prosecution of a common object.

Mr. Peel mentioned that, as to executing a treaty not approved there was a strong case in point, that of Mr. Fox, in 1783, who turned out Lord Shelburne by a vote of censure upon the preliminaries of peace, and then executed the treaty.

By intelligence from Paris it appears that the Emperor Nicholas will go on by himself, if his allies will not go on in concert with him, but he wishes to proceed with them.

The French Government recommends to our favourable consideration the proposals made by Eussia.

Dined at the Duke of Wellington's. Present, the Cabinet Ministers, and Lords Bexley, Beresford, Shaftes-bury, Maryborough, and Lords Strangford and Chi-chester, seconder and mover.

After dinner Dudley and I had some conversation about the course to be pursued, and agreed upon it. That the vague terms in which the treaty speaks of the settlement of Greece should be reduced to specific terras and then proposed to Turkey. Austria being invited to join in the proposal. It being intimated to Turkey that, in the event of her declining to accede to the terms, Greece would be recognised as an independent State. That is, we should proceed as if Turkey had acceded to the terms. The advantage of this, however, would be, that when we once recognised the independence of Greece we should proceed on the high road of the law of nations.

January 29.

At half past three Falmouth called upon me, and told me he had told the Duke that, with every disposition to support his Government, he so much feared Htiskisson, and so much disliked seeing all the minor offices left in the hands of the Canningites, that he must see how the Government went on before he could promise constant assistance.

At five went to the House. The impression produced by the Speech was that we came off with flying colours, but that Dudley would have a difficult task.

Lord Chichester and Lord Strangford ran very close to the sands and were very Turkish. Lord Holland made a speech of historical research, showing in what manner the Turks had been viewed and treated by English and other statesmen, and that they were not considered ancient allies. He spoke of them as anti-social, and said that what they conceded in the capitulations was given as an act of kindness; that they did not treat us as equals, and he observed, among other things, that in 1770 we allowed the Eussian fleet going against the Turks to refit in our ports. Upon all these points I may perhaps make observations hereafter.

Lord King asked a question as to what was to be done with regard to the Corn Law, which the Duke answered, and then said a few words in answer to Lord Holland's observations upon the words ancient ally and untoward the latter expression having been applied to the battle of Navarino.

Lord Grey declared he did not feel confidence in the Government, but was civil to the Duke.

Lords Lansdowne and Goderich upheld the treaty and Codrington.

The Duke had gone farther than we had agreed beforehand as to Codrington, and set him up too much.

Everybody seemed in good humour. Many congratulated me. All my old Whig friends, Darnley, King, Auckland, c., were quite cordial. The evening passed off as if the Administration had been established years.

Dudley just declared that the treaty would be executed fairly and faithfully.

The feeling manifested by Holland especially, and by Goderich and Lansdowne, convinces me that, had they continued in office, we should soon have been at war with Turkey. The change is just come in time, if in time.

January 30.

Went to the Cabinet room. Eead papers relative to the Greek question. Looked into what had been done towards the settlement of Servia under the 8th Art. of the Treaty of Bucharest. Nothing seems to have been finally decided till the Treaty of Akermann, when the basis of settlement was more specifically laid down. This basis is our best precedent for the settlement of Greece.

Cabinet dinner at the Duke of Wellington's. After dinner Dr. Jenner was spoken of as the fittest man for the office of Judge Advocate. Dr. Lushington being out of the question on account of politics. Phillimore m fitness comes third.

Lord Hill was fixed upon as first General on the

Staff, not as Commander-in-Chief. The saving is 3,000. a year. The other plan of having some one under the King, as Commander-in-Chief, a great object with his Majesty, was rejected at once; and likewise that of having a Commission.

We had a conversation which lasted till half past eleven on Greece. I think they will ultimately come to my first idea of reducing to specific terms the vague expressions of the treaty as to the basis of settlement for Greece, and endeavouring to get Austria to join us. We shall probably have a Cabinet on Saturday on this point. The Eussian Memoir is very stout and warlike. The French agree to it, even to the measure of the three Powers taking between them a Greek loan of two millions, to enable the Greeks to make war. The Dardanelles to be blockaded, and Moldavia and Wallachia occupied. Such are the proposals, which are, however, accompanied by the most solemn protestations of a determination not to extend the Eussian frontier.

January 31.

Went to the Foreign Office and saw Dudley. He told me more in detail the Eussian propositions, which I afterwards read. The Emperor proposed that his army should take Moldavia and Wallachia, and march on till the Sultan accepts the new proposals, which are to be sent in an answer to the Grand Vizier's letter to Nesselrode. These proposals are based on the treaty, the line of demarcation to run from the Gulf of Yolo to the mouth of the Aspropotamos. It is proposed that the allies should bombard the fortresses occupied by the Turks in the Morea, continue the blockade, and even extend it to the Dardanelles, and attack Constantinople. In addition to all this it is proposed that the three Powers should guarantee a loan of two millions to the Greeks. The Memoir is written with much ability and goes into great detail. It commences by throwing upon England the charge of having led the Emperor on to a point at which his own honour and influence forbid him to stop. There is evident determination in it.

I told Dudley I thought the only way in which we could possibly prevent the Emperor from doing what he threatened, was by placing in a strong light the real objections to the invasion of the Principalities, and obtaining the accession of France, Austria, Prussia, and the Netherlands, to a contre projet, which should have for its object the attaining, by military means, the evacuation of the Morea, c., within the line of demarcation.

All my feelings revolt at the idea of the cruel injustice to Turkey, of which we should be guilty even in adopting this limited measure; but the invasion of the Principalities would lead to such dreadful calamities, that, bound by the treaty, we are obliged to suffer a lesser evil in order to avoid the greater. My fear is, that should we, by taking on ourselves an act of injustice, prevent the invasion of the Principalities now, that having once collected a larger army the Eussians will, on the ground of their own peculiar (pretended) causes of difference, still carry into effect the invasion at no remote period.

The Emperor means well; but he has been taught to entertain high ideas of his imperial honour. His Minister, Nesselrode, and Lieven, his Ambassador here, entertain very dangerous designs, and the Eussian army, once engaged in Turkey, will make, if it does not find, reasons for remaining. The Austrians must be very cautious, or the march of the assembled army will be directed to Vienna, instead of to Constantinople, and the Eussians would prefer it.

After dinner at Prince Esterhazy's I had some conversation with him. He does not seem to think matters so serious as they are. I frightened him thoroughly without telling him any particulars.

M. de Bulow, the Prussian Minister, and M. Eoth, the French Charge d'Affaires, were introduced to me, and I had some conversation with them, more with Bulow than with Eoth. Bulow seemed to think there would be little resistance on the part of the Turks, and that the Eussians would attack by sea and Asia, as well as by the Danube.

February 1.

Drew out a line of demarcation for Greece, from Thermopylae along the summits of the mountains to the sea, a little beyond Lepanto. Aberdeen, to whom I showed it, thought the line should begin at Thermopylae, but that the line of the Aspropotamos was the best. This includes Missolonghi. Eead dispatches of M. de Eigny, giving an account of the state of Greece, the armistice of September 25, and the situation of Ibrahim Pasha, which show M. de Eigny to be a man of ability and firmness. Our man Codrington is a mere fighter. VOL i C

Dudley told me the Duke did not think so seriously as we do about the Eussian designs, and seemed to imagine the Emperor might be put off with the hope of getting Ibrahim Pasha out of the Morea.

February 2.

Found in Lord Collingwood's letters passages show-ng that the blockade of the Dardanelles would not affect the provisioning of Constantinople.

Cabinet at 1. The answer to be given to the Eussian Memoir, decided according to the idea I threw out in the paper I gave Dudley some days ago. He proposing it. My views and Peel's coincided entirely.

Dined with Lady Londonderry, where the first thing I heard was that Dudley was out of office, and Lord Stuart in his place. The lies of the day are quite wonderful.

February 3.

Called on Lord Kenyon, who told me the Tories were more dissatisfied at Lord Eldon's not having been consulted than at his not being in the Cabinet.

Sir Alexander Grant said that was certainly the case, and the Duke of Newcastle, amongst others, is gone out of town much disgusted.

I hear Frankland Lewis was more violent against the Duke and Peel than any one else, and he is made Vice-President of the Board of Trade. Not satisfied with having Huskisson, Grant, Palmerston, and Frankland Lewis in office, the Canningites are discontented at not having Wilmot Horton, too. This is really too much. I dined with Lord Cassilis, where this man was, and I have no doubt he repeated everything that passed. He has been down at Earsham, shooting with Huskisson the last few days.

February 4.

Went to the House. Nothing but Lord Hawarden's question of privilege. Dudley told me he did not think any one had a right to say that he knew Mr. Canning's views as to the mode of executing the Greek treaty, Dying words there were none. His last travail related to the Portuguese question.

February 5.

Went with Aberdeen to the Cottage. A Council to swear in Frankland Lewis. The Bishop of Llandaff there. Coplestone, the new political economist bishop. The King looked out of humour. He wants to have the Eecorder's report at Windsor, a thing never done before. The Chancellor had a long conference with him before we went in. He kept us waiting two hours.

February 6.

Went to the Foreign Office at 12. Saw Dudley. Bead his proposed answer to the Eussian note. A great part of it excellent. He had not stated as strongly as he might have done that the first suggestion of force did not come from iis. In fact, by Lieven's note, and a letter from Lord Granville, of February 23, 1827, it appears that the suggestion proceeded from Eussia.

Eead the Duke's paper relative to the line to be taken in a Conference, and the contre projet. Lord Howard seemed to be working against Dudley and ours, and to wish to show that the suggestion of force came from us, and was made first by the Duke of Wellington. I mentioned this to Lord Bathurst, who told me I must take great care what I said to Lord Howard, for he was very hostile to the Government. Young

Abercromby had had committed to him the copying of the Duke's memorandum. He is as constantly at Lansdowne House, and very young.

Dinner at the Duke of Wellington's for the roll of Sheriffs. While we were at dinner came the Speech of the King of France. He is to recall his troops from Spain, tres incessamment, and expresses his hope that the affairs of Greece will be settled sans le secour de la force. He calls the battle as we did, imprevue. This is the first fruit of the change of Government. A fortnight ago the French were acceding to the Eussian proposals.

February 7.

Eead Huskisson's speech. He makes use, as all the Canningites do, of the false phrase of Canning's foreign policy and Canning's liberal views as to trade, c., yet at the same time asserts the Duke of Wellington never thwarted the last or objected to the first.

As to pledges, the fact he states being so, he could require none as to the past, and he does not seem to have received any as to the future. The past is the pledge for the future.

The Duke told me there were no pledges, that it was untrue that he never differed from Canning. [1] That for [1] Mr. Canning, in reply to Mr. Hobhouse (February 24, 1823), who had spoken of the ' present' as opposed to the late Ministry, said that he should three years he prevented the recognition of the South American States. That if he was asked any questions he should say, ' There was much in the papers referred to that was untrue."

Unfortunately when things are asserted so broadly as these were by Huskisson, some will believe them.

At Lord Chesterfield's I met Arbuthnot, who told me he knew the whole detail of the negotiation, and that what Huskisson asserted was altogether untrue.

February 8.

There is a new dispatch from Nesselrode to Lieven, acquainting him with an interview M. Tatischof had with the Emperor of Austria, in which the Emperor expressed the greatest fears of the recommencement of a war of which he should not live to see the er d, and at the same time declared he would not mediate and would not assist the Turks, and this he had told the Vizier.

The Emperor Nicholas, upon the receipt of the letter from Tatischof, giving an account of the interview, act unfairly to that Government, of which he was so recent a member, if he did not reject any praise that was bestowed upon it at the expense of those of whom it was formerly composed. He was compelled in mere justice to say that upon his entering upon the office which he had the honour to fill he found the principles upon which the Government were acting reduced into writing, and this State paper formed what he might be allowed to call the political creed of the Ministers.

The speech in 1824 referred to was probably one on a debate on the Catholic question, when, in reply to severe criticisms on his position in a Cabinet many members of which differed from him on this subject, he pointed out that he differed entirely from the Opposition on the at least equally important subject of Parliamentary reform, which therefore must have been an open question in any Cabinet in which he had been associated with them.

wrote to the Emperor of Austria, expressing his satisfaction and repeating the expressions stated by Tatischof to have been used by the Emperor, in order to fix the Emperor to them.

February 9.

Cabinet at 3. Dudley's dispatch to Lieven considered. He had got into some confusion in the first part of it, and he did not state as strongly as he might have done that the proposal of force did not originate with us. He seemed disposed to speak of it as a simultaneous proposition, and said there was nothing in the documents to which he had access to show that it primarily and exclusively originated with this country. The Duke, with whom I dined, thought from his unwillingness to speak out on the subject that he knew privately that Canning had suggested it first. The Duke said Canning seemed always leaning to that point, but that he had frequently drawn him off from it.

The facts are these. The protocol was ours. We prepared it under the idea that the Conferences of Akerman were more likely to terminate in war than in peace, and that it was in that case something gained to bind down Eussia to the basis sketched in the protocol for the future settlement of Greece. Six months after the signing of the protocol Eussia declares that, having once begun, she must, to maintain her influence at Constantinople, go on. It is first proposed by France to convert the protocol into a treaty, and the additional articles are first proposed by Eussia. France acquiesces in them reluctantly. Our feeling does not appear, as

Lord Granville was then in England, and all the Conferences seem to have been carried on here.

On February 23, 1827, Lord Granville, not having then left Paris, speaks of the Eussian project which contained the proposal of force.

After Dudley's draft we read the Duke's centre projet, which is substantially mine, and his remarks on the effect of a Eussian invasion, seconded by France arid England, for the purpose of forcing the Porte to recognise the independence of her rebellious subjects. The latter paper is very ably drawn.

February 10.

Lord Chesterfield told me it was reported Lord Granville was to be Lord Chamberlain. I do not think this unlikely, as Paris is wanted for Lord Stuart de Eothesay. Dudley will not like having Lord Stuart forced upon him. I asked him if he had any reason to think Canning had first suggested force. He said no, but that the documents in the office did not enable him to charge the Eussians with having done so, or to put the thing stronger than he has done. He is nervous about the debate to-morrow, as Lord Carnarvon, who makes the motion instead of Lord Holland, means to go into the whole of our policy with regard to Greece.

February 11.

Lord Carnarvon made his motion; went into the policy of the treaty and its justice. Endeavoured to show the usage of nations was in favour of interference between a Sovereign and his subjects. Then called upon Dudley for explanations, and spoke of pledges and guarantees.

Dudley objected, on the ground of public expediency, to producing the papers moved for. Then said there were no stipulations, but there were understandings in conversation. He made a short discreet speech.

Lord Goderich then made a statement of the circumstances which led to the breaking up of the Administration, which he attributed entirely to the difference between Herries and Huskisson, throwing all the blame upon Herries.

Eldon spoke against the treaty as contrary to the law of nations. He did not speak well.

The House was nearly up, when the Duke rose. He said every member of the Government was as free as air, and might propose any measure he pleased.

Lord Clanricarde then attacked Dudley, called upon him to explain why he acted with those who were personally hostile to Mr. Canning, and asked him to whom he alluded when, in August last, he said he would not serve with Canning's personal enemies. He then read an extract from a letter of Canning's to the Duke in May last, in which Canning spoke of the impossibility of the Duke's being Minister, because he could not divest himself of influence over the army, and the union of military and civil patronage could not be borne.

Dudley answered him, and said, ' I had no personal hostility to Canning, and that my opposition last year had not interrupted his friendship with me, and Canning knew it had not." He instanced Canning's sitting in Cabinet with Lord Londonderry after the duel as a proof that Canning himself felt that enmity should not be eternal.

Then got up Lord Lansdowne, and attacked me. He supposed, sneeringly, that my adherence to the Government was honourable and conscientious ', but he likewise supposed that I had acquired information since I had become a member of the Government which had induced me to take new views, and now to support Canning's principles of foreign policy. He supposed, too, that I had disapproved of the expedition to Portugal, and now concurred in the expressions in the King's Speech which praised it.

I said that when it should become consistent with the public interests to lay the papers bn the table, and to discuss the Treaty, I should be ready to do so. In the meantime I declared my opinions, whatever they might be, were unchanged, and no one had presumed to ask me to change them. He presumed that I had disapproved of the expedition to Portugal, and yet could now concur in rejoicing that the objects of the expedition were accomplished, and that the faith of treaties having been maintained and the safety and independence of Portugal secured, his Majesty had ordered the immediate return of his troops.

I said," The noble Marquis is as incorrect in his fact as he is in his reasoning. I never did disapprove of the expedition to Portugal. I could not disapprove of his Majesty's keeping his plighted faith, and maintaining the faith of a treaty. I ridiculed the absurdity of those who spoke of that expedition as a master-stroke of policy. There could be no policy where there was no choice. We acted in strict conformity to the express stipulations of a treaty. But if I had disapproved of the expedition, how much more must I have rejoiced at the termination of an expedition of which I did not approve?"

The noble Marquis assumed that it had been promulgated that Mr. Canning's principles of foreign policy were to be persevered in, and that I, having changed my opinion, was to maintain the principles of which I disapproved. Even if I had changed my opinion I could not have pledged myself to maintain Mr. Canning's principles, for I really did not know what they were. No man had ever attempted to explain what they were, as contradistinguished from those of his predecessor and of his colleagues.

I then read an extract from a speech of Canning's, of Feb. 24, 1823, in which he rejected praise given to him at the expense of his colleagues, and said he had found the principles upon which the Government was acting reduced to writing. That State paper formed the political creed of the Ministers, and whatever credit he might deserve was for following it.

As to the recognition of South America, the principle of that measure was announced to all Europe at Aix-la-Chapelle. After that it was only a question of time. The principle, therefore, was not Mr. Canning's.

As to the expedition to Portugal I had already shown it was undertaken in strict obedience to the letter of a treaty.

If the foreign policy of Mr. Canning meant merely the treaty of July 6, undoubtedly it was not my intention to advise liis Majesty to violate his plighted faith. But I was yet to learn that it was a political crime in Mr. Fox to censure the preliminaries of peace in 1783, and yet carry those preliminaries into execution. Certainly I was prepared to execute that treaty fairly, in the spirit of conciliation and of peace, in which, if I might judge from the tone of some noble lords, they, at least, did not think it was passed.

As to commercial policy I sat by the side of the noble Marquis when the measures alluded to were introduced, and I did not oppose them. The principles of Free Trade I approved. I wish to carry them as far as I could with safety, but I thought that as some of those who in former times defended the Slave Trade by showing that the condition of the slaves was better in the West Indies than it had been in Africa, forgetting all the miseries and losses of the middle passage; so the political economists, satisfied that the country would attain greater wealth under their system than under the ancient order of things, overlooked altogether the miseries occasioned by the transition, and the ruin of all the existing interests which had grown up under the operation of the ancient law. For myself, I should, in considering the propriety of any commercial regulations, look, not only at the wealth which might flow from it, but at the more important moral and political consequences; for above all things I desired to maintain the independence of the country, the moral happiness of the people, and the safety of that constitutional system which was far more valuable than gold.

The noble Marquis can hardly censure me for belonging to a Government founded upon the same principle as regards the Catholic question, as that of which he was himself a member. It may seem paradoxical to the noble Marquis, but it was an opinion I expressed last year, and I have not changed it, that a Government, neutral on the Catholic question, was more advantageous to the Catholic cause than one united in its favour. I am convinced that a Government united in its favour would produce a reaction which would throw the question back many years. A Government united against it would produce evils of a different description. I am convinced that practically more good can be done for Ireland under the present Administration than under that which has just expired.

I had now only to confirm what had fallen from my noble friend (Dudley). I never was a personal enemy of Mr. Canning. I could not be, for I hardly knew him. The very few times I had met him, nothing had passed but the ordinary interchange of courtesy. I believed he was much beloved by his friends, and had many domestic virtues, but I looked at him only as a political character. I thought him a dangerous Minister. I think so still, and if he were alive now I should oppose him. But as this feeling never had interrupted the friendship between me and my noble friend, or prevented the most cordial communication between us, I could see no reason why it should prevent me now from sitting in the same Cabinet with him.

Aberdeen and Bathurst told me I did very well. I think the Duke thought I had been indiscreet. Beres-ford, Salisbury, Stanhope, Strangford, congratulated me.

They told me I never spoke better. I think I did right in saying what I did, as our best friends were alarmed by Huskisson's speech, and began to think there had been concession on our parts. I am satisfied with the matter of my speech; but I was neither so fluent nor as correct in my language as I usually am. I shall speak better the next time. It was new to me to speak from the Ministerial Bench.

After the debate Dudley said he could not object to my calling Mr. Canning a dangerous Minister, as I had called him so before.

Lord Eosslyn told me I spoke damned well, but Lord Wharnclhte did us most good. So he did. Our friends will now support us with warmth. Lord Wharnclhte said he saw the pledges were not worth a farthing.

February 12.

Cabinet at 3. Decided that there should be a Bill to enable the King to have the Kecorder's report elsewhere than in London. Lord Bathurst made great objections, and thought it would produce a very unpleasant feeling and much observation. The King is to be impressed with the necessity of availing himself of the power of having it out of London only in the case of illness. He is to be brought to London, if possible, for the next Eecorder's report, and then the Bill would proceed better on the ground of the injury done to his health. He did intend to come up on the 19th to the marriage of the Duchess of Kent's daughter, 1 and yet he will not come to a Eecorder's report, though there are 1 Princess Feodore, half-aster of her Majesty.

already two waiting for him, and a third coming in a short time, while Newgate is full, and the prisoners in a state of disorder.,

There was some conversation respecting the expediency of communicating our contre projet to France, before we laid it before the Ambassador here, that we might have the first communication to St. Petersburg made, if possible, with the concurrence of France. If the Russians receive our contre projet without at the same time hearing that France accedes to it, and that Prussia and Austria will assist in endeavouring to carry it into effect, they will express themselves so strongly against it that France will not venture to say anything in its favour.

It seems that from the beginning France has, in the first instance, gone with Eussia and then fallen back upon our more moderate propositions.

Some thought it would be unfair to Russia to let France know the contre projet before her. This seems to me absurd.

My impression is that the Russian army will move as soon as the roads are passable, and the grass springs up, and that all we can do is to place ourselves in a good position with the country.

Herries, before the others came in, complained that Goderich had omitted all mention of his own abdication and restoration, which made the whole difference. These events took place before Herries' letter, and were the reason why that letter was not written earlier. The first abdication was occasioned by the King's refusal to admit Lord Holland. I am inclined to think that

Herries saw the Whigs were strengthening themselves in the Cabinet, and took the first opportunity of going out. How he and Huskisson are to settle the matter on Friday I know not.

I walked with Aberdeen to the House. Lord Darn-ley was the only Whig there. He was saying there would, he saw, be no opposition. He told Aberdeen I spoke with more discretion and temper than they expected. The only expression I used which, when he first heard it, Aberdeen doubted about, was that of ' dangerous Minister' applied to Canning; but he said he was glad of it now he saw the good effect produced upon our friends. Stanhope, too, spoke of my speech as what satisfied them. Lord Winchelsea, who had looked quite cold before, was smiling afterwards. Aberdeen seems to think there may be a separation still between us and Huskisson. I do not. If there should be, I think Goulburn will be made Colonial Secretary and Herries go to the Exchequer. I think either Bexley or Lord Wallace would have the Mint.

I wrote out my speech of last night.

February 13.

Met Lord Grey at Lady Jersey's. He seemed friendly. Told me I made a very good speech. Ridi-culed Lord Lansdowne's geography, and appeared sorry he had not been prepared to go into the general question and answer Lord Carnarvon.

Every one seems satisfied with my speech, and our friends are now in good humour.

Cabinet dinner at Aberdeen's. The Duke, Dudley, and the Chancellor dined with the King after the Council. Dudley slept at the Cottage.

After dinner we had a good deal of conversation on matters of finance. Peel spoke of the absolute necessity of reducing expenditure, as we have no surplus, and cannot impose taxes. He spoke of reducing the number of seamen. There are now 30,000, of which 9,000 are marines.

Lord Melville insisted on keeping up all the marines, but allowed a reduction might be made in the seamen. They talked of reducing the whole rate to 25,000. That is 16,000 seamen and 9,000 marines. I do not believe we can protect our commerce with this force. The French have more than 20,000 men. It seemed admitted that the army could not be reduced. Three-fourths or more of the lives of our soldiers are even now passed abroad. There are but 2,500 men in London.

I am against all reductions of troops and seamen till we see daylight in the affairs of Greece. We should reduce what is not essential to national strength.

February 14.

The Duke of Wellington is decidedly in favour of the Rideau Canal, [1] which would, he thinks, so completely protect the communication between Upper and Lower Canada as to make all the designs the United States might entertain quite abortive, and induce them to be very quiet on all points of difference between the two countries, which they will not be while they think [1 For the protection of Canada]

they can easily annex Canada to their territory. If they see they can gain nothing by a land war, and must lose by naval hostilities, they will be tranquil enough.

February 15.

Mr. Peel made his statement of the financial situation of the country in moving the appointment of the Finance Committee. He concealed nothing, but exhibited things as they really are. This is the true policy. Explanations were expected from Huskisson and Herries, and it was said Tierney was desirous of making a statement. However, nothing was said. The House was taken by surprise by the motion for adjournment, and everybody went away laughing at the disappointment.

February 16.

Cabinet at 3. Information that Ibrahim Pasha had sent his sick and wounded and superfluous artillery to Egypt, together with from three to five thousand women and children as slaves. Great doubt was thrown upon the latter part of the statement, as it did not appear that Ibrahim had tonnage sufficient for such numbers.

The Duke of Clarence told me afterwards that the slaves, principally children, were between six and seven, and were sold in the market at Alexandria on their arrival. We went through Dudley's paper, but I was obliged to leave the Cabinet before it broke up, to go to a Charity dinner at the London Tavern, for the Seamen's Hospital, where the Duke of Clarence was to be in the chair.

VOL. i. D

February 17.

Esterhazy called. He brought the paper of advice Austria sent to the Porte. In this paper Austria speaks of retaining the fortresses for the Turks, but Esterhazy seems to think that will not be insisted on. I wish we could retain the fortresses, at least Navarino, which is the only good port, but Russia would never consent. Another point Austria wishes to obtain for the Turks is the preliminary submission of the Greeks. This, too, Esterhazy thought, might be held to be accomplished by the Greeks admitting the suzerainty of the Porte.

February 18.

Went to the Cabinet room at 4. Met Lord Bathurst there. Saw Dudley.

Went with Aberdeen to the House of Commons. Heard Lord Normanby's questions, and Huskisson, and Herries. Lord Normanby spoke miserably. The others very well. Herries made a statement which sets him up very much. Huskisson got out of the scrape. The letter of a Mr. Shepherd, who stood by him on the hustings, declaring he had not stated that he had ever demanded any personal guarantees of the Duke of Wellington, did him great service. Herries' speech was the best received. Herries, towards the end, which I did not stay to hear, having left the House when his statement seemed concluded, declared that he knew (this expression he qualified afterwards) that the difference between him and Huskisson was made the excuse for breaking up the Administration, but was not the real cause.

35

February 19.

Lord Goderich, in the House of Lords, declared that Herries' resignation was the sole cause of the breaking-up of the Government. So the two are at issue.

Lord Carlisle and Lord Morley spoke. The former said he was sorry to hear me use the expression of ' dangerous Minister,' [1] and the latter said that my having declared I did not know what the system of Mr. Canning was, was not a sufficient reason for his refusing to Support a Government of which I was a member.

In the House of Commons last night Brougham used some slighting expressions respecting me, and misstated my speech. Lord Normanby likewise misrepresented what I said, and then attempted to turn it into ridicule. Hobhouse began this line in a very impertinent manner the other night. Should this practice continue, I shall be obliged to select a strong case, and call for an explanation.

Nothing can be more contrary to good Parliamentary usage or more really inconvenient than this new custom of answering in one House the speeches made in the other. It is so unfair and unmanly, that should it be persisted in, it will oblige members of one House to make their answers in a third place.

February 20.

Cabinet dinner at Dudley's. After dinner very little conversation on political subjects till the Duke, Peel, Lord Bathurst, and Melville were gone, and Palmerston,

36

too, [1 In reference to Mr. Canning] [?] and Herries. Then Huskisson, Grant, Dudley, and Aberdeen, and I talked of the line to be adopted with regard to the repeal of the Test and Corporation Acts, and whether the Government should oppose the repeal, making it a Government question.

Huskisson and Grant seemed against making it a Government question, and Dudley too. So am I. Huskisson and I should vote against the repeal as prejudicing the Catholic question. I think Grant and Dudley would vote for it.

There is an awkward question with France as to an insult committed against our flag in the Gambia. It ' will be treated in an amicable way by us. Huskisson, to my great surprise, expressed great dislike of the Americans. He seemed to anticipate the breaking up of the United States from the divergence of interest between the Southern and Northern, the maritime and back States. It seems that at the moment we were concluding the Pacification of Ghent, the province of Massachusetts was sending proposals for separation, which arrived just too late. Huskisson thinks if we had pressed the Northern, instead of the Southern States, and taken Ehode Island, instead of attacking New Orleans, that the Northern States would have dissolved the Union.

It is thought Jackson, if he lives, will be President. He is seventy-three. They say he cannot be more hostile to us than Adams.

Huskisson seems to suppose the Americans feel a degree of awe and respect for this country, which I confess I cannot trace in their acts.

37

February 21.

Intelligence of January 10 from Constantinople. The Turks have issued a Hattisheriffe inveighing against all the Allies, but particularly against Eussia, declaring she will never acknowledge the independence of the Morea, calling upon all Mahometans to arm in defence of the faith, and giving over to the purposes of the war the sum which was to be paid to Eussia under the Treaty of Akerman. At the same time they have sent from Constantinople about 200 English, French, and Eussian subjects, and have closed the Dardanelles.

I fear after this there will be no possibility of preventing the Eussians from marching.

I see no reason why we should view what the Turks have done otherwise than we should have viewed similar acts on the part of Turkey at any other time, when we were desirous of maintaining friendship with them. We are bound by the treaty to co-operate with the others for the pacification of Greece, but the moment that object is accomplished we are free. We are not called upon to act with Eussia in her quarrel.

If States always made war when they could state as a cause and justification of war that which has at some time or other been made a cause or pretext of war, peace would never be established in Europe.

Lord Cowley represents Metternich as having been much affected when he heard the news.

Dudley seems still to feel that Metternich has contributed to bring the mischief upon us by encouraging the Porte to resist.

February 22.

There seems to have been a most violent attack upon Herries last night,", and Hardinge tells me he was damaged, and the House against him. He had declared the other night, with the most solemn asseverations, as he hoped to be saved," c., that he had consulted no one as to the line of conduct he should pursue. Brougham asked him ' if no one consulted with him? ' and to this he declined giving an answer. This is the only awkward point, for on all other points he stands well. The language of Wynne to Herries, and of Herries to Wynne, was violent and not Parliamentary. Lord Wellesley, as the Duke of Wellington told me, compared the discussion to the concluding chorus in ' Tom Thumb," where all the characters say, You lie 1 you lie!! you lie!!!"

It is reported Herries is gone down to Windsor to ask the King to allow him to disclose all he cannot state without the King's permission.

February 23.

Met Lord Clive at Lady Belfast's. He was in the House of Commons during the explanations on Thursday, and went there with a feeling for Herries, and was much distressed by the scene that took place. Peel's countenance evidently showed he felt Herries was damaged.

Ashley told me the wish at Lansdowne House was that Herries might be retained.

At the Duke of Clarence's dinner, where the Cabinet, c., dined, I asked Peel what his objections were to the repeal of the Test and Corporation Acts. He said that under the Acts there had been no difference between the Church and the Dissenters that there was no practical grievance, and that he had rather continue this sort of quiet and rest to the Church than open a new state of things which might not be accompanied with the same degree of tranquillity. He added that he thought the repeal would prejudice the Catholic question, and that if he was in favour of the Catholics he should, on that ground, oppose the repeal.

The Corporation of Nottingham is in the hands of the Dissenters, and I believe others are. The Duke of Wellington said the law as it stood practically now was not intended to prevent Dissenters from being in Corporations, but to prevent them from doing mischief when they were there.

We are to have a Cabinet on Monday to consider whether opposition to the repeal shall be made a Government measure.

February 25.

The newspaper contains the Turkish manifesto. It is a declaration of war at least Eussia will so consider it, and march at once. I fear Eussia will think herself released from the self-denying ordinance, and if she claims territorial indemnity, Austria will go to war, for she cannot permit the appropriation of the Principalities to Eussia.

Cabinet at 3. Decided that the repeal of the Test and Corporation Acts should be opposed by the Govern-ment on the ground that there was no practical inconvenience, that the thing worked well, and that it was unwise to change the relative position of persons who went on so well together. Huskisson, others, and I said we must object to the repeal, not only on that ground, but as prejudicing the Catholic question. This was assented to. The Duke cautioning us as Ministers not to urge the union of Catholics and Dissenters with the view of forcing the measure upon Parliament.

House at 5. Lord Clanricarde stated the grounds upon which he had made the observations he did the other night on the apparent inconsistency of Huskisson's conduct, and his declaration in August last. He spoke discreetly. Dudley answered him.

The Duke declared he was not the personal enemy of Mr. Canning, and even that he had no political hostility towards him.

This declaration, certainly in direct contradiction to what we all supposed, and indeed know, gave great dissatisfaction to Stanhope, Londonderry, Eldon, and indeed our best friends, those on whom we must depend in the event of difficulty, our body-guard.

There were at the Cabinet room letters of Lieven to Dudley, and of De la Ferronays to Eoth, both considering the Turkish manifesto as a declaration of war, and the French note urging us to sanction the entrance of the Eussians into the Principalities in order to keep Eussia to her self-denying engagements.

The Duke has received a note from La Ferronays to the same effect. The Duke read the draft of his answer, which was much like Dudley's paper, as regarded the necessary effects of allowing the Eussians to invade Turkey. The Duke thinks a Eussian army entering Turkey with the sanction of France and England would encourage insurrections everywhere, and create a state of things which would lead to the dissolution of the Ottoman Empire, and to irremediable confusion.

It seems it is not properly a manifesto of the Turkish Government; but a speech read to the feudatories, which some scribes of the Fanar reduce to writing from memory as well as they can afterwards. There are two versions of this. The most moderate is that in the; Moniteur," the other is that received by Esterhazy. These are not official documents. In 1821 and again in 1823 there were speeches made of violent character, but having no consequences, which Lord Strangford did not send home, knowing them to be unofficial. This circumstance the French do not seem to have known.

Cabinet. The Duke's answer to La Ferronays' letter decided upon.

Dudley is to answer Lieven's paper, put a new headpiece to the English project which is to be divided from the answer to Nesselrode, and answer La Ferronays' dispatch to Eoth by two o'clock to-morrow. He will hardly be able to do it all, for he works slowly. I have had half a mind to offer to recast the Duke's letter into an official answer to La Ferronays' letter to Eoth, but I am afraid of appearing to encroach upon Dudley's duties. I am not sure I should like to be Foreign Secretary, and have so much of the business taken out of my hands as is taken out of Dudley's by the Duke. Yet if I were Prime Minister I should do just what the Duke does.

I told the Duke I was afraid he would make some of our best friends dissatisfied if he used such language as he did last night, saying he had not any political hostility to Mr. Canning.

February 26.

Stratford Canning is come. He will not be sent back again. I think our best friends much dissatisfied with the Duke's speech.

I hear Planta did not send out the notes for the division to-night till yesterday evening, so that there was a general idea it was not to be made a Government question, and many men having dissenting constituents have pledged themselves. Others are not coming up. On the other side there is a perfect whip. I told the Duke this at dinner at Lord Londonderry's, and he was much annoyed.

February 27.

The Committee for considering the repeal of that part of the Corporation and Test Acts which imposes the Sacramental Test, was carried against Government last night by a majority of 44. The numbers being 193 and 237. It was clear from the beginning of the evening that Government would be in a minority, and even as it was many of their friends voted very reluctantly with them. The debate was dull.

Went to the Lodge to a Council. Met there Lord Melville, Peel, Lambe, Palmerston, Lord Maryborough. Dudley came late with Stratford Canning. The King had a conference of two hours with Peel before the Council on the division of last night.

Cabinet dinner at Lord Bathurst's. After dinner we talked of the course to be pursued as to the Test and Corporation Acts. Nothing was decided; but Sir T. Acland threw out last night that an annual suspension of the Sacramental Test would be better than an annual indemnity; and Peel seems to catch at this as a mode of getting out. It seems some of the influential bishops will agree to this.

The difficulty is to pass so modified a Bill through the Commons as we can carry through the Lords without displeasing our best friends.

The more I think of the repeal the more injury I think it will do the Catholic cause.

We had on the table some papers sent by Codring-ton. A letter of his for which he ought to be recalled; it is so like a partisan.

February 28.

Eead the last dispatches of Ottenfels, from Constantinople, dated January 10. Prince Esterhazy sent them to me. The Turks seem to have lost their heads from a sense of danger, but they are resolved to meet the danger like brave men. They consider that the cession of the Morea would lead to general insurrection, and that the Allied Powers desire the destruction of the Turkish Empire.

Eead at the Cabinet room Sir F. Adam's account of his interview with Ibrahim Pasha at Modon. Ibrahim acknowledged the correctness of the observations made by Adam upon his position and danger. Said he was ready to leave the Morea if ordered to do so by Mehemet Ali, the Pasha of Egypt, who would not order him to do so, without the consent of the Porte. For himself he said that what he most desired was military glory, and he was determined to preserve his military honour. He was a faithful servant of the Porte, and held his life at the Sultan's service. All the expressions used by him do him honour, and it is humiliating to see an English officer obliged to ask a Turkish Pasha to do what the Turk thinks, and the Englishman allows to be, inconsistent with his honour as a soldier. This is but one of the consequences of the fatal treaty.

I had some conversation with Lord Grey about the Test and Corporation Acts. He thinks that to gain the principle established by the repeal would, of itself, be of more use to the Catholics than the votes of the Dissenters they may lose.

I cannot help thinking the repeal will injure the Catholics.

I dined with Dudley. He read to me his reply to Prince Lieven, which is pretty good, but he is a slow worker. He has not yet replied to La Ferronays' letter to Eoth. La Ferronays seems to agree as to the effect of invading Turkey, but he thinks it better that Eussia should do so with the sanction of the Allies than by herself. The Duke thinks the insurrection will be encouraged by the idea that the three Powers have resolved on the destruction of the Ottoman

4.5
Empire. As to the self-denying ordinance, Eussia will hardly be able to adhere to it, even should she be inclined, which I do not believe.

February 29.

Peel seems to have lost his temper last night in the House of Commons. Lord Milton said what was very provoking. Peel endeavoured to get a little delay for the purpose of consideration. It was refused, and he did not divide, but seceded.

Cabinet at 2. Dudley's answer to Lieven read. It is excellent. We talked a good deal about what took place last night, and what was to be done in the Lords. The Corn Bill is to be considered on Monday next.

Lord Eldon means to oppose the repeal on the same grounds on which he has always done so.

A dispatch of Disbrowe's, from Petersburg, says the Eussians are to have three corps darmee on the Pruth, and expect to be at Constantinople in three or four weeks. Witgenstein commands in chief. Woron-zoff has one of the corps. Diebitch is chef d'etat Major, and will really direct under the Emperor. The general commanding on the side of Persia has only 14,000 disposable men, a force not considered sufficient to march upon Trebizonde, but some diversion will be made on the Asiatic frontier. The peace with Persia is not yet signed. The general, Paskewitch, is unwilling to conclude it, and wants more money. However, it will be concluded, the Persians paying 1,800,000. The Persian Empire is represented as falling to pieces. An

4.6
English officer, Macdonald, has been very instrumental in bringing about an arrangement.

March 1.

Eead Macdonald's diary and dispatches. Offers seem to have been made by the principal people in all the provinces of Persia to place the Empire under English protection. The Eussian General Paskewitch has 8,000 infantry, 7,000 very bad cavalry, and 1,000 artillery, with sixty guns at Tabreez. This army may altogether consist of 20,000 men. It seems to be wretchedly appointed in horses. All the chief officers spoke freely of their despotic Government, and against that and the service. I had heard before that the late Emperor sent all the corps most infected by Liberal principles to the Caucasus. The losses of the Eussians there have been very great. Macdonald's account is very curious, and worked up a la ' Walter Scott."

March 3.

In the House Lord Clifden began a talk about the Test and Corporation Acts, which Lords Eedesdale and Calthorpe took up. Dudley wishes to have the Acts repealed. The Chancellor seems to me to wish so too. Aberdeen, Huskisson, Palmerston, and Melville and Grant would, I should think, be the same way. The Duke is adverse. Peel indifferent. Goulburn rather for and against. Bathurst against repeal. Herries I do not know. By-the-bye it is said Herries is very unwell, and Huskisson too.

The Bishop of London[1] would be satisfied with a declaration or oath for the maintenance of the Church. So would my uncle.[2]

The Duke is to see the Archbishop and the Bishops of Durham and Chester on the subject.

It seems to me that our object should be to settle the question. I care not how.

March 5.

Council at 3. Eecorder's report. The first I have attended. The Duke of Buccleuch and Lord Eosslyn were sworn in as Scotch Lord-Lieutenants. The appointment of Lord Eosslyn gives offence to Lord Elgin and Lord Leven, both having larger estates in the country, but it was quite right to give the Lord-Lieutenancy to Lord Eosslyn. I never cease regretting he is not in the Cabinet. The King seemed souffrant from the first; but he was placed in a thorough air in a very cold room, which chilled even me who was nearest the fire. He fell asleep, and latterly seemed really ill. The Duke fell asleep, too, and looked like death.

The Duke of Leeds, Lords Winchester and Conyng-ham stood behind the King's chair. The Eecorder sits on the King's right hand on a stool.

We dined with the Chancellor. He gave us a good dinner, and bad plate. The Duke had so bad a cold he eould not dine with us; neither did Lord Melville nor Mr. Herries.

After dinner we had some conversation on the sub-[1 Dr. Howley, afterwards Archbishop of Canterbury.]

[2 George Law, Bishop of Bath and Wells.]

ject of the instructions to be sent by the Plenipotentiaries of the Allies to the Admirals, and of the instructions to be given to Sir F. Adam. Of the last, read by Huskisson, I entirely approved.

Dudley's proposed instructions by no means met with general concurrence. It was suggested that they should be remodelled on the plan of Huskisson.

March 6.

I made a draft of instructions to the Admirals on the plan of Huskisson's, and sent it to Dudley. On going to the Cabinet I found he had given his paper to be remodelled by Huskisson. This paper was read and after discussion approved. The Duke was not present, being still ill. I called to inquire how the King was, and was told he was quite well. The manner of the porter seemed to say, Why do you ask?

The Consul at Alexandria, Barker, says the Turkish fleet brought 5,500 slaves. The Captain of the Pelinus says 675. It was proposed that we should endeavour to get these slaves back, and agreed to; but we are not to assume a tone of war or menace.

Huskisson read a dispatch to Codrington, which, after stating the passage of forty-five sail of Turkish and Egyptian vessels from Navarino to Alexandria without interruption (of which forty-five thirty were vessels of war), refers Codrington to his instructions of October 16, and desires him to transmit forthwith a detailed statement of the orders he had issued in consequence, and of the measures he has adopted for preventing the passage of Turkish and Egyptian ships from port to port.

March 9.

Cabinet at 4. We were to have considered a new Corn Bill, but Dudley began by suggesting a relaxation of some strict resolutions not to allow the Eussians to cross the Pruth. The French seem to wish to permit the occupation of the Principalities by a small for ce, and to this Dudley seemed to be inclined to accede, under the idea that it might prevent the Eussians from going further.

The Duke objected. His objections rested on principle. We desired to effect the objects of the treaty in the least dangerous and most direct manner, and to keep within the treaty. I thought that by yielding at all we gave the grounds of argument for further concession and inducement to demand it. We gave up principle, and made a case for further concession on the facts. It was determined to adhere to our original answer.

It was considered whether Codrington should be recalled. Huskisson's proposed letter, with some corrections made by himself, was decided upon, and the letter is to be shown to Lieven and Polignac.

The proposed joint instructions to Sir E. Codrington and the others are in the hands of the Plenipotentiaries. I think the result of the letter to Codrington must be his recall. Lord Exmouth will be sent.

The Duke proposed that we should reduce the 6 vague extreme' of the treaty to specification (the French having desired us to do so), and his idea was 1. That the new Greece should be confined to the Morea.

2. That 200, 000*l*. a year should be fixed as the annual sum to be paid to the Ottoman Government as compensation for the revenue, and 2,500,000*l* in one sum as compensation for property.

3. That the Ottoman Government should select one of three names as the chief of the new State.

Some (Palmerston, Dudley, Grant, and, I think, Hus-kisson) were for a more extended limit than the Morea.

It was settled at last that Dudley should, in a conference upon another subject to-morrow, feel his way, and find how far the Plenipotentiaries, if he proposed any plan, were empowered to accede to it; and, further, should throw out that this was a matter which, under the treaty, must sooner or later have been decided by all the Plenipotentiaries, and therefore not one upon which they have a right to call for the projet of any one Power.

As to the compensation for revenue, he might suggest the average of the seven years before the war; and as to that for property, it could only be referred to Commissioners on the spot.

Thus the Duke was, for the present, overruled. He looks ill still.

While we were talking came dispatches from Corfu, which Huskisson and Dudley had not time to read at length; but it seems that Colonel Cradock's mission to Egypt has failed altogether, Mehemet Ali saying he is a subject of the Porte, and must take his orders from Constantinople.

Capo d'Istrias has been received well at Egina. He is in the greatest difficulty. There is no money, and the whole population of Napoli di Eomania, lately the seat of government, has fled to the islands, the forts being in the possession of men who do not acknowledge the Government. Upon this disclosure, which I was aware of before, Peel exclaimed at the state in which we are placed. Should the Porte accede to all we demand, how can we ever establish a regular Government in Greece? and what quarrels between the three Powers in consequence of this undivided and tripartite possession of the Morea?

March 10.

Cabinet at 3. Grant proposed his Corn Bill. The only relaxation he proposed of the Bill of last year was a diminution of duty shilling by shilling ', instead of two shillings for one from 62s. to 66s. imperial.

The Duke proposed a duty of 30s. at 55s. Winchester diminishing shilling by shilling to 65s., and then more rapidly so as to expire at 72s.

Huskisson was willing that, if 200,000 quarters should be entered for home consumption in any twelve successive weeks, during which time the average price should be below 64s., the duty should be increased one-fourth during the six weeks following, provided the price did not rise to 66s.

Grant rather objected to this.

Thus the difference is very wide. Peel is rather for the Bill of last year. This we cannot agree to who opposed it in the Lords; indeed we could not carry it. However, Peel would adopt the Duke's proposition.

The House was full, there being a general idea that there would be a message to communicate a Eussian declaration of war.

Aberdeen, with whom I walked home, seemed to think Dudley, who has seemed to give in on the subject of the Greek treaty, showed a different disposition yesterday, and was inclined to make a point of authorising the entrance of the Eussians into the Principalities. I do not think so. He seems to me to have gone on very heartily with us, and he easily gave up his crotchet.

Cabinet at 3. We should have begun at once on corn, but Dudley first wanted the opinion of the Cabinet oil some points in the proposed instructions to the Admirals. We then began on corn, and made no progress at all.

I do not see how this is to end. Huskisson will go out if the pivot is changed. He cannot agree to the Duke's proposal. Grant is with Huskisson. Peel is satisfied with the Bill of last year. Lord Melville seems so too. Goulburn, Palmerston, and Dudley, I think, incline for the old Bill; Aberdeen, Bathurst, and I are with the Duke. The Chancellor has not attended; Herries seems rather indifferent; but certainly we seem in a minority, and as Peel is the other way our position is awkward. I shall propose to-morrow an alteration in Huskisson's clause, which will make it more efficacious.

The Duke seems annoyed. Our position is difficult, mine in particular. I opposed the Bill of last year altogether. The others did not. I was willing to agree to make 646'. the pivot, rather than not pass any Bill last year; but below that I would not go.

The Duke depends on the agricultural interest. On the Corn Bill Lords Grey, Rosslyn, Lauderdale, and others are with the Tories.

March 12.

Before I went to the Cabinet I saw the Duke and asked him what he meant to do. He said he should adhere to his own plan. I told him, as I understood it, I thought I could hardly agree to Huskisson's clause with the Bill of last year.

In Cabinet an explanation was given of Huskisson's clause. It seems that it would be called into operation as soon as it should appear that 200,000 quarters had been sold in the course of twelve weeks, during which the average price should have been at or below 64s. imperial, and once called into operation it would last at least six weeks, and beyond that time, till the average had been 665. for six weeks; that is, it might be permanent.

The whole Cabinet, with the exception of the Duke, acceded to this. The Duke has given up his idea of half-a-crown on leaving the warehouses, in addition to the duty fixed by the Act.

Lieven last night communicated to Dudley the Bus-sian declaration of war against Turkey. It is motive not only upon the closing of the Bosphorus and the making of the Treaty of Akerman, but upon the Turks having induced the King of Persia not to ratify the treaty, and having marched troops on the Eussian flank.

The Emperor declares he will continue the war till he has received indemnity for all his losses, and for these hostile acts; and if the Allies will act in the manner demanded of them in his projet, he will then act towards Greece according to the existing treaty; otherwise, as he thinks accords best with his own interests and convenances.

The Duke saw the Prince de Polignac, and told him he did not apprehend much mischief if France and England would act together. Polignac assented. The Duke thought Russia gave up the treaty. Polignac said not entirely. The Duke said, c That is, one of the parties to a tripartite treaty declares that, unless the other two will act according to her dictates, she will give up the treaty." To this Polignac assented.

March 13.

When we separated last night there seemed every prospect of the Government being broken up. The Duke would not yield, though all were against him. I went at 12 to-day to Peel. He thought I should see the Duke.

Aberdeen, Melville, and Bathurst, whom I saw at the Cabinet room, thought so too. I went and found him disinclined to accede to the proposition I had grounded on Peel's and Huskisson's, though I showed him it gave more than the agriculturists themselves asked in the Commons last year, more than he asked below 665. (that is, after the introduction of 300,000 quarters), and a practical advance of 8s. (under the circumstances) upon the duty as proposed last year.

He renewed his proposition, which I modified in this way. I closed with his idea that, as a basis, Grant's plan might be adopted (which makes the duty diminish Is. for Is. for four turns after 62s. imperial), and suggested that, after 200,000 quarters had been entered in twelve weeks, during which the aggregate average had been below 64s. imperial, 5s. additional duty should be laid on. This he acceded to.

I took this to Huskisson, and succeeded in obtaining his agreement, with the slight alteration in his original clause, that the duty should cease when for twelve weeks (commencing after the imposition of the duty) the aggregate average price had been above 64s.

The original proposal was that it should cease when for six weeks the average had been at or above 66s.

The only difficulty is with Grant, who doubts whether he can propose this plan to the House of Commons.

I must say Huskisson has behaved very fairly, and has made great concessions. The Duke thought yesterday that there was an indisposition to make any concessions to him, and a desire to demand them of him, and he said to me, to-day, ' This shows how imprudent it is to coalesce with those with whom there have been recent subjects of difference."

Huskisson said he was willing to make great concessions, and to expose himself to much attack, rather than break up the Government on such a point at such a time.

Dudley, whom I met in the Park after the House was up, was both surprised and delighted to hear the matter seemed likely to be arranged.

March 14.

Eeceived a note from Grant, stating that at present he did not think he could propose in the House of Commons either Huskisson's amendment, or that which I took to the Duke yesterday.

Eeceived a letter from the Duke expressing his reluctant consent to the plan agreed to yesterday by Hus-kisson, but adding that it was very important to make the high duty cease on the conditions contained in Huskisson's proposition, not on those contained in the plan agreed to yesterday.

I went to Huskisson and endeavoured to persuade him to accede to this; but he, having in the meantime seen Grant, had ascertained there would be great difficulty in getting him to agree to either; instead of conceding what I asked, he seemed disposed to wish to go back from what he agreed to yesterday; but I would not let him. I failed in inducing him to make any concession. I then went to the Duke; used every argument in my power, but could do nothing with him. Aberdeen, Bathurst, Melville, and the Chancellor and Dudley are all very much annoyed. In fact, the point in dispute is worth nothing. I am not sure some farmers would not prefer the plan Huskisson agrees to that the Duke wishes to have. It might certainly be more beneficial to them under certain circumstances.

After dinner I wrote to Peel, Grant, and Huskisson. It will not be my fault if we break to pieces.

Aberdeen thinks Huskisson will not stay in if Grant goes out, and that Dudley would go with Huskisson.

The King is said to have been abusing us all to the Duke of Devonshire; and Aberdeen and Bathurst think the King will send for Lord Lansdowne at once.

The Duke has been ill all the week. He is disappointed at not carrying his own plan at once. He feels he is looked up to by the great landed interest, and he is afraid of being reproached by his friends. He thought a strong Corn Bill would give us a weight in the House and the country and strengthen the Administration. He imagines Huskisson and the others will make no concessions and expect them from him. In fact, they have made great concessions, and, I believe, really wish to keep the Government together. They have behaved very fairly. If we break up, it will be the Duke's fault, and his agricultural friends will be furious. The new Government would force a worse Bill upon the country. The Duke thinks they could not; but he is mistaken, and overcalculates his strength. He has only been approached by those who think as he does upon the Corn question, and he mistakes their voice for that of the nation. However, I believe public opinion is less favourable to the Bill than it was.

March 15.

Cabinet at 3. The Duke gave up his objection to the clause as agreed to by Huskisson; but, Huskisson acknowledging he was bound by it, argued against it, and said that, if Grant did not agree to it, he could not. Indeed, generally he said he could support nothing Grant did not feel he could propose, and must go out if Grant did.

Grant was very obstinate; but Peel and Huskisson told him they were as much responsible as he was for the Bill of last year, Huskisson more so, and [1] more so still.

Peel suggested, in order to obviate one of Grant's objections, that, instead of adding 5s. throughout, Is. 5rz. should be added to the duty; and, in order to get rid of another objection, it was agreed that the new duty should cease if the aggregate average price for, say, six consecutive weeks, commencing after the imposition of the duty, should not rise to 66s. before December 31 next ensuing. This was to prevent the duty lasting, as it might, for years. The other change was to prevent the fall of duty being too sudden at last.

Grant has taken these plans into consideration, and I conclude we shall agree now.

I had some conversation at dinner with Gosford, Carnden, Stanhope, Falmouth, and the Duke of Newcastle, on the Corn Bill and politics generally. I find much is expected a change of pivot to 67.

The Duke of Newcastle seemed more reasonable than the others, and talked more sense.

I should say, from what I heard from all these peers, and particularly from Camden, who is very moderate, and Gosford, who voted for the Bill last year, that we cannot propose to one House less than we seem now to agree upon, without creating much dissatisfaction, and perhaps losing the Bill.

[1 A name omitted in the Diary.]

March 16.

Cabinet at 4. In the morning I sent to Lord Bathurst and the Duke a clause I had drawn out for the additional duty of Is. 5J., and wrote a note to the Duke to explain the mistake I had fallen into in supposing 5s. had been agreed to. The Duke wrote in answer that he was much surprised, and had imagined 5s. had been acceded to. On asking the different members of the Cabinet, I found most had thought Is. 5d. had been agreed to.

Huskisson seems inclined to back out of this too. First he agreed to 5s.; yesterday to Is. 5c., and now he says 20s. is too high a price at 66s. imperial.

I do not think the Duke will make any further concessions, and I do not feel inclined to make any. It must be settled to-morrow.

After that we talked about the Eussian war. I strongly urged the expediency of declaring the Treaty of London to be at an end whenever Eussia issued her manifesto, on the ground that, being at war, she could not give a joint instruction. Besides she has plainly declared that, if we will not agree to the mode of operation she proposes, she will not consider herself bound by the stipulations of the treaty; and the real object we had from the beginning having been the prevention of a Eussian war, the commencement of that war makes the attainment of that object quite impossible, and therefore absolves us from the obligation of the treaty. However, I did not find the others agree with me.

I said our object now should be to get back our

60   Ministers to Constantinople, and to connect ourselves with France for the purpose of checking the advance of Kussia by our joint influence. Absolved from the strict obligations of the treaty, we are still morally bound by our language to Greece and to Turkey. We must pursue the same object, that of the pacification of Greece, but in the spirit of peace and conciliation in which the treaty was formed.

Dudley and the Chancellor seemed to think with me that the declaration of war by Russia would absolve us from the treaty as regards Russia. I doubt how far it would as regards France.

France seems disposed to go all lengths with Russia. The change of Government there has been most unfortunate. The Chambers are masters of the country. The King is unpopular, and has no power; the Ultras desire war to strengthen their Government, the Bona-partists to regain what France has lost. I believe they will send troops to Greece. If they act by themselves, the treaty will be quite broken.

March 17.

Cabinet at 3 on Corn. Agreement of all except Grant on the plan of adding Is. 5d. to the duty on Grant's scale. Grant still obstinate. If he goes out Huskisson will. I now think Grant's going out, even if followed by Huskisson's, would do no harm. Grant would not return for some time. Huskisson would come back in six months. I dare say Lord Bathurst would hold his office for him for that time with the Presidency of the Council.

61   At 10 we had another Cabinet on Greek affairs. I wrote in the course of the day a paper containing my views on the subject, and, to put them more clearly, a draft of a reply to Nesselrode's letter, and of a letter to Polignac. What was settled was this, that we should say to Eussia in effect, 4 We are very sorry you are going to war. We will not. We refer you to what we have already said on that subject. We do not see how you, who are going to war, can co-operate with vis who will not go to war; but we do not admit that your going to war absolves you from the self-denying obligations you have contracted with us. We are as desirous as ever of accomplishing the objects of the treaty, and we will endeavour to concert with France measures for that purpose It was determined at the Cabinet in the morning that a Bill should be brought in authorising the giving to the son of Mr. Canning the pension his father had but never enjoyed. The Duke inclined to leaving the measure in the hands of Spring Eice. I suggested

it should be taken up by the Government, and this will be done. It is but a matter of common justice.

The worst possible accounts have been received tonight from Lisbon. The English troops will have begun to embark on the llth. Their sailing will be the signal for violent reaction. Villa Real has no hopes.

March 18.

Found Aberdeen at the Cabinet room. He did not know whether Grant yielded or not; nor did anybody in the House.

Lamb has written doleful accounts of the state of things at Lisbon, but he states no facts. It is all panic. He has taken upon himself to detain the troops, that is, 3,000. The rest are gone, three regiments to the Mediterranean, and the cavalry and artillery horses. The 3,000 others left have only four guns.

We had a Cabinet at 10. At first all seemed for withdrawing the troops immediately, till Huskisson came in, and endeavoured to persuade us to keep them there. He said we should do so for the protection of the Constitutionalists to whom we had promised our support, and for the security of British property. In fact he made an insidious attempt to obtain a continuance of Canning's policy. We had a skirmish. At last it was carried that the troops should return in forty-eight hours; that a line-of-battle ship should remain, and the marines (300) keep fort St. Julian, while the ship remained. That the strongest language should be used to Miguel.

The objections I felt and stated to keeping the troops were, that they were not enough to act with effect, even had they a right to interfere, and orders to do so. That to interfere would be in violation of our declared policy, and unwarrantable. That such interference would lead to the continued occupation of the Spanish fortresses by French troops. That it was impossible to see all the consequences of the measures, and it was most dangerous to take a first step without being able to see our way to the second and third.

We went to Portugal to execute a treaty. We had no right to promise our support to the Constitutionalists.

Sir F. Lamb reasoned against the troops remaining on the 8th, and detained them on the 12th. He seems quite panic-struck, and has fallen into the hands of the Constitutionalists.

Palmerston said if we allowed the Constitution to be overthrown, we should appear to have been so many dupes. I said I did not believe there were three dupes in England. Dudley, who was on the other side, there being some noise at the time, thought I said he had been a dupe and was very angry. He desired to know why he was a dupe? c. It was some time before the noise allowed of his hearing. I had said the reverse of what he supposed.

In fact I think he has done all that could be done to maintain the tranquillity of Portugal by maintaining its existing institutions. The perfidy of Miguel, if he be perfidious, of which we have as yet no proof, is an element over which we had no control. I always expected the Constitution would be practically overthrown.

Huskisson receives communications of which he makes use, which he does not lay before the Cabinet. I imagine that the chief business of his office is conducted through private letters, a bad practice which has recently grown up, and which deprives a successor of the knowledge he ought to possess.

March 19.

Cabinet dinner at Peel's. After dinner some conversation about the mode of dealing with Penrhyn and East

Retford. Peel proposing the first for Manchester, the second for the Hundreds. I only object to establish-i ing a principle which may concede the necessity of) Parliamentary Eeform. Whatever the Government adopts in the Commons the Government should support in the Lords; but the Lords must first treat each question judicially.

Peel does not much like his position in the Commons. He is not sufficiently well supported. He will fight anything, but then, he says, if he is defeated, he will resign. I said I thought there had seldom been circumstances under which there was less of personal pleasure in belonging to a Government; but there had seldom been circumstances under which to abandon the administration on trifling grounds would have been more criminal. The Corn question, the Eussian question, and that of Portugal would all have been decided differently had there been a Whig Government.

It is very odd Grant never shows himself. He says nothing to the Duke. He was not at the last Cabinet, nor at the dinner to-day. They think he will go out. It would be a god-send for us if he would, and do more than anything else to strengthen the Government.

March 20.

Grant has made no communication yet to the Duke of Wellington.

In the House Lord Strangford asked some questions of Dudley respecting the war between Brazil and Buenos Ayres, which is a war maintained on both sides solely for the purposes of piracy, under the name of blockade. Lord Londonderry took occasion to attack Canning's foreign policy. I walked home with Eosslyn, who is very friendly to the Government. We talked over Canning's legacies.

March 21.

Cabinet at 3. Dudley's answer to Lieveri. Very well written, but too long, and going into some unnecessary points.

The Duke has written a letter to Grant to bring the matter of his staying in or going out to a point.

March 22.

Grant is not yet brought to a point, and his conduct is most contradictory. He never comes to a Cabinet, and yet he sits on the Treasury Bench, and was present when there was some objection made to some business coming on on Friday, the 28th, because Corn was fixed for that day. There was only a majority of thirty-six for throwing the representation of East Eetford into the Hundred. This is not agreeable.

Cabinet at 4. "We finished Dudley's paper. He writes well, but he never embraces the whole reasoning at one grasp of the mind. He writes one day what is inconsistent with what he wrote ten days before. His papers give a great deal of trouble. In this paper he has omitted the strongest point. He wanted to insert a sort of defence of the Treaty of London, a defence certainly gratuitous in a paper addressed to Russia. I am afraid now that he will not argue the point of Russia being pledged to abstain from conquest, high enough. He is strangely obstinate sometimes. VOL. i. F

66

March 23.

Wrote a note to Dudley, urging him to introduce the passages in Nesselrode's note of Dec. 25, which pledge the Emperor to abstain from conquest dans aucun hypothese, in extenso. He called upon me in the course of the day, and I understood from him that he had done so. He told me, in answer to a question, that he thought Grant meant to bolt; but I gathered from his expressions that he intended to stay.

Lord Stuart de Eothesay called upon me. He told me the questions Lord Strangford put to Dudley the other night had no other object than that of raising the price of Brazilian Stock, in which Lord Strangford has invested all his property. Indeed Lord Strangford confessed as much to Lord Stuart. Lord Stuart thoroughly hates Canning, and so does every one who served under him.

March 24.

Found Aberdeen at the Cabinet room. Walked with him to the House. Met Lord Bathurst, who had been to see the Duke, and found him well, notwithstanding the accident he had on Saturday night. He fell out of his cabriolet on his face and found it necessary to be cupped.

Grant was waiting for an audience. He saw the Duke yesterday, and brought some inadmissible proposition. Aberdeen asked Dudley about it, and rather understood he meant to go out if Huskisson did, and he said he must if Grant did. Aberdeen thinks

67

we have hardly a day to live, and that the King will take the first opportunity of turning the Duke out, and getting back Lansdowne and Lord Carlisle. The worst of it is that our friends are out of humour and go away. They will not vote. Some of them wish us to dissolve Parliament. They are all out of humour with Peel. They think he does not take a line high enough. I had a long talk with Falmouth and endeavoured to soothe him. He is more out of humour than any. Amongst other things he wished Penrhyn to be thrown into the Hundred. They say we should have had a better division for throwing East Eetford into the Hundred if we had endeavoured to throw Penrhyn into it too; but the idea of a compromise cooled all our people.

Dispatches of the 15th have been received from Lamb. He seems to think both parties are in such a fright that they are ready to run away, but the Constitutionalists are most frightened. Miguel has dissolved his Chambers, and has not instanter convoked a new Chamber, which it seems is contrary to the foolish Charter. Lamb talks of forcible interference on our parts, sanctioned, as he expects, by the rest of Europe, as a matter of course; at least a measure of policy and honour. The fact is, he, on his arrival, fell into the hands of the Constitutionalists, and has seen onlytwith their eyes.

March 25.

Cabinet at 3. Before the Cabinet entered upon other business the Duke read a letter from Grant, notifying his resignation. Huskisson will resign too. Whether Dudley and Palmerston will is uncertain.

68

Probably they will. They have no excuse for doing so, and will be scandalised in the House.

The Chancellor thinks the King will regret Dudley, but that he will hold to the Duke, and that the Government will be recomposed. If it should be, it is doubtful how we can get on in the House of Commons.

After we had received this communication, and the Duke had expressed his regret, and Huskisson, in a low tone of voice, spoke of the consequences, Palmerston made a feeble attempt to reconcile the difference, which is in itself small. Grant wishes the new duty to cease in sixteen weeks. The Cabinet agreed it should cease on the first of January.

We then proceeded to other business. France withdraws her proposition to assist Eussia, and only wishes to send a few troops that we may get Ibrahim Pasha out of the Morea, and then speak with authority to Eussia and Turkey, and unite with Austria and Prussia. A note is written to Granville expressive of the wish of our Government to continue united with France, and in another note he will be desired to draw out their opinions as to union with Austria and Prussia.

Codrington has instructions to decline acting with Count Hey den, should he receive orders to act as a belligerent. We do business quickly as we come near our dissolution.

Dined with Janet at the Duke's. The Duke and Duchess of Clarence were to have dined there; but the Duke of Clarence has been ill the last few days. He has a rupture. He is exhausted, but upon the whole better.

69 There were at dinner the two Peels, two Aberdeens, Lady Westmeath, Lady G. Bathurst, Lord Bathurst, Lord Beresford, Lord Hill, Sir Byam Martin, Sir George Cockburn, Sir E. Owen, Dudley, the two Lyndhursts, the two Arbuthnots.

After dinner we had some conversation about our situation. Grant has written to Huskisson saying that, as he heard nothing, he supposed the question was still open, and proposed taking a duty of 23s. at 62s. imperial, instead of 20s. Sd. This duty to fall and rise by two shillings. This duty would give less at 65s. and 66s. than he proposed before.

Grant. 62

Peel wrote to Huskisson, suggesting that we might still find a permanent duty which would be equivalent to the plan the Cabinet had now determined on, and more simple, and which Grant might accede to.

Huskisson is to see the Duke at eleven to-morrow on this point. I do not expect they will come to an agreement. If we are to break off, we cannot break off at a better point than where we are now.

The Chancellor is confident the King will be firm and faithful to the Duke. If he be so the sooner we break off the better for us, and I hope Dudley and Pal-merston will accompany Huskisson. Huskisson we shall get back by himself at the end of the Session. If Huskisson alone went out, Lord Bathurst would be Secretary for the Colonies, and President till tlie end of the Session, and the Board of Trade would be filled up permanently.

March 26.

Heard from the Chancellor in the House that nothing was yet settled, Grant having till late on Friday left to him to decide.

Lord Carlisle and others have had a meeting at Holland House.

Dudley told the King to-day in what a state we were. This he had no right to do. To tell the King the Cabinet differences, which have not yet had any result, is either betise or treachery. The Chancellor saw the King too, to-day. The Chancellor's only wish is to keep Dudley in.

We dined at Huskisson's. Not a word said about corn. The dinner excellent, and tres recherche. The plate, c., very handsome.

The House to adjourn only to Easter Monday week, as the business is much in arrear.

March 27.

Called on the Duke at 11. Eode down to Downing Street with him. He told me Huskisson agreed yesterday to the proposal he made, which is that of making the duty at 62s., Is. 4d., and rising and falling by Is. Peel saw Grant yesterday, but made nothing of him. Palmerston saw him to-day.

The Duke said he should speak to the King to-day, as Dudley had done so. We thought when this was over we should go on better, as Huskisson and the others must feel they could not act as a party, and say, There are four of us." The Duke will speak to Huskisson on the subject.

I went over to the Cabinet room and began drawing the resolutions. If Grant goes out they will not be moved till Monday. I think they should not be moved till after Easter, when the Government will be resettled, and all our friends in London. The Duke seemed to doubt whether Frankland Lewis w r ould remain if Grant went. I have no doubt of his staying, and he will do the business better than Grant.

"Went to the levee. The Duke had an audience, and told the King in what state we were, saying he should not have mentioned it unless he had known that Dudley had spoken of it to His Majesty, as he was unwilling to trouble him with a difference which might have no result. He reminded the King that Huskisson had not stipulated for Grant, and that therefore there could be no reason for his going out with him. He told the King they would all support the Bill. The King said then Huskisson might go out, support the Bill, and return. The Duke said he had rather not think yet of the measures to be pursued if an event occurred which he still hoped would not take place. The King seemed satisfied. I saw him receive Huskisson very graciously, and he seemed to desire him to remain to speak to him after the levee.

Huskisson, the day before yesterday, wrote to Grant, and told him his conduct would be the occasion of his terminating his public life in bitterness.

Madame de Lieven says of Dudley's last paper that it was, ' tres peu satisfaisant et tres dilatoire." Lieven, when he got it, took out his watch and said ' quinze-jours!"

March 28.

Went at 3 to Downing Street. The Duke, whom I saw, had not yet heard anything decided from Grant; but expected him to go out. Huskisson was to go to the King at 3, to be talked into staying if Grant bolted (this is Dudley's expression). At half after 3 the Duke sent Goulburn to Grant to know his final determination. His answer was that he was too unwell to bring forward the resolutions to-day, but that he would on Monday. The Duke sent to me to tell me of this, which surprised him very much, and I told Lord Bath-urst and Aberdeen, and afterwards, in the House, the Chancellor and Lord Melville. The Chancellor had written to Huskisson at one, and had for answer that Grant's mind when he last heard from him was in a hopeless state.

I much regret this termination. I had rather lead the Opposition than continue Privy Seal; and if the Canning leaven had gone out we should have gone on so comfortably together, and have been so much stronger. It was a great error ever to admit them. The

King has a weakness for Dudley, but pretended he only wished to keep Huskisson. Dudley amuses the King.

In the House there was much disappointment at the Corn question being put off, and there was a report we were all quarrelling about it.

March 29.

The Duke dined with me, and told me he had had a very satisfactory conversation with Polignac. The King of France and the French Government entirely agree with us that, if France and England continue united, the invasion of Turkey by Eussia becomes comparatively harmless. They now seem to intend to direct their powers against Algiers, instead of the Morea. They must be moving, and they care little where.

I had some conversation with Arbuthnot after dinner. He thinks the Duke is much annoyed at the conduct of the four, and will be very glad to get rid of them, or to break their union, whenever he can. He thinks Grant will resign at last. So do I, and I doubt his bringing the question forward on Monday. I think he will be indisposed. That Peel will do it, and when he sees his retirement cannot bring with it the resignation of the others, he will go out. I think he can hardly show his face in the Cabinet after all that has passed. He has shown such weakness!

I do not think Dudley is comfortable. The King returned to the Cottage to-day.

March 30.

Cabinet at 10. Neither Grant nor Huskisson there. Aberdeen made an ineffectual attempt to have the duty on oats raised.

March 31.

In the House the Duke, in moving for papers relating to corn, opened the new Bill. Upon the whole the feeling of the House was favourable to the plan. Goderich expressed his wish to take the most favourable view of the measure, feeling the necessity of settling the question. This sentiment was cheered by Lansdowne. Falmouth said he was disappointed. King was outrageous, and did no good by abuse of the measure. The Duke of Newcastle, Delawarr, Salisbury, were satisfied. So were others who voted for the Bill of 1827, not liking it. Lauderdale and Eosslyn do not seem satisfied. Upon the whole things looked well. The Duke made a very judicious speech, and said much in favour of the agricultural interest. This soothed many who would otherwise have been hostile. The Duke of Newcastle is more reasonable than most of the Ultras.

April 1.

The Corn resolutions were moved by Grant in the House last night, in a speech which concluded by a foolish flourish about that great man Canning, and which showed he proposed the duties contre gre. In short he showed we had gained the victory.

The civil war in Mexico is over, the Vice-President General Bonar, who was at the head of the insurrection, being taken. A Bill was brought in, in order to try him for treason, and carried, but by a small majority, and it seems the people are surprised he is to be tried at all. So natural are revolutions in that country that treason is hardly considered a crime.

Peel told me the agriculturists were well satisfied in the House of Commons. I met Grant at the Foreign Office. I believe he means to stay in altogether now.

75

April 2.

The Turks have proclaimed an armistice for three months to enable the Greeks to consider terms of submission offered to them. The Turks offer amnesty, relief from taxes for a year to come, all former privileges, c. The Duke thinks much may be made of this, and that it will at any rate prevent the intended expedition of French troops to the Morea. I think the chief advantage is that it makes all co-operation on our side with Eussia still more impossible than it was before.

After the Cabinet dinner, which the Duke gave, as no one had sent out invitations, thinking, I suppose, that the Government would break up, we heard a paper of Dudley's, addressed to Prince de Polignac, proposing a definition of the Treaty of London. There was a disposition on Huskisson's part to accede to a proposal of Austria, received this day, to effect the. entire independence of Greece, if the Turks refused to accede to our propositions for a qualified independence. The Duke declared he would not go beyond the treaty. We had a good deal of discussion respecting the meaning of the word suzerainete. Some wished Greece should not follow Turkey in peace and war. Huskisson wished to give more than a commercial character to the agents of Greece. However, we ended by keeping within the treaty, and where we could not agree upon a definition we repeated the words of the treaty, and left it as obscure and as vague as before.

Huskisson reproduced a suggestion he made a week ago, that the clause of the Foreign Enlistment Bill should be repealed, which prevents shipbuilding for foreign Powers. I hate the whole Foreign Enlistment Bill, but I believe it is a right measure. The Duke objected to the proposed amendment, and at half-past twelve I left him and Huskisson with a few others still talking upon the subject. It seems Mr. Palmer intends to put a question on the subject. There are orders from Egypt and Algiers, c., to the extent of 500,000., which cannot be executed as the Act stands.

Grant reappeared at the Cabinet dinner. I think the Duke is disappointed at his remaining, and heartily repents having ever brought him and the Canningites into his Cabinet. I wish they were out.

April 3.

I sat as a Commissioner to give the Eoyal assent to some bills. While I was there the Chancellor said to me, ' We should have no Cabinets after dinner. We all drink too much wine, and are not civil to each other. Last night Huskisson went away much annoyed, and declaring if the repeal of the clause in the Foreign Enlistment Bill was proposed lie could not oppose it. The Duke, too, was rather out of humour."

I think Huskisson is annoyed at his position. Every one was disgusted with Grant's speech, and it was foolish, for it showed we had not only brought the horse to the water, but made him drink too.

After the House I went to the Foreign Office with the Duke, Aberdeen, and Dudley. Esterhazy is to see all we have done since the Eussian note of December 25, and so is Bulow. The Austrians, having held back a long time, are now, in ignorance of what we have been doing, inclined or rather prepared to go further than we wish. A very little douce violence will bring them back; but if they should communicate their readiness to declare the independence of Greece, and effect it by force, should the Turks refuse to accede to our propositions, they may undo all we have been doing during the last fortnight. As it is, France and England agree almost entirely. This has been effected by the Duke's good sense and influence.

Miguel ordered his troops not to play the Constitutional Hymn. Our troops continued to play it, and to gather crowds around their barracks. This is very offensive and very foolish. The Duke is very angry with Clinton about it.

April 4.

The Cabinet met at 3. The first thing brought forward was the question of the; Canning Pension." It seems Canning's son was well satisfied with the arrangement made by the Government, but his mother was not. She wrote letters and made her son write letters in a very improper and intemperate style to Huskisson, and they now insist on having the same provision made for Canning's son that was made in the case of Lord Chatham a most extraordinary instance of infatuation. Lord Morpeth is to make a motion on the subject on May 13, unless something satisfactory should in the meantime be done by the Government. He wants to make a flashy speech, and it seems gave notice of this motion without communication with his father and his friends. Lady Canning treats Huskisson as a traitor to Canning's memory.

We had then a long discussion about the definition of suzerainete, which may mean anything from the palfrey[1] of the King of Naples up to real dominion. Peel was particularly desirous that Greece should not follow Turkey in war. The Duke's idea was that the power of Turkey over Greece should be the same as that she had over Eagusa. That indeed was the idea of those who signed the Protocol.

Certainly it would be an embarrassment for Turkey to be followed in war and in peace by Greece unless she held the fortresses, which she is not to do; and if Turkey were to be answerable for all the piracies of the Greeks she would be involved in continual quarrels. Turkey, however, has a right to demand that Greece, separated from her dominion, shall not be made a place d'armes for Eussia.

Polignac asks, ' Is Eussia considered to have placed herself out of the treaty? Do you refuse altogether to act in concert with her?" Dudley seemed to think we must answer directly these questions. Palmerston inclined to act with Eussia. Generally there is an indisposition to declare Eussia oijt of the treaty.

I said, ' We have told Eussia we think she has made co-operation difficult, if not impossible; but that by declaring war on her own grounds she has not absolved herself from the obligations of the treaty." We have told France ' This is the language we hold to Eussia;[1] The kingdom of Naples was held of the Holy See by the tribute of a white palfrey.]

but we are ready to discuss immediately, in concert with you, the measures necessary for carrying the treaty into effect." Let us wait till we receive answers, and in the meantime refer France to what we have said to Russia, telling her, if she can propose any mode of co-operation with Russia, Russia being a belligerent, we are ready to consider it." This seemed to be the opinion of the Cabinet.

Peel wanted orders to be sent to Codrington; the Duke especially objected to our giving joint instructions with Russia.

Dudley has sent Esterhazy's memorandum to Lord Granville, without any directions. He will communicate it to the French Government; and, if he does, he will undo all we have been ten days in accomplishing. Esterhazy and Bulow have seen the papers which have passed since the changes of Government. They are well pleased.

After we had disposed of these questions, Huskisson stated the various questions connected with slavery. The first is that of compulsory manumission. The second that of allowing slaves to be transferred under certain restrictions from one island to another. The third that of fugitive slaves.

He was inclined to adhere to the course to which the Government is pledged, and to enforce compulsory manumission. He was of opinion that the Privy Council might be enabled to authorise the transport of slaves from one colony to another, on the condition of their not being employed in opening new lands. It seems that, as to the third point, Lord Bathurst had proposed that the fugitive slaves should be sent back to all countries where the offence of running away was not punished with death. 100 slaves have gone over from the Swedish Island of St. Martin's to our little Island of Arquilla. These men are not slaves, and they have no means of subsistence.

April 7.

The revenue is improving. The receipts of the year just ended are one million beyond the receipts of the last, and the receipts of the last quarter half a million. I read Lamb's last dispatches of the 22nd. The order of the day to the troops, issued by Miguel, is violent; but his appointment of a commission to arrange the mode of proceeding to the election of the new Cortes is not contrary to the Charter, as Lamb says. He cannot have read the document he encloses, or he must be quite twisted by the representations of the people into whose hands he fell on his arrival. He wishes to kidnap and remove the Queen.

Esterhazy is delighted with the papers we have sent to Paris and Petersburg. He told me Lord Londonderry was talking very foolishly at Paris, holding very anti-liberal language, and giving out that he was in the confidence of the Duke of Wellington, and that the feeling of our Government was anti-liberal. This before

Pozzo.

April 8.

In London I met Peel, who told me the Corn Bill was succeeding very well.

Lord Hertford, whom I met at dinner at Esterhazy's, said he was quite satisfied with it; but wished to have something done in the matter of wool. They would be satisfied with raising the duty from Id. to 36?. It was once 6d. If we had no Huskisson in the Cabinet this would be done.

Bulow told me he was very much pleased with what we had done about Greece.

April 10.

The French regret our determination not to employ any military force in the Morea, but they follow our example. They regret, too, that we should think the co-operation of Eussia impossible.

April 12.

Went to Downing Street. While I was there Dudley returned from Windsor.

Eead Lord Granville's dispatches of April 7. M. de la Ferronays is earnest that we should act with the Eussian fleet in ' the prosecution' of the Greek treaty, and so hold Eussia to her engagements, otherwise he says we shall be obliged to make war to prevent her aggrandisement. He has asked from Eussia an explanation of what-she means by the word ' indemnity ' used in Nesselrode's letter.

Eead Lamb's dispatches. The troops are arrived, thank God! Lamb says the English are very unpopular with both parties. The continued occupation of the forts is a subject of much dissatisfaction.

Lamb saw Miguel on the 31st. He heard him quietly, but when he asked him to dismiss his ministers, Miguel said decidedly, ' Je ne les changerai pas. Je VOL. i. G. suis content d'eux. Je ne crois pas ce qu'on m'a dit de'vous. Pour les Miriistres, je ne les changerai pas." His answer was so decided that Lamb made no further observation than one of regret, and came away.

April 13.

Cabinet at 4. Orders are to be sent out immediately for the evacuation of the forts, and the return of the ships from the Tagus. A brig is to be left cruising about, to return to Lisbon every now and then. Lamb is to go to Cintra, leave his secretary of embassy in Lisbon, have an eye on what is going on, but take no part. If Miguel declares himself King, his powers expire of course. If he commits any act of outrage Lamb is to report, but not come away.

Dudley thinks Lamb is in a passion. Huskisson did not say a word for him. He is very anxious to return; but he must not do so yet. Huskisson expects Don Pedro in Europe before twelve months are over. I think it very likely. I suggested to Dudley that this was his time for pressing Don Pedro to make peace with

Buenos Ayres.

April 14.

At Lady Hertford's Lord Beresford told me we had done very wrong in keeping the forts in the Tagus, and had made ourselves very unpopular by it, and put ourselves in the wrong for no purpose, for the occupation of them was of no use. However, at the time the order for retaining them was given, we could hardly have exposed English property to the risk of being quite unprotected, and it was thought the ships could not remain unless we had the forts. We were obliged to a certain extent to give credit to our Ambassador's opinion. However, the orders are gone out for withdrawing from the Tagus altogether.

Lord Longford told me he was satisfied with the Corn Bill, but he believed the Irish generally were not.

Littleton and Lord Talbot told me the Government was gaining great strength in the country.

April 15.

House. Lord Grey moved the omission of an amendment, introduced by Lord Lansdowne into the Criminal Law Consolidation Bill, by which the bodies of murderers were not to be dissected.

Told the Duke of Wellington I had been looking into the facts relative to the wool question. Lord Harewood has written to Leeds for the information I want relative to the price of woollen manufactures at different periods, the expense of the manufacture, and the quantity and cost of the wool, contained in a given quantity of the manufactured article.

April 17.

Committee on coins and silver currency at 12. It is proposed for the purpose of affording a market line to the silver of South America (which cannot be said to exist now, as little is used for plate, and silver is not received for coinage at the Mint), of extending the metallic basis of the currency, and facilitating the adjustment of the exchanges, to receive silver at the Mint, and to give for it silver notes, the silver to be estimated at to the gold of our currency, which is the proportion established in France.

The officers of the Mint will be examined, and the Governor and Deputy-Governor of the Bank.

I am to read a paper of Huskisson's on the subject; and several books on coins. It seems to me that these silver notes may displace a portion of our paper-currency, but I do not see how they will afford solidity to what remains. They will be exported in preference to gold, to adjust the exchange, and so far prevent a run upon the Bank, and a panic. Silver is not to be made a concurrent tender by law, but the Government and the Bank will receive silver notes.

House at 5. Eepeal of the Sacramental Test. Lord Holland made a long historical speech; he exaggerated the grievance, and forgot the Indemnity Bills. Lord Eldon exaggerated the security and forgot the Indemnity Bills too. Durham, 1 Chester, 2 York, 3 and Kaye. 4 Kaye best. Chester, like a schoolmaster. Durham in rather a slovenly manner. Eldon was very solemn, but he would not have divided ten. The Duke did not explain the grounds on which the Government had acted very clearly. Goderich spoke, and all about himself. He seems to think it necessary he should always speak. On the whole it was a dull debate.

Before the debate Dudley showed me the dispatches he had just received from Lord Cowley and Lord Gran-ville. Lord Cowley hears the Eussians mean to attack Turkey at all points, and to bring the army from Persia 1 Van Mildert. 2 Bloinfield, afterwards Bishop of London. 5 Hon. E. Vernon. 4 Lincoln. ED. upon Trebizonde, which is a place valuable from its position, and the copper there. The Emperor of Austria has written to the Emperor of Eussia deprecating war, expressing a hope that the great Powers united may still obtain from Turkey the concessions required by the Treaty of London, and likewise the necessary satisfaction to Eussia.

Lord Granville represents La Ferronays as very desirous we should allow the Eussiari fleet to act with ours under common instructions (those before agreed to). La Ferronays seems to think that the refusal of Eussia to do this would leave her bound by the self-denying obligations of the Greek treaty. We have already said she is so bound, her own act having made co-operation impossible, or at least nearly so. La Ferronays puts a case which would certainly present much difficulty that of our having induced Ibrahim to leave the Morea, and the Hussions attacking him on his voyage to Egypt. It is not very likely to occur, but certainly the inconveniences of not acting with the Eussians may be as great as those of acting with them. We must have a Cabinet on this point. Dudley is for acting with them.

The French are going to increase their army and navy and raise a loan of four millions.

The Duke, whom I saw in the House, is rather annoyed at the naval as well as military preparations of France. He is very unwilling to consent to the cooperation of the Eussian fleet, now Eussia is at war.

The French army is to be increased 70,000 men.

April 19.

Committee on Coins at 12. Mr. Bingley, of the Mint, examined. We had afterwards some conversation about granting a Committee on Wool in the Lords. Huskisson has pledged himself against it in the Commons. He thinks it would create great alarm amongst the manufacturers, and that to lay on a duty would ruin our export trade, which, even now, can hardly maintain itself.

Littleton, whom I saw at Devonshire House last night, says the Duke of Wellington's examination on military points struck the Finance Committee very much. Hardinge did himself great credit, and the general opinion was that he should hold a higher situation than he does.

Brougham and the Whigs seem in better humour than they were at first.

April 21.

House at 5. Sacramental Test Eepeal. We wished to keep the Bill as it came up from the Commons without alteration; but the feeling in favour of giving some more solemn sanction to the declaration was so strong that we were obliged to yield, and did it well. The Duke moving, first, ' in the presence of God," and afterwards, ' upon the true faith of a Christian."

We resisted converting the declaration into an oath, and had 100 to 32. This decision, and our introduction of the words, c upon the true faith of a Christian," enabled us to resist Lord Winchelsea's amendment, ' in

Jesus Christ the Son of God," and another foolish amendment of Lord Tenterden's, which we did not think it worth while to speak against. We managed to keep the bishops with us, to divide with a great majority, to resist successfully amendments which would have nullified the measure, or converted it into a penal law, and to have all the grace of concession.

I had to speak twice. I believe I spoke at the right time, and did well.

April 22.

Committee on Coins at 12. Examined the Governor and Deputy-Governor of the Bank. The latter, a man of some understanding; the former, a dolt.

House at 5. The Eussians have sent a threatening note in answer to our reply to theirs of December 20. It has been read to the Duke and Dudley; but not yet delivered to them. It is of great length refers to conversations between Canning and Lieven objects altogether to our limitation of Greece, and to the proposed connection of Greece and Turkey, but still offers the co-operation of the Eussian fleet in the blockade, to which, however, objections are taken on the ground of its insufficiency. The passage of the Pruth is deferred till May 10, on account, it is said, of the state of the weather.

April 24.

The Duke told me the Eussians had written in a softer tone to France.

Young Prince George of Cumberland was behind the Woolsack in the House to-day. The Duke of Wellington said he never saw a boy look so mad.

We went into the Test Eepeal Bill. Eldon proposed a new preamble to the clause containing the declaration, taking his preamble from the Act of Union with Scotland and announcing that he meant to move the insertion, in the declaration, of the words, ' that I am a Protestant." The Chancellor was not ready in putting the question of the first amendment, and consequently we got into an irregular discussion, some talking of one amendment, and some of another. Old Eldon fighting hard and well. The argument was that without the words he proposed Catholics might be admitted to Corporations, as many of them would take the Oath of Supremacy. We rejected the alteration of the preamble by two to one, keeping our bishops. It was then proposed to adjourn the further consideration till to-morrow, to give further time for considering the other amendment. The Bishop of Chester wished to adjourn till Monday. On a division we had two to one for tomorrow, but only three bishops voted with us. The others went away.

On coming home I wrote to the Master of the Eolls, informing him of our difficulty, and asking his opinion as to the best way of getting out of it.

Eldon is gathering strength, and, as he always does when he is not well opposed in the first instance, he becomes more mischievous and grasping.

89

April 25.

I wrote to the Master of the Kolls and Lord Eosslyn suggesting that the words might be admitted, and the Test repealed only as to those who took the declaration, leaving all others under the Bill of Indemnity as before. This would not touch the Catholics and the Jews, who are now excluded by the declaration, and it would give the Dissenters all they ask; that is, it would relieve them from the necessity of being indemnified.

Saw Eosslyn, Leach, and Lord Holland. All of opinion this amendment should not be received. Blount and Battie say no Catholic can take the Oath of Supremacy, worded as it is now, without legislative explanation. They are willing to give the State the same assurance of loyalty, but in other words.

Cabinet at 3. The Chancellor decidedly of opinion that the declaration against transubstantiation ought to be taken by the governing members of Corporations by the Test Act. The proviso excepting churchwardens, c., shows others than those deriving their authority from the King must take it, and the enacting words might bear that interpretation too. He had found, too, by enquiry, that practically the Common Councilmen, c., in London, do take it. The Catholic therefore would be effectually excluded by the declaration against transubstantiation if he were not, as he is, by the Oath of Supremacy. We had just determined to resist the amendment when a letter came to the Duke from the King, expressing his wishes for the introduction of the words. We got the Duke and the Chancellor to go to the King instantly. The Duke thought it was too late. It was a quarter to four, and the Chancellor seemed rather unwilling to take upon himself the responsibility of an interpretation contrary to Eldon's, and talked of referring the question to the law officers. This would have created delay, and we should have had general defection and much clamour if the idea had got abroad that there was a difference between the King and the Government upon this point; so I fairly pushed the Chancellor out of his chair, and off they went.

L90

They came back in an hour, the King having declared he was satisfied to take the line approved of by his Ministers.

The Duke of Cumberland had do. ne this. In the House the Chancellor made an admirable speech in answer to Eldon. Eldon could not touch his argument, but spoke very well and frightened the bishops; so on a division they all ratted except three Fowler, Jenkinson,[1] and Ryder.[2] Bloomfield and another went behind the Woolsack. Almost all our friends voted with Eldon. We had only Salisbury, Thomond, Clarendon, Ormond, and two or three others beside the official men. I do not think we had twenty in all of our own people, but in the House we had seventy to forty-three, and with proxies 117 to 55. We had another division better than this on another point.

Huskisson and Grant wished to take some resolutions on Corn proposed by Benett, instead of ours, saying they should be pressed. These resolutions gave a higher duty at the low prices, and a lower duty at the high prices than ours. I said I would not yield unless 1 Bishop of St. David. 2 Bishop of Lichfield.

to a division. That it weakened a Government to recede lightly from what it had adopted on full consideration. That the reasoning in favour of our own scale of duties was unanswerable. That Huskisson's own speech could not be touched. That if we yielded we should on every occasion have our friends advancing their own conundrums. They went to a division upon it, and had 230 to 32!

Cabinet at 4. It was decided, in consequence of the receipt from Polignac of a dispatch informing the Government; that the French charge d'affaires at Petersburg had received assurances from Nesselrode that Eussia, notwithstanding France and England should not join in the war with her, would still consider herself bound by the treaty, and act with them in it, giving to her Admiral in the Levant the same instructions as should be given by France and England to theirs, and further that Eussia would only ask indemnity for the losses of her subjects;' to ask Polignac's permission to communicate this dispatch to Lieven, and to enquire from Lieven whether- he had authority to confirm these assurances. On obtaining such assurances from Lieven the conferences would be renewed. They were broken off when the Eussians declared in their note (from Petersburg), of February 26, that, if England and France did not join in the war, the Emperor would arrange the affairs of Greece ' selon ses interets et ses convenances."

The Eussians say the treaty can only be defined as to the limits of Greece after an armistice, and in concert with the Greeks and Turks. They are correct in point of strictness. They likewise say the tribute must be fixed after the limits are fixed, and that the only thing to be reserved to Turkey is the part determinee in the choice of the Chief of Greece.

The Duke told me at dinner that, after the House on Thursday, he wrote to the King to tell him the Household were not present. The King in his answer, received while we were at the Cabinet, first expressed his opinion as to Eldon's amendment. The Household did not come on Friday.

April 27.

G. Fortescue, whom I met riding in the Park, told me the report in London was that the King would refuse his assent to the Sacramental Test Eepeal Bill. I laughed at the story. However, the Chancellor, who dined with me, told me he had been a long time with the King, and that it was of the utmost importance we should get the Bill through to-morrow. The Catholic question, which was to have come on on Tuesday the 29th, is put off for ten days. This is to keep it clear of the Dissenters' Bill.

April 28.

Cabinet room at 3. Bead dispatches till near five. House. Sacramental Test Eepeal. The Duke had a satisfactory conversation with the King upon the subject. Lord Grosvenor made a most foolish speech, connecting the Bill with the Catholic question. Lord Eldon was delighted. I was obliged to speak a few words to restore the Bill to its right position. The debate was not very good. We had in the House 100, to 42, and with proxies 150 to 52 on Lord Eldon's motion to insert in the declaration " I am a Protestant." We had nine bishops to seven, I think.

April 29.

Went at 3 to the Cabinet room to read a paper transmitted by Lord Cowley, on the present state of Greece. It is written by an agent of Metternich's. There is nothing very new in it. It represents Capo d'Istrias as having managed with much adroitness to deprive Grivas, Colocotroni, and some other chiefs of their power. Capo's plan is to throw troops into the country north of the Morea, to excite insurrections there, that there may be an excuse for desiring the limits of Greece to be carried north of the Isthmus.

In the House I found from Dudley that Lieven had no instructions which enabled him to give the assurances we required; of course, therefore, we do nothing.

The Duke told me the sum of 250,000, respecting which there is some talk now, was the surplus of the French compensation to British subjects after the settlement of all claims; it belonged to the Crown as a droit, and was lent to the Woods and Forests for the completion of Buckingham House. Lord Liverpool, Canning, and Goderich were the only Ministers privy to this disposal of the money. An account should have been laid before Parliament. By a former Act the surplus of the Woods and Forests was given to Buckingham House, but the expenses in the parks have been so great that there has been no surplus. I am very glad the Duke had nothing to do with it.

The Eussians have fixed the day for passing the Danube, and for the attack on Shumla. They have about 120,000 infantry, 23,000 cavalry, and 400 pieces of cannon for the active operations. There is besides an army of reserve of 50.000 men. They have eight sail of the line, four large frigates, and four or five ships in the Black Sea. Dudley tells me the Turks have only 51,000 men, and that the infatuation at Constantinople is as great as ever. I think he much underrates the Turkish forces.

I look forward with horror to the war, not only as affecting the general interests of Europe, but as a war shocking to humanity.

April 30.

Cabinet dinner at Palmerston's. Huskisson ill, and not there. It seems that under Canning's Administration it was agreed to submit the question of American boundary in Maine to some European Sovereign. As the question goes to the security of our Canadian possessions, it should never have been let out of our own hands. This was one of Canning's follies. Dudley proposed the King of the Netherlands and the Swiss Cantons as one name, to be sent in sealed; it being agreed, to avoid all discussion, if possible, that in the first instance each party should send in two names; if both have chosen the same name, that Sovereign would be the umpire. The Duke objected to the King of the Netherlands, who, he said, was the most crotchety of men. He proposed the Emperor of Austria and the King of Sardinia as the only two Sovereigns who would do us justice. He said he should have been very well satisfied with the King of France if he would decide for himself, and not leave it to his Ministers. The Duke said M. de la Torre was a very clever man, and an honest man. He is the King of Sardinia's Minister.

They had a division in the Finance Committee today on a vote of censure on Lord Bathurst, containing the words; culpable neglect," moved by Mr. Stanley. The motion was negatived by a good majority.

At 3 met four woollen manufacturers at the Board of Trade. Their information made me doubt very much whether it would be prudent to lay any duty upon wool. They were much alarmed at the idea of a Committee. They said a Committee published all the secrets of trade, and this Committee would induce the withholding of orders, and disturb the trade, which was going on slowly but quietly. They said the raising of the price of English wool would lead to the greater use of cottons. That by keeping back their wool the wool-growers had given a premium upon foreign wool, and were now obliged to take a lower price. That there was now little pure Southdown wool. The Southdown sheep has been crossed with the Leicestershire for the purpose of enlarging the carcase and increasing the quantity of the wool. They have succeeded in both objects, but the wool is of an inferior quality. The sheep produces three-and-a-quarter, or three-and-a-half pounds, instead of two-and-a-half, and the wool has more staple, but it is coarser. Machinery invented last year enables them to comb this new Southdown wool, and it will be made into worsted. This is a new trade. The wool has lost its clothing qualities and acquired combing qualities. The manufacturers said the trade scarcely maintained itself. That the smallest addition of price would turn the market in favour of the German and American. Including duty, 33 per cent., and freight, woollen manufacturers must sell in America 50 per cent, beyond the cost price, to remunerate. They say men look more to price than to quality. A man continues to give 12.9. a yard for cloth, because he has been accustomed to do so. He does not pay a lower price for the same article he formerly used. The lower the article the greater the fall of price. All this shows the increase of wealth and luxury.

Afterwards came on Lord Darnley's motion for a Committee to enquire into the state of the distressed people of Ireland. He made a long desultory speech, and was answered by Lords Limerick and Longford. His object was to have an equal assessment on the land for the lame, sick, impotent, and aged. Lord Lorton talked of the Association and of the Catholic question. The Duke spoke discreetly and well. He did not say a word as to the Catholic question. We had no division.

Cabinet at 2. We first decided that the Catholic Association Bill should be allowed to expire. It has been ineffectual, and no attempt has been made to carry it into effect. It is too late to do so now. A stronger measure could hardly be devised. For renewing it there is no case, as this lias not been executed, and latterly things have been quieter in Ireland. Should the state of things become worse during the autumn we can come to Parliament with strong ground for new powers; especially if means are taken for enforcing the Common Law and the Convention Act. Orders will be sent to the Irish Government to this effect. It is considered in itself objectionable to renew a temporary Act. It naturally excites the jealousy of Parliament.

The Duke of Portland has had communications with Huskisson on the subject of the Canning pension. The family want to have an address to the Crown, and on that a Bill giving 3,000. a year for the Kves of Canning's two sons. The family have the precedent of Lord Chatham in their heads. They want the pension for two lives, because the eldest son has bad health, and they mean to sell the pension for 50,000. It was decided to adhere to our original plan. Huskisson said he must vote for the other measure if it was pressed. Palmerston and Grant seemed to intimate the same intention.

We then entered upon foreign policy. Polignac saw the Duke this morning. It seems the Committee to which the pro jet of the loan was referred in France have expressed a wish that a portion of it should be given to the Greeks. The French Government is quite in the hands of the Chamber of Deputies. The Liberals have got an accession of twenty or thirty more votes by the last elections.

We cannot renew the Conferences till we receive a written answer to our last paper. The Russian threat that, if we would not adopt hostile measures in conjunc-
tion with them, they would dispose of Greece ' selon leurs interets et leurs convenances," still remains unexplained. Neither have they given us any official explanation as to the nature of the ' indemnities ' they ask. France agrees with Eussia as to the limitation of Greece being a subject for the three Powers with Greece and Turkey to decide, and so it is in the treaty.

We send the commercial agent, contrary to our rule and the law of nations, but according to the treaty. As to money we cannot think of it, and troops we shall not send. We have a Cabinet on Sunday to consider what detailed reply shall be made to the French note.

Thus Eussia has gone to war and has thus virtually put herself out of the treaty. France, driven on by the Liberals, adopts for herself the measures she proposes, before she can receive an answer. The treaty, in as far as it was intended to be tripartite, is at an end. Each Power pursues her object in her own way.

The Duke complained to me in the House of the manner in which the four hang together. He hoped they would have ceased to do so after the Corn business. He would not be sorry to get rid of Dudley, Grant, and Palmerston. Our meeting with the manufacturers tomorrow is not to take place. Lord Bathurst thought there was no object in it, as the Duke of Eichmond was resolved to bring on his motion and have his Committee, at any rate. The Duke of Eichmond did not care about it, so the meeting will not take place.

Sunday ?, May 4.

I met Hardinge at Battersea and brought him to town. He told me I had disappointed the Whigs, They prophesied I should try to have everything my own way in the Cabinet, be quite impracticable, and go out in a huff in three weeks. They are much surprised at hearing I have given no trouble.

Went to the Cabinet room to read Polignac's last paper. It is quite in a different tone from any we have yet received very Eussian evidently written under the fear of the

Chamber of Deputies, and for them. The French say they received avec etonnement our proposal for communicating our limitation of Greece, c., to other Powers.

They consider it to be a violation of the treaty. They say, as the Eussians did, that by the treaty the Greeks and Turks must have a voice in fixing the limits of Greece, the tribute, c. They object to our limitation. They say nothing can be done without Eussia. They propose sending commercial agents, giving money, and sending 6,000 men each. In the meantime they have named their agent and given their money.

I did not like the tone of Dudley's. It was not sufficiently dignified it was too long and diffuse. Substantially it was right, because the Duke had sent him sense. Peel wished to relever that expression of the etonnement of the French Government. I thought the best mode of answering the expressions to which we objected was not by touching the expressions themselves, but by the general tone of grave dignity which should pervade our reply. Dudley had omitted altogether to notice the observations of the French upon our proposal to communicate what we decided upon as to Greece, to the other great Powers.

The arrangement now is that the pension should be given for the life of the younger son of Mr. Canning, the amount of it to be disposed of by Lady Canning and the eldest son. They can sell the pension for 30,000. We are, as a Government, to oppose any further proposition on the part of Canning's friends. Huskisson and the others are satisfied with this arrangement.

The Duke gave me a long letter to read from Sir F. Lamb. He is evidently thoroughly out of humour, and very desirous of coming home. The latter part of his letter has little to do with the subject, and is half mad.

May 6 House at 5. Game Bill. The Duke told me there was a letter from Codrington declaring he had no instructions. It seems Nesselrode is satisfied with our answer to the Russian declaration! This is inexplicable, as he was dissatisfied with our answer to his dispatch of December 25, and is at the same time irreconcilable with the tone of his last communication.

I went with Dudley to the Foreign Office to look over his answer to Polignac. It was afterwards sent home to me, and I made many alterations in it, raising its general tone, giving it, as I told Dudley, a little more of the toss of the head than it had at first, and making it shorter. There was a conversational, argumentative tone in it at first, which was not suited to the occasion or to the importance of the subject. It remains to be seen whether he will adopt my suggestions.

May 7 Called on Dudley at half-past twelve. He approved of all my proposed alterations except one, which on further consideration I disapproved of myself.

Eecorder's report at 3. The King apparently very well. The report very heavy. There were at least ten cases in which the punishment of death ought to have been inflicted. We chose six.

Cabinet dinner at Goulburn's. Codrington has written to say he has no instructions, and particularly that he has none on some specific points. His instructions were given on October 15. He acknowledged the receipt of them on November 7; said he should particularly attend to them, and actually issued orders on the specific points on which he now says he had no instructions. He will be recalled. Lord Melville mentioned Sir Thomas Williams as a fit man to succeed him. It seems Lord Exmouth is gone by.

Miguel has in some instances, it seems, taken the title of King; but at the critical moment his courage failed him, and he is as undecided as ever, saying one thing and doing another.

Dudley read his altered dispatch to the Duke, after dinner. The Duke approved of it highly.

Peel mentioned the circumstance of the King having signed no commissions for more than two years. He will not sign parchment. There can be no reason why the commissions should not be on thick paper; but they say the King would sign them for the first few days and then give it up.

May 8 Went to Dudley's to finish the paper, then to the Cabinet room. Codrington has written letters of defence and inculpation to Dudley and the Admiralty. They are well written; and as far as regards the question of the Greek slaves he has the best of the argument.

Lamb has written a letter to Dudley in rather an impertinent tone, and is much out of humour.

May 9 Foreign Office. Wrote a paper in reply to Codring-ton's, as a ground for recalling him. He will be recalled without reasons assigned. Probably Sir P. Malcolm will succeed him.

Lamb complains of Palmella's having communicated to his Government the first intelligence of the intended withdrawing of the troops from the forts, and of his attributing it entirely to his requisition, to bring the whole credit of it to himself. From the whole tenor of Lamb's dispatches he seems very much out of humour, and desirous of picking a quarrel with the Government. He wants to come back, having got the rank of Ambassador, and thus the claim to the higher pension.

May 10 It was decided not to bring away at once our Ambassador from Portugal, but to present a remonstrance and order him not to go to Court.

May 11 I sent Dudley a draft of a reply to Sir F. Lamb. It shortly answers his observations, and then says, ' that His Majesty's Government do not think it fitting that dispatches of a controversial nature, addressed by His Majesty's Ambassador to the Foreign Secretary, should remain on the records of the office, and therefore has directed that they should be withdrawn."

Dudley read his protest against the events of April 25 at Lisbon, and a paper on Campazana's proposal for drawing some Spanish troops to the frontier, and releasing Miguel from his obligations to the Courts of England and Austria on the subject of the Constitution. Of course we cannot hear of either plan. This paper, too, was well done, but there were some alterations to make in it.

Just as we were coining away Huskisson began to talk about co-operation with Russia, a point settled long ago, and on which we are pledged to one line of conduct by solemn public declarations of our views. This was got rid of; but the never-ending return to the same point annoys the Duke very much. I had some conversation at Countess St. Antonio's with Arbuthnot on the subject. He says the Duke is broken-hearted about his Cabinet, and deeply regrets having taken in the Canningites. Palmerston is always pecking. Grant is obstinate and useless. However, he is seldom there, and takes little part. Dudley would never give the least trouble if it were not for Huskisson, who sets him on. Huskisson is not to be trusted.

May 12 Lieven has communicated the Russian declaration of war. It expresses an absence of all ambition, and declares the Eussian territory is large enough, a very obvious truth. It claims pecuniary indemnity, not only for the Eussian subjects (as they had told France), but for the expenses of the war. This may be extended or contracted at their pleasure. They must have security for the maintenance of treaties, and the free navigation of the Black Sea. The Duke thinks they mean to keep the forts on the Bosphorus and the Dardanelles. Some fortresses, too, may be said to be necessary for the first object. As to the Treaty of London they are to use their influence to effect its objects; but then they wish to extend the Greek frontier, and their notions of suze-rainete seem different from ours.

Thus commences a war of which no statesman can see the end or calculate the consequences; but which, whatever may be its result, will inflict upon the population of the Turkish Empire calamities at which humanity shudders.

I find Bathurst and the others very angry indeed at Huskisson's revival of the old proposal for acting with the Eussians.

105 *May 13* Sir Francis Burdett's resolution in favour of the Catholics was carried last night by 6 272 to 266. Last year the number for was the same against, 276. I always had a presentiment the question would be carried. They say Peel was much annoyed at the division. The resolution is to be sent up to the Lords for their consideration.

Wool Committee. A very intelligent Lincolnshire farmer was examined. The newspapers report Don Pedro's having completed the act of abdication on March 3.

The French papers have a telegraphic account that Miguel was declared King in various places. The dispatch is dated Bayonne, May 10. We ought to have had a Cabinet to-day, for really the affair of the Admiral will not bear delay. I hear Huskisson begins to think he cannot make a good case against the Admiral, and is afraid of pressing his recall.

I had a long talk with Aberdeen about the state of the Government. The Russian circular says," No Power has disputed the justice of their right of going to war!" They want the approbation of other Powers. We should send a circular declaring our views, and repeating the language we have held.

There was a good deal of opposition, led by Lord Althorp and Bankes, to the proposed pension to Canning's son. They divided, more than fifty against it. I am not sorry for it, though I consider the measure to be an act of justice; but I like to see men
106 consistent, and anything is preferable to the humbug with which we have been so long disquieted. I find Salisbury does not like it, and, as for Lord Londonderry, he is mad about it.

May 14 Cabinet at 3. Decided to recall Sir E. Codrington. Dudley read his answers to Lamb on two points, and a dispatch explanatory of our conduct with regard to the Constitution and its supporters. All good and satisfactory.

May 16 The Duke has seen the Duke of Clarence, who approves of Codrington's recall, and thinks Sir P. Malcolm the best man to succeed him, but has some trifling objections which the Duke will get over. They relate to some difference he had with Lord Melville, relative to the duration of his command at St. Helena trifles.

May 17 Much talk about East Retford. No decision come to. Doubts how far Peel is pledged to give the representation to Manchester if Penrhyn should be thrown out.

Huskisson said he must vote for a town. Grant and Palmerston seemed the same way. Dudley is so too.

The Duke is very much dissatisfied with Planta and Palmerston. The former has taken the measure of publishing his eulogy on Canning on the occasion of the Pension Bill, and Palmerston took occasion to say, "A Government would only be entitled to support as it followed the principles of Mr. Canning." This has given great offence to our friends, and the Duke fears that, if Lord Grey should oppose the Bill, it may be thrown out in our House. I have no fears of that nature.

The Duke called the conduct of Planta and Palmer-ston a mutiny. I think he will do nothing while the Session lasts, but take the first opportunity of getting rid of Palmerston and Grant. That is Arbuthnot's idea. Hardinge, with whom I had some conversation after dinner, says Sir E. Knatchbull is the best man to be got in the House of Commons. V. Fitzgerald is the cleverest and is useful but he is unpopular, and would rather discredit a Government. Lord F. Leveson seems disposed to work and likely to do well. I never heard him speak. Hardinge told me the Duke said I was the most reasonable man in the Cabinet, and Arbuth-not, some days ago, told me the Duke was charmed with me. I was always ready to work for him, c.

Went at one to Sir G. Cockburn. Made alterations in the letter to Codrington by leaving out passages. Bead Nesselrode's letter to Lieven. Cabinet at 4. Dudley, c., wish to renew the conferences and allow the Russians to co-operate. The Russians propose that the Plenipotentiaries should meet near the seat of the Greek Government, and arrange in concert with Capo d'Istrias the limits of Greece, c., and that the treaty should, thus defined, be proposed to the Turks. Eussia says she will carry forward her military operations till Turkey consents to what is proposed, and conclude a general treaty, including the settlement of her own quarrel, and the Greek question. If we acceded to this proposal, Capo d'Istrias might, by refusing to acquiesce in what we thought right, prevent Eussia from making peace he might enable her to avoid making peace. Eussia might prevent the settlement of the Greek question till she had settled her own quarrel (which is her object), or, having settled her own quarrel, she might, by obstinately resolving to settle both questions at once, make war for the Treaty of London. We cannot sanction a war for that object.

Let the conditions on which the co-operation of the Eussian Government with ours is to rest be what they may, the moral effect will be the same. The various nations of the Turkish Empire will see the three greatest Powers of Europe apparently acting together for the subversion of the Ottoman Empire.

After dinner I had some conversation with Lord Grey. He said Palmerston's and Spring Eice's speeches would make it necessary for him to explain the grounds of his vote on the Canning Pension Bill. He thought it indefensible. He said he approved of all he knew of the Duke's measures, and differed from him only on the Catholic question. He thought the Duke was too sensible a man not to see that that question must make its way, and that he would not make a pertinacious resistance to what was inevitable.

Eosslyn and Lord Grey were both desirous that, if possible, all discussion should be avoided on the Catholic question this year.

Sir H. Parnell had suggested that a Committee might be moved for ' to report in what manner the Roman
Catholics of England, Ireland, and Scotland were effected by the existing laws." This would be a proper preliminary to the discussion of the question, and last long enough to make the discussion impracticable this year. They wished to know what the Duke thought of their measure. I promised to ask him to-morrow.

Saw the Duke at half-past twelve. He said he would think of the proposed Committee. He seemed rather against it. The King is very eager on the subject of the Catholics.

I read to him a paper I wrote this morning on the subject of the Eussian propositions. He said it was all true, but some part of it could not be said to Eussia. He is angry with Palmerston for his speech, but there is an awkwardness about coming to an explanation with him about it, and he does not wish to come to extremities. That speech has endangered the success of the Pension Bill. The letter to Codrington he approved of entirely, and has sent it to Huskisson.

Cabinet at 3. Determined that the Penrhyn case not being yet settled in the Lords, all those w T ho voted in the Commons for throwing East Eetford into the Hundreds should vote for it to-night.

Dudley brought two sentences to the Cabinet and no more! He complained bitterly that we talked of things of no real importance, while his concerns, which affected the peace of Europe, were left unsettled; and yet he comes to the Cabinet himself, with no fixed ideas, and with nothing done. I gave him the paper I wrote this morning. The Duke said he would write a paper on the subject. Dudley said it would be better to put some person who had more weight than himself into his situation. I think so, too. I advised him to go at once to the Duke. He could settle everything with him in half an hour, which in the Cabinet would not be settled in five hours. He will take my advice. I did not add, as I might have done, that I advised him never to go to Huskisson.

The Duke saw the Lord High Admiral to-day. He agrees to send Sir Pulteney Malcolm, but reluctantly. He wanted to send Sir J. Gore, who really could not have accepted the situation. It would have led to an accusation of intrigue.

We had our Conference with the Commons, and received their resolution respecting the Catholics. Our managers were the Lord President, Duke of Devonshire, Earls of Eldon, Grey, Vane, Bishop of Durham, Lord Colchester. Debate fixed for this day three weeks.

At Prince Leopold's Apsley told me there had been a complete smash in the House of Commons. Peel with a majority of only 18 for the Hundreds against Birmingham Huskisson and Palmerston voting in the minority contrary to the understanding come to at the Cabinet. G. Bankes told me he considered it a complete break up. If things are allowed to go on in this way our friends will not support us. Indeed, in the division I hear they said there was no use in their coming down to support a Government which was divided.

Lord Howick and a number of men are for giving the two members to Yorkshire, and then dividing York- shire into three. Apsley said he thought this was the best course and the most likely to succeed.

May 20 Called at the Treasury. The Duke out. Went to the Wool Committee. Afterwards called again on the Duke, who was gone to the Horse Guards. Lord Bath-urst seemed to treat lightly the affair in the House of Commons last night.

House at 5. Aberdeen told me Lord Bathurst had told him that Huskisson resigned this morning. The Duke, as I afterwards learnt from Apsley, called on Lord Bathurst early, so Lord Bathurst knew Huskisson had resigned when he affected to treat the division of last night lightly.

The Duke was in the House for a short time and left it with Palmerston. I suppose Palmerston has resigned too. If he has, I do hope the Duke will not ask him to remain. I do not think he will. As for Huskisson, his going out would make all our friends rejoice, and give us better divisions, but he is an able man. Should he resign I know not where we could get a proper person to hold his office. There are four or five important questions pending in that department which it would be impossible to bring forward this year. Sir Edward Knatchbull, Leslie Foster, the Speaker, and Calcraft, and Hardinge are the only men we can bring forward in the Commons.

Salisbury, the Duke of Newcastle, Lord Shaftesbury, Lord Cassilis, were all indignant and delighted hoping this would end in the retirement of Huskisson and Co.

May 21 Called on Aberdeen. He had heard nothing. He told me when Huskisson was going out before, Lamb would have gone too. I should be sorry for that. It would be difficult to replace him. Frankland Lewis would be a good man.

It seems there are reports about of changes. It was said Peel had resigned. He will, I dare say, be unwilling to go on without Huskisson; but still he is out of humour with Huskisson, and may be disposed to try it now.

Huskisson, Hardinge,
Palmerston, Knatchbull,
Grant, Leslie Foster,
Lamb, Calcraft,
Lord Francis Leveson, Littleton.

Mansion House dinner. The Duke was received extremely well. He looked ill, and as if he had been annoyed; but he was quite in good spirits with his reception, elated. Huskisson and Palmerston were not there, nor Dudley, but he never meant to go. Lord Melville was ill and could not go. The Chancellor was engaged.

May 22 At Epsom races. Lord Eosslyn came and had a long conversation with me. I gathered from it that there would be little or no difficulty, if Huskisson went out, in obtaining his accession and that of Lord Grey to the Government. In any case they would support the

Government if the secession of Huskisson should embarrass it. Eosslyn seemed to think there would be no difficulty in getting Brougham, and that Mr. Stanley could not refuse the Irish secretaryship. I thought it right to write a note to the Duke on my return to tell him this.

The disappointment will be universal if Huskisson and Palmerston do not go out. I do not see how we can go on comfortably and cordially with them again-As the Duke certainly repented of having brought them in, I should hope no want of firmness on Peel's part will induce him to keep them now they have themselves offered to go. How he will fill their places I cannot imagine. Palmers ton's loss can be easily supplied, but Huskisson's not so easily.

I have not heard a word from the Duke, so I conclude nothing is settled definitively. The idea on the Course was that Huskisson and Palmerston would go; Grant and Dudley remain. I may be mistaken, but I cannot help thinking that if Dudley and I were to change places the country would be no loser; but the King likes him and dislikes me, so I suppose things will remain as they are as far as regards us.

May 23 Called upon Aberdeen at 10. The Duke dined with him yesterday. Nothing was settled at eleven o'clock last night. The Duke had determined not to make any advance or recede a step. If they are willing to withdraw their resignations, he consents. If they choose to go, he thinks he shall stand better without them. Peel has made up his mind to try the House of ~~VOL. i. I~~

Commons by himself. Dudley has been much with the King, and then with the Chancellor. The King is infatuated about him.

The Duke said yesterday, ' I am no speaker, but if I was in the House of Commons I think I could set things to rights in three minutes."

Just as I was setting off for Epsom I received a note from the Duke desiring me to call upon him in the course of the morning. So I gave up Epsom. The Duke read to me the letters which have passed between him and Huskisson. Huskisson walked home from the House of Commons on Monday night with Planta, who held very strong language to him on the vote he had given, and told him the only thing he had left to do was to resign. Under the influence of this conversation Huskisson wrote to the Duke at two o'clock in the morning, stating the vote he had been obliged to give from a regard to his personal character, and placing his resignation in the Duke's hands if he thought it necessary to the character of the Government that lie should be replaced. I do not remember the words, but the meaning was this; and it was evident from the terms of the letter that Huskisson thought his vote did materially injure the character of the Government. The Duke in his answer said he had received the communication with surprise and concern, and should lay it before the King. On Tuesday morning Dudley went to the Duke and said Huskisson's letter had been quite misconceived; that he did not intend to resign. Would the Duke see Huskisson? but lie was not desired by Huskisson to express a wish to that effect. The Duke said he had no objection to see him, but since Huskis-son did not desire it he did not see why he should.

Then came a letter from Huskisson telling the Duke he had been misunderstood; that all he intended was to remove any difficulty of a personal nature, should the Duke think it necessary to remove him, in consequence of his vote. The Duke replied. Huskisson retorted rather angrily. The Duke had the last word. The Duke's letters are excellent. The King is quite satisfied, and regretting Huskisson's conduct stands by the Duke firmly. The Duke will take no further step, nor will he point out to Huskisson what step will be sufficient on his part to replace things as they were. The King enters into this feeling, and will suggest nothing.

The Duke's spirit is up, and he is quite determined. He means to let this day pass over without doing anything, and to-morrow he will consider what measures to take for the purpose of replacing Huskisson, should he not knock under. One thing the Duke said struck me much. It was, ' I have done in this case what I have observed in all things it is safest to do. I have taken a moderate line to which I can and will adhere. When an exaggerated position is taken there is no holding it."

He said he knew the men he had to deal with. The Canningites all entertained an erroneous and exaggerated view of their own consequence, which existed in the minds of none but themselves. They were always endeavouring to lord it. In this case, if he had solicited Huskisson to remain, Huskisson would have been Minister instead of himself.

116 The Duke is completely roused, and seems to feel as he did at Waterloo.

In riding home through the Park I passed Huskis-son and Dudley. Dudley made a face, as much as to say, ' Here's a pretty foolish business!" The Duke saw Palmerston on Tuesday in the Painted Chamber. Palmers ton two or three times said his resignation was in the Duke's hands, of which the Duke took no notice. He told me Palmerston must follow Huskisson, and he did not choose to fire great guns at sparrows. How pleased this expression would make Palmerston!

Called again on Aberdeen and went down with him to Downing Street. He went on to the House to a Commission. I read dispatches from Codrington, just arrived. On April 19 he did issue orders in the spirit of his instructions, but not till then, and then only to two ships, the ' Glasgow' and Dartmouth," the latter off Candia, the former off Alexandria. The Turkish fleet went to Candia for the purpose of sending supplies in single vessels to Mod on. Two of these (corvettes of 20 guns) the Warspite turned back.

There was a letter, too, from Stratford Canning to Huskisson, written on hearing Codrington was to be recalled, and expressing an opinion that his recall would induce the Turks to think we did not mean to proceed with the treaty. He says the Turks look only to facts; when they look to the fact of the Morea being more strictly blockaded under a new Admiral, they will be satisfied we do mean to go on with the treaty.

Codrington's letter is in a better tone, and perhaps, had it been received sooner, he 117 might not have been recalled. The letter is not yet gone to the Lord High Admiral, nor that to Codrington!

Saw the Duke again in the House. He told me the fact of Codrington's recall being in agitation was known on Sunday last at Holland House at dinner, and Lord Holland told Captain Spencer, who told the Duke of Clarence. I took the dispatch to be copied to Backhouse. Lord Howard must have seen it, and told Lord Holland. The Duke said he had frequently spoken on the subject to Dudley, but just at present he did not like to mention it again. The Duke complained of some proposition made to him, I did not understand whether by Huskisson or Grant, to export bonded wheat in the shape of flour. He complained propositions were made to him which seemed at first sight plausible none of the objections were stated, and he was obliged to cast about and endeavour to discover all the bearings of the question himself. He is thoroughly out of humour with Huskisson and Co., and if any accommodation takes place now it cannot last long.

The Chancellor asked Aberdeen whether anything had been done, and hearing nothing had been, concluded Huskisson was out. He said the King would be very sorry to lose Dudley. Really I think Dudley should be Lord Chamberlain, and then he would be always about the King's person.

Dudley was in the House to-day. People are much on the qui vive. All very anxious. The Tories in very good spirits at the idea of Huskisson's going out.

I have not the most remote idea how the Duke will fill up the vacant office. I have some suspicion that I 118 ~~DIARY. 1828.~~

have been mentioned in the newspapers as Colonial Secretary, but I should never have thought of it. The office is one of great labour and importance, and there are many questions now pending which require much consideration. I should not like the situation, but it is a great object of ambition. Will the Duke place Goulburn there and make Herries Chancellor of the Exchequer? Goulburn knows the business, for he was under-secretary in the Office. Will he make Lord Melville Colonial Secretary, and give me India? Or will Lord Bathurst take the office again? Aberdeen says not. I have exhausted all the propositions which occur to me, and I dare say whatever is done will not be any one of the things I have imagined. As for Palmerston's office I rather think Hardinge will have it without the Cabinet, and very well he will do it.

Grant and Dudley will, I conclude, stay. At Lady Londonderry's party saw the Duke, who at that time had received no direct communication from Huskisson; but Dudley had been with him, and Lord F. Leveson had written to him, and they both wished to get the Duke to suggest to Huskisson some mode of getting out of the difficulty. The Duke said when a gentleman got into a difficulty he ought to know how to get out of it; and he would do nothing which would appear like collusion to the public.

Arbuthnot, whom I saw before the Duke came, was as very anxious I should tell the Duke what I thought was the present state of the question, and the impression on the public mind. I promised to do so, and had the opportunity when the Duke

[119] came. I told him the thing had gone on so long that there would be an universal feeling of disappointment if Huskisson and Palmerston did not go out. That it would be impossible to make the country understand how the difference arose or how it ended. That the result of a reconciliation would be weakness in the House from want of character, union, and confidence, and in the Cabinet from the recollection of what had passed. He agreed in this, but said, which is "true, that if Huskisson said he was sorry for what had happened, and made a proper excuse, he could not refuse to take him back, though he should be sorry to do so.

I should not be surprised if Dudley, Grant, F. Leve-son, and the others, as a last resource, threatened to go out if Huskisson went. The Duke is not to be bullied, and he would tell them to go. I cannot imagine how the offices will be filled up. Several modes occur to me. [E here sketches out two alternative reshuffles of the Cabinet.]

We want strength in the Commons, and I think the Duke will prefer keeping the Colonial Secretary there. He might have an equal number of Ministers there by sending the Duchy down.

[119] If the Colonies were in the Lords, a good deal of business might begin there which will now begin in the Commons. I am sure we should do well to make the Lords of more importance by beginning more business there.

May 24 Went to the Cabinet room. Met Lord Bathurst there, who told me there had been a most extraordinary proposal that morning, that Huskisson and the Duke should go together to the King and state their case. This was, of course, rejected, and cannot have facilitated a reconciliation by showing Huskisson considered himself on a par with the Duke.

Met Aberdeen in the Park and told him what I had heard. Aberdeen's opinion is that the King will impose his commands on Huskisson, and that so some concession will be made, and the matter settled. God forbid!

At Salisbury's dinner I met Bathurst, Aberdeen, Lothian, and the Duke of Dorset. The women are all violent against Huskisson and Palmerston.

Went to Lady Cowper's, and met there Lord and Lady Tankerville and Gwydyr. They are all for the Duke, and, as far as I can judge, if Huskisson remains in office, the world will think the Duke has lost the battle of Setford (the name I have given to the affair). There will be no means of explaining the matter to the country. Our friends will be breast high with us again if Huskisson goes out. If he does not, there will be a degree of irritation which will make it very difficult to carry on the Government. Besides I do not see how after all that has passed there can be unity of purpose and cordiality between the members of the Cabinet. The world begins to be very impatient for a denouement. The inconvenience to the public service has been great already. The case is not the same as it was on Tuesday morning. A new case has arisen which makes a change still more essential to the character and efficiency of the Government. The country looks to the Duke alone, and cares little who are the other Ministers; but, should Huskis-son remain in, it will not be easy to make it clear to the country that the Duke is really Minister.

May 25 I wrote a note to the Duke giving him the opinion I have expressed above; telling him I fully approved of all he had done, and I was sure I should approve of all he might do; but I should be very sorry if it should not be as evident to the public that he was right as it would be to me. Eeceived an answer from the Duke to say he concurred with me in thinking delay an evil and a concession in itself. He should have made his communication to the King yesterday, had he not found it necessary to postpone it till he could make known to Dudley that he intended to speak to the King about an arrangement before he made it. Dudley had been apprised, and the Duke was to see the King at two o'clock.

As to our friends the Duke said they must allow him to look at all the circumstances attending the situation of the country, in all its relations at home and abroad. He did not mean to say that a quarrel with Huskisson would do the Government much harm if Huskisson should be in the wrong in the circumstances and details of the affair from its commencement to its termination; but of this lie was very certain that we and the country should feel severely the consequences of any harsh or precipitate step. We must not take such a one. His belief was we should be in a better position after this affair, be its result what it might; and he added he was very little anxious about the result although within two hours of the solution of so important a question.

May 26 Heard nothing all the morning. The day very bad. I did not go out. At 9 P. M. heard from Aberdeen that Huskisson, W. Lamb, and Palmerston were certainly out. Grant, being in great affliction for the death of his sister, has taken no step yet; but Aberdeen expected one or two more resignations. Lord F. Leveson, I should think, would certainly not remain in as Undersecretary. Dudley will make a motion as if he wished to resign; but I doubt his going out.

Went to the ball at St. James's. Saw the Duke, who told me he had done it at half-past two yesterday. A letter had come from them in the morning, which was quite inadmissible. I am to go to-morrow morning to read the letters. Sir G. Murray succeeds Huskisson. A better man could not have been found. He is able; a good man of business; a good speaker (as far as he is known), and he brings a high established character into the service of the country. He is, besides, a Catholic. My expectation is that next session he will be the most efficient man in the House of Commons.

Mrs. Arbuthnot told me she had suggested Hardinge to the Duke for the Irish Secretaryship. The Duke was thinking of Wilmot Horton, who would be very unfit he is a bore full of fancies. Hardinge had not occurred to him; but he was much struck with the idea.

Lady Jersey told me Lord Grey was only afraid the Government might assume a Tory character, and make it impossible for him to support it as he really wished.

The Tories were all in high spirits, but Lord Mansfield is not satisfied yet, and will never be satisfied till he has a pure Anti-Catholic Administration, which he never will see in this country again.

May 27 Went to the Duke. He showed me the last letters. Huskisson sent through Dudley a letter which the Duke returned unopened, because it came too late, that is, after he had seen the King. Huskisson returned the letter, which contained the substance of what he had intended to say to the King, and requested the Duke would lay it before the King, as he had not had an audience. The Duke did so, and answered the letter. Huskisson afterwards had an audience and delivered up the seals. I told the Duke how pleased I was with Sir G. Murray's appointment, and said I hoped he would be able to do something for Hardinge. He said he thought of him for Ireland, but the appointment of Sir G. Murray, as a military man, created a difficulty. I said it might occasion a debate, and be talked of for three days; but if the man appointed was a fit man, as Hardinge is, he would soon put down party clamour. He agreed with me. I then said something against Wilmot

Horton, Hardinge's competitor for Ireland, and the Duke said he thought he was a man full of fancies, &c &c.

I told him what Lady Jersey said about Lord Grey, and about Lord Howard's going out.

Went to Mrs. Arbuthnot to tell her what had passed, and found Hardinge with her. I said nothing on his subject before him.

May 28 Seeing in the ' Times ' that Dudley had resigned, I drove to town from Eoehampton. Called at Aberdeen's, who was out, and then went to Downing Street. I read the last papers from Lisbon, till Mr. Greville came to call me to the Duke. I went, and he began by telling me they were all gone, except Lord F. Leveson, about whom he was not yet sure. I said Lord F. Leveson followed me into the office, and proposed his seeing him at once, which he did. The result of the interview was that Lord Francis gave in his resignation. Personally, he would have had no objection to remain, but Lord Stafford objects. The Duke asked if he thought Lord Stafford would equally object to his being at the Foreign Office. Lord F. said his father was old, and he did not like to trouble him any more about it.

Dudley gave no opinion upon the letters, but said he could not continue a member of a Cabinet constituted in so different a manner from what it was when he first belonged to it. The King expressed no particular regret at Dudley's going out. He told the Duke he would stick by him.

The Duke, told me Peel was very anxious to have all he could in the Commons; that Wilmot Horton would have the Secretaryship at War, not in the Cabinet; V. Fitzgerald be President of the Board of Trade; Calcraft is to have the office of the Paymastership; Lord Low-ther the Woods and Forests; Arbuthnot, the Duchy; and Aberdeen the Foreign Office. V. Fitzgerald¹ is to be in the Cabinet, which will thus consist of eleven instead of thirteen.

The Duke said Lord Stuart and Lord Heytesbury had been thought of for the Foreign Office, but they thought on the whole Aberdeen was the best.

I expressed my opinion of Wilmot Horton's appointment, and Calcraft's, un-favourable to the individuals, as they were mentioned. When the Duke had done speaking I told him I would fairly say I had never liked the office of Privy Seal; that I accepted it with reluctance, after long consultation with Hard-inge, that the rank was irksome to me, and that I particularly disliked having nothing to do. That while Dudley was at the Foreign Office I could do something, because he was an old friend of mine, and had no false pride, and was willing to receive any hints or suggestions. In fact I had almost written the last dispatch to Polignac. That no proposal having been made to Grey or Eosslyn, I was now separated from them without the chance of reunion.

The Duke said Lord Grey had no people in the House of Commons, and that he did not like to make an offer which would probably not have been entertained without some concession on the subject of the Catholics which he could not make.

[1 Vesey Fitzgerald, afterwards Lord Fitzgerald.]

I told him I understood from Rosslyn that Althorpe, Tavistock, Duncannon, and others would willingly act with the Government if Lord Grey belonged to it. I thought I had told him so in my note, but I suppose I did not.

As to myself the Duke said he felt all I said about the Privy Seal. That he acknowledged I had been as useful as any member of the Cabinet, both in discussing all questions, and in concocting the papers; and he should take the first opportunity of placing me in an efficient situation. That the object was to bring me into the Cabinet, and there was no other place at the time, and my position was not altered.

I asked about the Irish Secretaryship, and it seems that is not yet given. The Duke thinks Hardinge the fittest man by far, and agrees with me in considering the fact of his being a military man one of little importance. It will be a subject of debate one night, and Hardinge's good services will bring all round. But Peel is afraid of that one debate. The Duke told him to point out some other man. He is determined not to appoint an unfit man, for he feels it to be one of the most important situations in the country.

When the Duke said he had no office to propose to Kosslyn, as Peel wanted them all in the House of Commons, I said he might take the Privy Seal it was really disagreeable to me to hold it. I said the little work I did with Dudley would be lost to me now, for Aberdeen was by no means the same sort of person, nor would he receive good-humouredly any suggestions which might be given to him.

127   The Duke said the business of the Foreign Office, however important, was but a portion of the public business; that there was a great deal to do in the Colonial Department, with the matters relating to the slaves. I said that was not business I liked. That the foreign business I had always attended to.

The Duke asked what I thought Lord Grey would do. I said I thought he would be much indisposed towards the Government. That he would be disgusted with Wilmot Horton and Calcraft, and that he would have been gratified by an offer, even if he had not accepted it.

The idea of Lord Lansdowne seems to have suggested itself only to be rejected. I told the Duke I would not have served with him.

Had Lord Heytesbury, Lord Melville, or Lord Bath-urst, been made Foreign Secretary, I should have acknowledged their superior claims. Had either of the latter been made, an office of some work might have been opened for me, and Aberdeen, taking the Privy Seal, his office would have gone to the Commons as now. I cannot think Aberdeen a fitter man than myself. He has been useless to the Duke in the Cabinet, and he failed as Ambassador to Austria. He cannot speak at all.

I do not think the Duke acts wisely. I am more popular with the Tories; the Whigs would have considered my appointment (I mean Lord Grey and c.) one of good omen for them, and as far as a man is capable of judging himself, I could have done the duty of the office well.

128   Aberdeen being- known to be quite Austrian, his appointment will create suspicion in the minds of Eussia and France. I have no idea of his being able to do the business even as well as Dudley, who, after all, did all the ordinary business very well. He only failed in his great papers, and he would have done them better in time.

The Duke has thrown away an opportunity of making a strong Government. He might have had Lord Eosslyn, certainly, probably Lords Grey and Stanley. I could have supported such a Government in any situation, but I have no satisfaction in supporting Aberdeen as Foreign Secretary, and such men as Wilmot Horton and Calcraft. Now Stanley will lead the Opposition and terrify Peel, Lord Grey will soon join the Opposition in the Lords, and I shall have to fight against all my old friends in a cause I dislike. For the Duke I have the greatest regard, and in him, personally, I place great confidence. I cannot desert his colours while the enemy is in the field; but my present feeling is to fight by his side manfully while the session lasts, and to resign on the day of the prorogation.

May 29 Wrote a paper detailing my personal views of the recent changes, and the draft of a letter to the Duke of Wellington, stating my intention of resigning at the end of the session, but accompanying that statement with the warmest expressions of regard for him, and of respect for his character, and assuring him I would stand by him during [129 the session. This I intended to leave at Hardinge's, should he not be at home, asking his frank opinion.

Went to London and met Aberdeen. Walked with him through the Park, and avowed to him my dissatisfaction with the arrangements made, with the exception of that of Sir Gr. Murray. I explained what seemed to me the disagreeable circumstances in my own position, both in the Cabinet and with regard to my old political friends. He endeavoured to show the Duke could not have done otherwise. His own appointment he spoke of as a bore, and said he would not have accepted it had he had the Privy Seal. It seems Wilmot Horton has refused the Secretaryship at War and Calcraft the Pay-mastership; so the Duke, who feared a repulse from Lord Grey, has received it from W. Horton and Calcraft. The whole mischief arises from Peel's not taking a manly view of things.

Called on Hardinge. Told him in substance what I had written in the paper. He saw the Duke yesterday. He expressed great regard for me; said I had ten times the ability of Aberdeen: that I was as certain of rising to be a Secretary of State as he ever was of rising in the army; that I had more talent than any man in the Cabinet, and had showed great temper and judgment but why are persons placed permanently in every office I could occupy? It seems Peel wishes to have one Cabinet Minister less in the Lords. This might have been managed otherwise had it been desirable.

Hardinge said the idea was that on Lord Anglesey's resignation (but he will not resign), either Aberdeen or Melville might be induced to go to Ireland, and then

~~VOL. I. K~~ the office of whoever went would be left for me. But so was Dudley's, so was Huskisson's, so was Grant's office left for me now.

I showed Hardinge my letter to the Duke. He said it was very kind, but would still hurt him very much, and, if known, do great mischief to the Government. I might resign, if I pleased, on the same grounds two months hence. I believe he is right. My doubt was between resigning, if circumstances required it, then, and intimating the resignation now. I must fight fairly for the Duke now, so I had better defer my resignation.

Erankland Lewis is to be proposed to the King as Secretary in Ireland. Hardinge will, I conclude, be Secretary at War; but he must ask Lord Londonderry about his seat, and Lord Londonderry is dissatisfied because Sir G. Murray is preferred to him, and may dislike two elections in one year. There are still to be filled up the Paymastership, the Vice-Presidency of the Board of Trade, and the two Under-Secretaries for Colonies and Foreign Affairs. Hardinge cannot see daylight, or guess where these are to be found.

Hardinge wishes the offer had been made to Lord Grey. He thinks it might be made even now.

Went to town. First to Downing Street, where I saw Peel and his brother-in-law Dawson, and brother William at the Cabinet room. I told Peel I thought he had managed ill, that he had united the Opposition, and made a weak Government.

I find Frankland Lewis resigns too. He mars his fortune at the very moment when it would have been made.

Came up with Lord Londonderry. He had been with the Duke, to say he did not like Hardinge's vacating his seat. It would cost him 10,000. now, and then there might be a general election soon. The object was not sufficient to Hardinge, and he got nothing for Castlereagh or for himself. He had been putting forward his own claims. He wants an embassy.

Went to the Council. Arbuthnot was there for the Duchy. Lord Lowther for the Woods and Forests. Hardinge as Secretary at War, Courtenay as Vice-President of the

Board of Trade, and Sir George Murray as Colonial Secretary. I had never seen Sir George Murray before, and was introduced to him by Lord Melville. I told him no one could rejoice more than I did in his accession to the Government. I had some talk with Aberdeen. He gave me to understand that I should succeed him in three or four months.

Hardinge told me the Duke said he wished Aberdeen would take the Privy Seal and give me the Foreign Office. He had much rather see me there.

Aberdeen received the Seals to-day. He seems disposed to give me as much business as I like. He asked me, as we were going away, if I had thought of any body for Paris in the event of Lord Granville's coming away. I said I was afraid the Duke was hampered with Lord Stuart de Rothesay, but I thought Lord Bristol a good man. He would go into Opposition if he was not prevented, for he was a Canningite. Aberdeen thought Lord Bristol would do very well. He had imagined Lord Londonderry might have been proposed by the Duke. I am afraid Lord Bristol would not go.

The King gave but short audiences to Dudley and Huskisson. The latter told him he should be in the House of Commons on Monday. Dudley wanted to enter into a long detail, but the King stopped him by saying ' that has nothing to do but with private feeling. I think you were quite wrong."

The King was not very well. He had taken some laudanum, and when we went there at two he was in bed.

I suggested to the Duke that we should do well to get some young men who stood well in society, such as H. Corry, or W. Ashley, that sort of man. He said, ' Peel complains they do nothing besides all the women are with us. I sat between two at dinner yesterday, Lady Conyngham and Lady Cowper. I do not believe Lady Conyngham likes me, but I have never enquired into that. I have always disregarded Court intrigues. Well, I was good-humoured with them both, and sent them both away in good humour. I called Clanwilliain to me and said, "See what a little good humour does look at those two women."

Speaking of Lord Londonderry, the Duke said, ' I believe few men know their own position. He thinks I can make him an ambassador to-morrow. I could do no such thing."

The Duke will keep the offices undisposed of, the Paymastership, Clerkship of the Ordnance, and Secre-taryship for Ireland, in his own hands, till he sees his way a little, and I hope he will go to Lord Grey, talk cordially with him, and practically place the Irish Secretaryship at his disposal. Then Lord Howick might be made Clerk of the Ordnance, and Eosslyn might be inclined to go as Governor-General to Canada.

If something is not done to conciliate Lord Grey the whole Opposition will be united in both Houses.

I fear it will be too late to induce Stanley to go to Ireland.

Sir George Clerk is thought of as a possible man for Ireland.

We all seemed to feel comfortable at being so few. Sir G. Murray was there for the first time. I like him.

We considered the heads of a letter to Lieven, and determined on reopening this Conference. Our letter is to restate the reasons for which we suspended them, and to declare our understanding of the practical retractation contained in Nesselrode's last dispatch. It is likewise to deny that we ever declared our opinion of the justice of the War undertaken by Eussia.

We must observe, too, upon the very insidious propositions of Eussia, as to the mode of fixing the limits of Greece, the suzerainete, c. as to marching forward till the Turks accept the terms proposed, and as to settling simultaneously the differences arising out of the treaty of July 6, and the separate differences of Eussia. Co-operation is to be refused. I wrote a note to Dudley him to send to Aberdeen a paper I gave him on these points. He was at Wimbledon at the Chancellor's.

He is much pleased at Aberdeen's taking Wrangham as his private secretary. Aberdeen was, after the Cabinet, to see Lord Douglas and declare him Undersecretary. He is a friend of the Duke's and a relation of the Buccleuch.

Goulburn got through fifty-one estimates last night. The House seemed in good humour. They did the business of a week.

In returning through the Park I met Arbuthnot, who began to talk about Lord Grey. He is very anxious something should be done about him. He had heard Lord Durham was outrageous at no proposal having been made to Lord Grey. I am not surprised. The Duke has no objection, but Arbuthnot says the King would say, ' Send for Lord Lansdowne if you want a Whig." I am to see Arbuthnot to-morrow about it.

I am told that the Whigs say the Government cannot stand, and there will be a great opposition. I expect it. It is our own fault. [1] We might have mollified it. However, the King is firm.

June 1.

Went to the Cabinet room. Met there Sir George Murray, whom I put aufait of what had been done. I like him of all things.

[1 i. e. By not offering office to Lord Grey or Lord Rosslyn.]

Aberdeen came in and said there were accounts from Portugal, and Miguel seemed to be in a bad way.

June 2.

Wool Committee. Eead dispatches from Portugal. Miguel wants courage to meet the dangers of his position.

The Spanish Government is alarmed. We must prevent their interference by telling them at once we will not permit it.

In the House of Commons Huskisson made his explanation, and spoke in a tone of exacerbation, which will do him no good. The Opposition did not take him up. On a division we had 258 to 152, a majority of 106. The last majority was 18. Huskisson threw out insinuations that his dismissal was to clear the way for a change of measures. This was denied.

June 3.

Went at 11 to the Cabinet room to finish the second letter to Codrington, which I took to the Duke, who approved of it. I then got the two copied. Aberdeen read to me his first dispatch. It is not as well written as Dudley's were. I thought he would have been at least correct, but he is not, and, like Dudley, he does not hold his object steadfastly before him, and give one unbroken chain of argument. I altered the dispatch very materially.

The Foreign Ministers paid their compliments to him to-day in grand costume, and each had his petit mot a dire There were twenty-one of them. I met Esterhazy and Polignac as I was going in with drafts.

L 136

Aberdeen asked me to write a dispatch to Madrid, which I did. Its object is to do everything short of threatening war in the event of Spain's interfering in the affairs of Portugal by force. I sent it to the Duke, and we are to have a Cabinet upon it to-morrow. The Duke goes to Ascot and will not be at the Cabinet. I wrote another dispatch to Madrid on various matters.

The Duke is to look over the Portuguese dispatches to-night, and make memoranda which we are to throw into the form of dispatches to-morrow. I shall do as much of the business of the Foreign Office as I can.

I had a long conversation with Eosslyn to-day. I told him I communicated to the Duke the impression produced upon my mind by my conversation with him at Epsom. He said the Pitt dinner, and some of the appointments had induced people to apprehend the Duke intended to go into extremes, and form a Government on exclusive principles. I assured him it was not so. He told me Huskisson's speech was very bitter and offensives in its tone. Brougham seems to have thrown him over.

The ' Turks ' have risen one per cent, upon the majority.

There was a telegraphic dispatch to-day to say that all the regiments but one in the north of Portugal had declared for Don Pedro.

Dudley and Huskisson have advised Lord Granville not to resign. Lord Bathurst thinks this advice was given that Huskisson may know ail that is going on.

137

June 4.

Wrote a dispatch to Lord Granville, desiring him to send full information as to the changes taking place in the disposition of the Chambers, and two dispatches to Sir F. Lamb. I took them to Aberdeen, but he was engaged with Stratford Canning, Lord Heytesbury, c., and I did not see him till the Cabinet met at quarter to four.

I found he had retained his defective phraseology, though he had adopted all my suggestions of real importance in the letter to Lieven. However, the Cabinet was of my opinion, and struck out the very words I thought objectionable.

The dispatch to Madrid the Duke approved of; but he thought a paragraph should be added to point out the danger of contagion, should a Spanish army be placed in an inactive state upon the frontier. This I have added, and I have struck out a passage which I believe the Duke thought too strong.

The Portuguese Government has ordered a blockade of Oporto. It seems it would be very inconvenient for us to acknowledge this blockade. If Miguel has assumed a title which is not his, his blockade has no value, but he calls himself Infant Regent in the decree establishing it. The King's advocate is to be consulted, and he is to receive a hint as to the opinion the Government wish him to give. This, it seems, is the usual course. So much for law!

The letter to Codrington was at last signed and taken to the Lord High Admiral. Aberdeen was to read it to him, but not to give him a copy. He seemed to think he might have a difficult business, and Dudley shrank from it.

L 138

Dudley so much committed himself to Lawrence's proposal of sending two names on each side for the purpose of choosing the arbiter, that Lawrence says he wrote to his Government to acquaint them with it.

Lord Anglesea certainly stays in Ireland.

June 5.

Saw Lord Bathurst at the Cabinet room. I told him what Arbuthnot had told me, that the King was in high good humour when the Duke saw him yesterday, and very staunch. Huskisson's speech and the majority of 106 have together done this for us.

Aberdeen saw Ofalia this morning. He is quite of our mind as to sending Spanish troops to the frontier. Aberdeen showed him the dispatch to Bosanquet, and he approved of it. He was desirous of receiving an assurance that we would use our influence to prevent the troubles in Portugal being made use of for the purpose of reviving political divisions in Spain. This assurance was willingly given to him.

The Duke of Clarence approved of every word of the letter to Codrington.

Lord Granville has resigned. This is a godsend. The Duke wishes it not to be known, that he may see if he cannot make some political arrangement out of it. Ireland, the Pay master ship, and the Clerkship of the Ordnance are still undisposed of.

I had some talk with the Duke about the language he should hold on Monday. He says he has never been committed strongly either way; that he thinks the practical difficulties of the question have not been sufficiently adverted to; and that the King is now the most Protestant man in his dominions.

Had some conversation with Lady Jersey at Lady Eoosebery's. She told me Stanley had wished to have an Opposition meeting to organise assault upon the Government; but Lord Lansdowne and others had objected to it, and begged he would at least wait till after the Catholic debate. They imagine the elimination of Hus-kisson and the others will lead to ultra-Protestantism, being quite ignorant of the real state of things. I hope the Duke will be very cautious in what he says on Monday.

June 6.

Canning's Pension Bill in the House. Lord Londonderry had the bad taste and imprudence to accuse Canning of refusing him his pension from personal motives. Dudley answered him very well, but was rather too long. His speech should have ended at the words, 'Lord Liverpool when he showed that the pension was refused not by Canning, but by Lord Liverpool.

The Duke placed the Bill on excellent grounds. Lord Liverpool's was a dull, prosy speech. Groderich's was pompous and inane. We had no division. Lord Plunket was in the House. I expressed my hope that he would be very temperate on Monday.

Lord Londonderry wants to go to Ireland as Lord Lieutenant!

June 7.

Cabinet room. No new papers, and Aberdeen engaged with Polignac, so I did not see him.

A large political dinner at the Duke of Newcastle's. Peers and Commoners mixed. Lords Thomond, Londonderry, Melville, Kinnard, Hill, Strangford, Beresford, Eolles, Salisbury, Wallace, G. Beresford, Brookes, Sir Byam Martin, Sir Edward Knatchbull, Sir Alexander Grant, c. Lord Beresford told me to-day he must vote on the Catholic question in the House as heretofore, but he was desirous of a settlement, and would be satisfied with the arrangements made in other Protestant States with Catholic subjects. It is my firm belief that the general tendency of men's minds is to a settlement.

June 8.

Lord Durham told me at dinner (at Prince Leopold's) that he had asked Lord Grey some time ago whether he would refuse to belong to any Government which did not make the Catholic question a Cabinet measure. Lord Grey said all he asked was that the Government should not be decidedly against it. That the Government should be neutral. I told Lord Durham I really believed no Government could be more entirely neutral than the Duke's, who would, in the distribution of offices, never consider whether a man was for or against the Catholics. Lord Durham expressed the astonishment every one else has at Huskisson's throwing the affairs of Canada into the hands of a Committee of the House of Commons.

June 10.

House at 5. Catholic debate. Lord Haddington made an excellent and very agreeable speech. The Duke of Sussex spoke well. The Chancellor followed him acknowledged the difficulty and embarrassment of our present position; asked securities, and said those given to Prussia were ample. Lord Plunket answered him. He did not speak as well as I have heard him speak in the House of Commons, but still very ably. Then Eldon. I should say Lord Plunket declared the strongest opinion in favour of securities and of the Irish Church. Eldon spoke well, and said he was not one of those who thought the concessions would never be made. Lord Wellesley declared his increased conviction of the necessity of the measure. The Duke of Wellington lamented he must differ in his vote from Lord "Wellesley, but said he did not believe their opinions upon the subject were very different. He would not hold out hopes till he saw his way. Deprecated the frequent agitation of the question. Eeferred to the securities given to Hanover, and other countries, and said they were not applicable to the peculiar circumstances of this country. Thought our present securities sufficient for the present, and that when we proceeded to admit the Catholics, we should do it by legislation, fearlessly, and with determination.

Lord Lansdowne congratulated the House on the altered tone of debate, noticed Lord Salisbury's speech (in which he said he only asked the Eoyal nomination of the hierarchy), and then of the Chancellor and the Duke. He said he could not but feel that it was admitted there was an intention of endeavouring to accomplish a settlement, since it was admitted we were in a difficulty, and that those were securities by the obtaining of which we might extricate ourselves. The Government, which would not let the House take up the question, was, admitting these things, pledged to take it up itself.

Below the Bar. I told Lord Lansdowne I thought his conclusion fair. Lord Grey said after this the Duke was bound to take it up, and he expected some measure next year. I told him I thought he was hurrying the Duke too much, and forgot the King. The Chancellor admitted to me the King was the real difficulty.

I see we shall ask more securities than any other State has. The Catholics will not give the same securities. Will the Pope? It will be a very difficult negotiation. It must be done by previous arrangement with the Pope, and by a Bull, of which the provisions will be suspended till the Bill is passed. But without repealing the laws against intercourse with Eome, we cannot come to a regular agreement with the Pope.

"With the Pope on our side we might laugh at the agitators. They might bluster, but the measure would work its way. I must get the Duke to look at the question practically.

The Duke improves very much as a speaker. I did not speak, and I believe I was right. I do not desire securities, and the desire of them is the fashion of the day. Besides, the King might have been irritated, and I should keep myself unpledged to any particular views of the question. Thus, should I ever have the power, I shall be able to do more good. The majority was 45 against the motion. The last majority was 48.

Lord Southampton, who thought it a bore to get his writ, was brought down to take his seat and vote for. Lord Forester, whose father died very lately, voted against. Chesterfield for; 319 voted, and there were 215 in the House, of which 92 for. All voted who were in the House in the course of the night. There was no pairing, but a word was said as to the division of the Government upon the point, and generally the debate was conducted with discretion.

June 11.

Cabinet dinner at the Duke's. The Duke said he believed there was no one who desired the settlement of the Catholic question more than he did; but he confessed he did not see daylight.

The conversation after dinner turned upon the improper tone of Lamb's dispatches, and the co-operation with the Eussian fleet. Nothing was absolutely fixed, and we are to have a Cabinet to-morrow.

The King gave a party at the Palace, and invited fifty or one hundred people, leaving me out, and others of the ministers. I know he cannot love me. He has not spoken to me since he gave me the Seal. I care little about this. If I should ever hold a situation which brings me into contact with him, I shall get on very well with him, and his personal feeling will not induce him to refuse to give me such an appointment.

Lady Jersey and G. Anson, whom I met at Almack's, expressed regret that I did not speak on the Catholic question. I said I was ready, but I could not have been of use; there was no good opportunity, and upon the whole I thought it was better I should not speak. I am still of that opinion. I find people are not so well satisfied to-day with the debate as they were yesterday.

Vesey Fitzgerald was at the Cabinet dinner to-day for the first time.

June 12.

House at 5. Lord Dundas put questions to Lord Beresford as to his letters to the Duke de Cadaval. Lord Beresford answered satisfactorily, but at length, and in a long, twaddling manner.

At the Cabinet we understood from the Duke of Wellington that he had seen Lord Beresford this morning. Lord Beresford had not answered the Duke de Cadaval's last letter, and promised to discontinue the correspondence.

At breakfast I wrote two or three paragraphs, reprehending Lamb for saying to M. Campazana, the Spanish Minister at Lisbon, that ' we had been misled by the lying assurances of Don Miguel, and that he hoped our eyes would be opened."

These I sent to Aberdeen, and he adopted them and inserted them in his dispatch. They were rather strong. We decided on co-operating with the Eussians in the Levant, under the Treaty of London, provided the Eussians would place their whole fleet under the orders of the Conference, and permit a communication to be made to the Turkish Government of the circumstances under which the co-operation took place. The Eussians are to be required to consent that their Admiral shall not command the allied fleet.

By communications from Baron Ottenfels, at Constantinople, the infatuation of the Turks seems to be miraculous. They have made no adequate preparation, and have hardly 30,000 men of regular troops.

I had a meeting with the Chancellor, Peel, and the Lord Chief Justice on the compensation clause in the County Courts Bill. My clause, taken from the Writ of Error Bill, was agreed to, and to be proposed in the House of Commons. The measures to be adopted in consequence of the Eeport of the Commissioners of Legal Enquiry will probably lead to alterations in the mode of proceeding, which will make it necessary to compensate many officers for loss of fees. Peel is disposed to take the Patent Offices into the hands of Government, giving compensation as in Ireland. I have no objection.

June 13.

Lord Stuart de Eothesay succeeds Lord Granville at Paris. This is the King's appointment. He insisted upon it, and the Duke did not think it worth while to make a quarrel about it.

Everything is very nearly settled for Lord Francis Leveson's going to Ireland as Secretary. His father wrote that the Duke should be impeached for getting rid of Huskisson, so it is rather awkward for him to consent so soon to his son's serving under the Duke;

VOL. T. L. but ambition carries it. The appointment is not a bad one.

Lieven did not much like the proposition that the renouncing of belligerent rights on the part of Eussia in the Mediterranean should be declared. The Duke spoke to me of this as his proposition, and seemed pleased with it, as doing away with all the great objections to a cooperation. It is odd, but if I am certain of anything it is that the proposition was mine, that I first mentioned it to the Cabinet.

There were but twelve in the House for Stanhope, and fifty-three for us. [1] He would divide, and had but seven proxies. So we had 86 to 19. At one moment the House was so thin that they had a majority. Lords Grey, Eldon, and Holland were not there.

Lord Bristol made a speech of much feeling in allusion to Lord Liverpool.

June 14.

Cabinet at 3. Aberdeen read his instructions to Lord Heytesbury. He fell into the same fault he had imputed to Dudley, that of writing an essay. I could not understand the reasons for which our Minister might attend Eussian Conferences for peace as a witness, if the French Minister did, but not otherwise, and might not attend at all if the Frenchman attended otherwise than as a witness.

1 proposed that, as Lord Heytesbury was directed o endeavour to ascertain the instructions of the French

Ambassador, and to act with him, he should pass by] On the Corn Bill.]

Paris, and see La Ferronays. It seems Lord Heytes-bury does not wish to go by Paris.

I suggested that, as in all probability the progress of events would bring Lord Heytesbury and Stratford Canning near each other, Lord Heytesbury should have given to him powers superior to those given to Canning, that he might control him, and make our diplomacy march mero intuitu. This will be done.

By the instructions, should Eussia propose the settlement of the Greek question, Lord Heytesbury was to say he had no orders. I suggested he should have at least the power of acceding to the preliminaries of a treaty, that is, that he should be empowered to accept from the Turks their accession to the principle of the Treaty of London, and to communicate that accession, with orders to desist from blockade, to the English Admiral. This will, I believe, be done.

I endeavoured to make the Cabinet feel that Lord Heytesbury would arrive at head-quarters about two months after our last intelligence from them, and that, as events would proceed rapidly, he should have instructions as ample as possible. The Duke seemed to think there. was time enough.

As to attending the Conferences, he will never be invited to assist at Conferences relating toeussian objects. He will be invited to attend at Conferences on the Greek question. Our orders, therefore, should be precise.

It seems Stratford Canning doubts about going.

We decided on accepting from the Spaniards 750,000. for the claims of our merchants, and giving them 200,000. for their claims. At first the Spaniards offered 700,000., and claimed 250,000.

June 15.

Lord Stuart de Eothesay dined with me. He told me the King promised him the situation when he saw him at Ascot, provided Lord Granville resigned. His Majesty must be more careful in future. This will not do.

House at 5. Penrhyn Bill put off till Friday, on account of Lord Carnarvon's having the gout. The Chancellor complained of the Bill being put off. He had taken down the evidence to Wimbledon, yesterday, and had read, as I have done, the 500 folio pages. The whole substance of them might be comprised in ten or fifteen.

June 17.

On Eldon's speech the House refused to suspend the standing orders as regarded the Earl of Shrewsbury's Estate Bill.

The Duke of Wellington and most of our side went behind the Woolsack. The Whigs had not the same tender conscience, and all voted for suspending the order.

The Duke begged me to see the declaration of neutrality we call upon Eussia to make. It seems the commissariat of the Eussian army is very bad. The Danube is swollen so much that they cannot throw a bridge over it. They cannot get to its banks. It is hardly expected they will be able to do so before July. In the meantime the troops are crowded together in Wai-lachia, a country intersected by streams in all directions, and they have little to eat. The Emperor is said to be ill already. The troops must suffer horribly. They will be obliged to move at last in the hot season; there is but one road; they will have no water, and malaria, probably the plague. It will be the judgment of Providence on unprincipled ambition.

Croker is made a Privy Councillor, because he felt himself passed over by the late appointments, and thought his conduct last year had made him a marked man. Calcraft is Paymaster.

June 18.

From what Lady Aberdeen said at the Duke of Clarence's breakfast this morning, I do not think she has the least idea of Aberdeen's having the Foreign Office only for three or four months. He has lent the house to Sir George Murray, and should I succeed, it would be very awkward for me to put him out. This I know, that I could do the business of the office better than Aberdeen, and I know that the Duke thinks so. It is very unlucky for me that there has been no business in the House this session, because business is my forte, and I should have stood forward prominently for the office if I had had the opportunity of speaking much in defence of the Government.

June 20.

Wool Committee. Mr. Gott examined, who is one of the men we had at the Board of Trade. A very clever man.

House. Penrliyn Disfranchisement Bill. The Chancellor made an excellent speech and showed there was no ground whatever for the charge of that extent of corruption which would alone justify a remedial measure. No division.

I have advised Aberdeen to write two circular letters to all the Foreign Ministers, and to desire them to send copies of all the dispatches of which the receipt has not been acknowledged. The other, to order them to write only official letters upon all matters connected with their public functions. The inconvenience of not adopting this course has been often felt. There is frequently a lacuna in the public correspondence, which leaves the Government in ignorance of important facts, and of the chain of events.

Dispatches have been received from Portugal. Don Miguel seems to be triumphant at the troops going over to him. What a contemptible people!

The Eussians have no forage in Wallachia, and the peasants are already made hostile by their extortions. They have no money, everything having been calculated for an immediate advance. They must be in great difficulty.

June 21.

We had some conversation about Portugal. Lamb has resigned. He has written as intemperately as ever. The Duke is lor accepting his resignation. The Cabinet in general seems disposed to think he must, under present circumstances, be retained. Lamb says it is expected that the Cortes will declare Miguel King, and that he will refer the question to the foreign Courts, before he assumes the title. Lamb wants to come away on the latter declaring Miguel King. The captain of the English brigs at Oporto has violated the blockade. We must disown him.

Aberdeen says the American Minister has sent in a most warlike note on the subject of the punishment of a subject of the United States by the British authorities in the disputed districts in Maine. We say we have always exercised authority there. The Americans say not.

The Turks have shown, through the Minister of the Netherlands, a desire to see the Ambassadors return to Constantinople, and to have a reconciliation with the Greeks. To the Eussians they say they are ready to do all that can be required under the Treaty of Aker-man, if the Emperor will tear up the Treaty of London. We shall propose that through one of the Turkish Commanders it shall be communicated to the Turks that we are ready to treat, but only on the basis already proposed. They must in the first instance accept the mediation and declare an armistice.

June 23.

The Duke is for recalling Lamb, and for withdrawing the mission on the declaration by the Cortes that Miguel is the rightful King of Portugal. I gave him a draft of a dispatch, with two ends, one recalling Lamb, the other telling him he will be recalled as soon as the public service permits. I gave Aberdeen a dispatch desiring Lamb, if Miguel declared he should not assume the Eoyal title till he had ascertained the sentiments of foreign Courts, to decline becoming the channel of a communication to that effect, but not to come away, leaving it to his Government to decide under all the circumstances. I think this the safer course, for it would be very embarrassing, if we should bring away our Minister, and other Powers should leave theirs.

June 24.

The Duke was desirous of recalling Lamb for his offensive letters. Lords Melville, Bathurst, and I agreed with him; but Sir G. Murray, Peel, Aberdeen, and Goulburn were the other way, and so was Herries. So a letter is to be written to Lamb, telling him the Government have long thought his functions could be better performed by another; that they hoped the long forbearance with which he has been treated would have corrected his contentious tone and temper. That he was only not recalled because it was proved his recall at this moment might expose the policy of the Government to misconstruction.

Aberdeen had prepared a dispatch, much too civil, requesting him to remain. This we all disapproved of. I then asked if he had mine, which he had, so I read it, and it was approved of. I have since made some amendments in it, and dressed it up a little.

Another dispatch of Aberdeen's was unnecessarily severe. It intimated a doubt whether in one of his dispatches Lamb had been serious.

The Duke was very earnest for Lamb's recall, and said we should find him quite unbearable, and counteracting us in every way. That no public servant he ever knew had written half so offensively as Lamb, and all others had been severely reprimanded for it. That Lamb had ventured to use offensive expressions to Canning once, and Canning had put an end to it at once; that in the same way the late Lord Melville had silenced Sir G. Street, and Lord Londonderry Sir John Moore.

June 25.

In the park Glengall told me O'Connell intended to start for the County of Clare, and would come in; that Fitzgerald would be thrown out.

Cabinet dinner at the Chancellor's. Great discussion about keeping or giving up the Lieutenant-General of the Ordnance. Peel and Goulburn for giving up. The Duke strongly for keeping him. I was for fighting it boldly. I can see our friends want a good party division. It would besides be very unwise to yield to the Finance Committee a point fought in the Committee by the Government, and carried by two against them. I know the feeling of the House is against abdicating the power of Government, and its responsibility, and placing both in the hands of a Committee. However, Peel is quite of another way of thinking, and I think I see that whatever I say against his opinion annoys him. He answers captiously. He was delighted to have me as a member of the Government. Perhaps I did not meet him with enough cordiality, but he does not suit me. I get on better with all the other members of the Government than with him.

The Duke seemed much annoyed at Peel's indisposition to fight the question. I do not think he was quite well. Aberdeen has made a dispatch to Lamb, out of his own and mine. It will do, but I do not think it is all on the same level. He sometimes goes too far, and sometimes not far enough. He did not at all like writing the letter, as Lamb is a friend of his. He is no friend of mine.

June 27.

Cabinet on the Lieutenant-General of the Ordnance.

Peel strongly against the Duke's wish to maintain the office, but ready to fight it if it is thought that as head of the Government the Duke is pledged upon it. The Duke thinks he is, for he has given the strongest evidence in favour of it before the Finance Committee, and really thinks it ought to be maintained. We have to read the evidence and decide on Monday. I think the thing is decided, and that we shall endeavour to maintain it.

Peel [1] certainly has not the character suited to the leader of a party, or to the command of a popular assembly.

June 28.

The Eussians passed the Danube at Isatzka on the 9th.

Eecorder's report. Four people ordered for execution. One for forgery, one for burglary, two for beating and robbing a man in a house of ill-fame. There was a woman engaged, who was spared on account of her sex, but she was the most guilty of all. I do not like Eecorder's reports. I am shocked by the inequality of punishment. At one time a man is hanged for a crime [1 Referring probably to his cold and stiff' manner, which was always admitted to be a drawback to his otherwise great parliamentary talent.)

which may be as two; because there are few to be hanged, and it is some time since an example has been made of capital punishment for his particular offence. At another time a man escapes for the same crime, having the proportion of five to two to the other, because it is a heavy calendar, and there are many to be executed. The actual delinquency of the individual is comparatively little taken into consideration. Extraneous circumstances determine his fate.

July 1.

House. Lord Grey presented a petition on the subject of the currency, and made a short speech. We shall have a debate on the subject on Thursday.

Peel's manner was better to-day, but he has been very disagreeable lately, and the Duke is annoyed. I wish we had some one else to lead the House of Commons.

July 2.

Cabinet dinner at Lord Bathurst's. The Chancellor not there. I suspect he thought we should have an angry discussion, and chose to be absent, and so clear of it.

Doubts are thrown on the evidence affecting the two men ordered for execution for the robbery in the house of ill-fame, and I conclude they will be transported for life and not executed.

It was decided to ask for money on account of the Canal, and the works at Kingston and Halifax, and to explain the extent of the estimates made; but to say no one was pledged to anything beyond the works on account of which an advance was now asked. We had a great deal of useless talk, a large portion of which originated in Lord Bathurst's being rather drunk. His wine was excellent, and he is a generous host. Peel was in better humour; but he is not the man for his station.

I wish Hardinge spoke a little better. He would lead the House if he did. I hope Sir George Murray will next year.

July 4.

O'Connell is returned for Clare. The Attorney and Solicitor-General have been desired to look into Acts of Parliament to see the law, and state it to the Cabinet, that we may learn what we are about, and have everything arranged. He is expected to attempt to take his seat on Monday. No riot.

Lamb's dispatches received to the 21st. He is in very bad humour, and in one of them says that ' Seeing what he does, to remain there is a disgrace."

He is very angry with Dudley for having sent to Paris and Madrid some dispatches of his marked secret and confidential, communicating a conversation with Campazano. It has come to the knowledge of the Spanish Court. Campazano has had a severe lecture, and went to Lamb to reproach him. I dare say it is by the indiscretion of Lord Granville or Bosanquet that the substance of the dispatch became known. To send it to them was a matter of course.

Lamb knows nothing, or tells nothing; but from the joy of the Miguelites he concludes things are going in their favour. Some English subjects have been arrested.

After all the bugbears Peel raised about the Lieu-tenant-General of the Ordnance, we carried his salary by 202 to 95. I hope confidence in our strength will not lead us to do things we ought not; but we are very strong.

July 5.

At the Cabinet room read Lamb's last dispatches, and letters from several persons at Ennis, giving an account of O'Connell's election. The freeholders to a man deserted their landlords. They marched into the town led by the priests in perfect order. They committed no outrage. If any one seemed disposed to offer insult, others pinioned him, and carried him away. They bivouacked in order in the neighbourhood of the town. At night there was no one in the streets. The police were stationed at every entrance to the town. They put in motion the whole male population voting and not voting. All the gentlemen supported Fitzgerald. No whisky was allowed to the people, and the priests had influence enough to prevent their drinking any; but it was said that at the end of the election they would be permitted to drink. Fitzgerald spoke well. The others ill. O'Connell like a blackguard.

By Lamb's dispatches it appears that several Englishmen have been thrown into prison and ill-treated. In this the Portuguese Government seems to have acted in contravention of treaties, and the Englishmen will be claimed.

July 7.

The Russians have lost 2,000 men in the assault of Brailow. However, it surrendered afterwards. The Turks fought well.

158   Cabinet room. The Miguelites say they entered Coimbra on the 25th, but this was not believed at Lisbon on the 28th, nor known at Oporto on the 27th. The Cortes declared Miguel King on the 28th. A servant of Lamb's had been seized, and he threatened to go away if he was not given back, yet he asks for his instructions to authorise him to declare England would protect the person of her own subjects!

It is reported that O'Connell is returned. They went on polling as long as they could, and polled many more than was thought possible. By far the most serious position in the present state of the country is the state of Ireland.

July 8.

The Duke showed me a letter he had written to Aberdeen, and a corrected letter to Itabayana, declining to have any other than an unofficial communication with him on the subject of Portugal.

Codrington has written an able answer to the letter recalling him. I have not seen it yet.

Lamb was to leave Lisbon on last Monday week. He may be expected immediately. Aberdeen is nervous about the recall of Codrington and Lamb. Madame de Lieven, who sat not far from me at dinner at the Prince de Polignac's, said responsibility always made men nervous; that Canning became quite timid when he was Prime Minister.

Neither M. nor Mde. de Lieven would look my way.

I hear from all quarters that Hardinge has done admirably and is gaining weight in the House. I am delighted at this.

159   The account of Sir George Murray is uniform that he is pleasing, and will be popular, but he has no power as a speaker.

July 9.

Cabinet dinner at Aberdeen's. Peel not there.

The Lord High Admiral dates an order from his yacht (he being at Bushey, and the order dated three days hence), with the object of trying whether he cannot do acts without his Council. He may by the law; but there was an understanding that he was to execute the office in London, and with the Council, there being a counter-signature to all his instruments. This was settled in the presence of the Attorney-General last year, and the Chancellor declared the necessity of counter-signature in answer to a question from me last year. We resist the Lord High Admiral's attempt. It is a delicate business, but it is a duty which must be executed.

July 10.

At the Cabinet room read Codrington's letter. It is not very dangerous. As soon as I have finished the wool question I shall write a memorandum upon it.

It seems the return of O'Connell is carried. The election concluded quietly, and with civilities on both sides.

July 11.

The Miguelites are within two leagues of Oporto. Saldanha has taken the command, and holds out hopes of being able to maintain himself. Taipa has gone mad. The Oporto merchants are in a terrible fright.

The accounts from Ireland are awful. It seems there are deputies from all parts of Ireland present in Clare. The organisation is perfect, the obedience implicit.

The Duke read to me his letter to the King explaining the difference between the Lord High Admiral and his Council. The Lord High Admiral has written a very harsh answer to Sir George Cockburn, who has sent a very proper and respectful reply. I got from Sir George Cockburn Codrington's letter, and all the papers which throw light upon it, and was occupied in writing a memorandum upon the subject till 3 o'clock in the morning. It seems to me that our answer to his letter is complete.

The Chancellor said to me, ' We must try if we cannot set up the Duke during the vacation to endeavour to settle the Catholic question." He said, too, ' What do you think of our seeing Hardinge some day leading the House of Commons? '

July 12.

A very rainy day, with a westerly wind which we hope brings rain in torrents to Ireland, and damps the Orangemen.

Cabinet at 2. A very important letter read from Lord Anglesey, pressing upon the Government the danger of the present state of the Catholic question, expressing his repugnance to yield to the appearance of force, and his opinion of the unpropitious circumstances of the present moment for making any concessions; but still declaring his conviction that things cannot remain as they are, and will become worse. The letter

~~THE CATHOLIC QUESTION~~. 161 will be laid before the King. The Duke says the King will be very little moved by it, and will swear a little.

On the subject of the Duke of Clarence the King is breast high, and says the attempt must be resisted in limine.

It is evident to me that nothing but the occurrence of the most untoward events, and the utmost misconduct of the Catholics in Ireland, can prevent the early carrying of the Catholic question.

Lord John Bussell's motion for an address to the King will be met by the previous question, and an attack upon himself, for having by a motion calculated to provoke discussions mischievous to the question, endeavoured to give the effect of a party vote to one which does not in reality bear that character.

July 14.

At the Cabinet room read the Consul's account of the entrance of Miguel's troops into Oporto. Had before read the captain of the ' Cordelia's." The cowardice of Palmella and his friends seems to have been extravagant; 4,600 soldiers were ready to fight, but they had no leaders. Even Saldanha left them. [1] The troops marched through Oporto towards Braga.

Eead Lawrence's letter on the subject of the differences on the borders of Maine. It is rather a warlike 1 According to the Conde de Oarnota, Saldanha intended to remain to the last with the troops. But having gone on hoard the Belfast' to confer with Palmella and the Junta, who had taken refuge there, he found to his surprise and indignation that while he was asleep the vessel had dropped down the river en route for England. Memoirs of Marshal Saldanha, vol. i. p. 195.]

162   VOL. I. M. letter. This subject is one of great importance, and must be deeply considered.

At the Chancellor's. Had a conversation with Baron Bulow about the imprisonment of Alcndia's servant. It seems Kae, the magistrate, was foolish enough to say publicly he should have treated his master in the same way. This had alarmed all the Ministers, and they mean to send their little notes. It seems they would be satisfied with this that in the event of a servant of theirs committing a criminal offence, he should be taken up, notice given to them, they would dismiss him, and then we might do as we liked. This is fair enough. Dudley had settled a similar affair.

Had a long conversation with Polignac. He is very anxious about getting Ibrahim Pasha out of the Morea, and wants to send troops to establish a land blockade. He thinks without that we shall not get him out, and that both he and his father only want an excuse. He feels, as I do, that what we have to do now is to get our ambassadors back to Constantinople the sooner the better.

Lord Duncannon told me he thought O'Connell would, not be quiet. That he found it necessary to keep the lead. He is not coming over this year. Lord John Eussell does not bring on his motion. He gives way to his friends' opinion without changing his own.

July 15, 1828.

Cabinet at 3. Vesey Fitzgerald gave an awful account of the state of Ireland. He
163 said, in addition to all we already know of the organisation of the Catholics, that the universal opinion was that a Catholic might sit in Parliament. He was very desirous that measures should immediately be taken for vacating O'Connell's seat, on the ground of his declining to take the oaths. This measure to be followed up by a Bill making Catholics ineligible. The unanimous opinion of his colleagues was against Vesey's.

We have now the chance of quiet; we should then have the certainty of convulsion. Next session O'Connell must take the initiative, and then the course is easy. Parliament must be kept sitting for the purpose.

I said I had more than the conviction arising from a course of reasoning; I had that of intuition that the line he proposed was wrong. In fact it would be madness.

The Duke of Clarence has desired Cockburn may be turned out. Lord Brecknock and Clerk will resign if Cockburn goes out. Sir E. Heron would stay, but reluctantly. The way in which they had been going on has long been disagreeable, the Duke endeavouring to do all without his Council. Cockburn will be retained, happen what may. The Duke of Clarence is a little mad.

July 16.

Lord Heytesbury finds he cannot pass through Wallachia. The plague is there. He is obliged to go by Yassy, and thence by Ismail and Galatz, to headquarters. The whole army of the Eussians encamps. They are afraid of entering any Turkish house. Lord Heytesbury is obliged to take with him a complete camp equipage.

164   Lord Cowley says the Kussians at Yassy acknowledge a loss of from 10,000 to 12,000 men at Ibraila. This is hardly possible. The Turkish women came out with

axes, and the Turks made six sallies during the storm. The Turks had only 3,000 men left when they surrendered Ibraila on condition of retreating to Si-listria. It seems their plan is to defend all their places.

House. Lord Holland made a motion for papers relative to Greece and Portugal in order to speak at length on both subjects. He said he made no charges, but he insinuated a great many, and in speaking of the Protocol was very bitter against the Duke.

Aberdeen answered him, and said all that was necessary, and made a safe speech, but he rendered the debate dull by his heavy manner. Then Goderich spoke; then the Duke, who was rather animated, but did not answer the attack on the Protocol powerfully. Then Dudley a few words; then Lansdowne, who made a speech intended to close the debate, and on which it was impossible to hang an accusation. Thus I had no opportunity of speaking, and the Session has passed over without my having done anything. I certainly do not like my situation. However, next year it is evident there will be opposition enough.

The King has written an admirable letter to the Duke of Clarence. He tells him he has been in error from the beginning; that as a Privy Councillor Sir G. Cockburn could not have done otherwise than he did; that the Duke must give way.

L165 It seems the Duke of Clarence's family are desirous he should give up his office. He does too much. His late illness is not by any means overcome.

The idea is that the Duke is rather mad.

He must be so, or very ill-advised. He treats Sir G. Cockburn's last letter to him as impertinent. It was the most respectful letter a man could address to a Prince.

The Duke's resignation would be inconvenient; but consistently with our public duty it was impossible to act otherwise than we have done.

July 17.

Cabinet at 2. Considered whether we should accede to the French proposal of sending troops to drive Ibrahim Pasha out of the Morea by a land blockade; a thing by-the-bye absurd. They must have fighting.

There is an objection to this measure on principle. It is clearly a measure of war. However, the necessity is so urgent of finishing the Greek business (which we can never do while Ibrahim is in the Morea, for the Turks will never cede what they hold), and of getting back our Minister to Constantinople before the Eussians approach it; and it is so expedient to continue to act in concert with France, and more especially not to prevent a step which the French Government evidently propose under the idea that it will be of advantage to them in their position at home, that we have overlooked all objections and given our consent. The French said they would not send the troops without our consent.

All men begin now to see that this war will last more than one campaign. The L166 Eussians are much irritated by the opposition they have met with, and spoiled by the bad example of the gratuity of 1,500,000. given to the troops in Persia out of the sum paid by the Shah, that they talk of still larger gratuities and of pillaging Constantinople.

Pozzo says the Emperor is no longer the master of his army. There has been some sedition. It is even said desertion.

The French think 8,000 men will be enough. The Duke thinks they should have 20,000, and that 15,000 is the smallest number with which they should go. Ibrahim has at least 20,000, some accounts say more than 30,000, and his army rests upon Navarin, Modon, and Coron, three fortresses open to the sea. Mahomet Ali has sixteen ships ready for sea at Alexandria.

I suggested the expediency of blockading Alexandria, and of bringing Church 1 from Dragomestre, 2 and the 2,000 men Capo has at Egina, to the Isthmus of Corinth, where we might feed them and support them on both sides. This would prevent Ibrahim Pasha from leaving the Morea for the purpose of going to Eoumelia, and the Turks about Missolonghi from joining him in the Morea. More ships are to be sent for this purpose.

We have eleven battalions in the Mediterranean, and could not spare above three for any operation; that is, 1,500 men. If we sent them from hence we could not send above 6,000 men, and they would be too late. Besides, we do not wish to burn our fingers. The French will find it very expensive, and probably get the plague, and some few hard blows.

1 The-well-known General Church. 2 A port opposite Santa Maura.

(67

I advised Aberdeen to look at our despatches and the language we have held on this subject, to keep our present language as much the same as possible, and, if not the same, to assign good reasons for the change. We should appear to consent to a measure of war with reluctance.

Metternich takes our view, and wishes to settle the Greek question as soon as possible by getting Ibrahim out of the Morea, no matter how.

House. The Duke looks very pale, and I think he is by no means well. He is worn out.

I suggested to Aberdeen that we should come to an understanding as soon as possible with France and Austria as to what shall be done with regard to Miguel, and as to what advice should be given to Pedro. We must follow Pedro in recognising Dom Miguel.

There is a report of a Eussian general having deserted to the Turks with 7,000 men. It is incredible.

July 18.

Polignac is pleased at being allowed to send a French army to the Morea, but he would rather have had English co-operation.

I find there is no objection to English officers going as volunteers, and I shall apply to Prince de Polignac for leave for Henry to join the French army. I shall make him write full details of what he sees.

I gave Aberdeen some memoranda on the subject of this French expedition.

The Duke of Clarence came to town immediately on receiving the King's letter,

[168

and to-day he had an inter-view with the Duke of Wellington, who soothed him by showing him that even the Duke of York as Com-mander-in-Chief could not move ten men without a Secretary of State. However, the Duke of Clarence went home, rather resigning than not, piu si chiar. He had then a conference with Sir George Cockburn, which ended stormily. However, after that he wrote a hasty letter to the King, consenting to remain, and saw the Council, told Cockburn to behave more properly in future, and gave directions for business to be done in his absence. He sets off for Portsmouth again to-morrow.

I gathered from Aberdeen that he expected Melville would have been restored.

Had some talk with Eosslyn about the Catholic question. He showed me a letter of Lord Donough-more's to Sir E. Wilson, by which it seems that the priests, who are described as being not more enlightened than the peasants, are carried on by their flocks.

The Chancellor is very desirous of having the question settled, and has hopes of the King.

As long as the Duke of Cumberland is in the country I fear we shall do little good with the King, unless by unanimity and resignation if he resists.

Eosslyn said we let Holland off very easily the other night, and that Aberdeen made a very weak speech. He acknowledged I had no good opportunity of speaking. In fact, I was so exhausted that I could not have spoken well; but I really had no opportunity at all. I do not like my position at all. If there was a. regular opposition I should be useful, and stand forward; but in calm times I have nothing to do. I feel my situation a disparagement. I shall remain for the present and do what I can for the Catholics; but if I find I can do nothing for them with the Cabinet, or if any move should take place and I be left where I am, I shall probably resign. I say probably, because I cannot foresee all the possible combinations; but my first feeling will be to resign.

July 19.

Cabinet room at 3 to read papers relating to the American question before the Cabinet met. The Americans demand the release of John Baker, a man who settled on land we claim, and over which we say we have always exercised jurisdiction. He created a riot, if it was no more, erected the American standard, c., and detained the English mail. They demand compensation for him, too. This is their first demand. The second is, that the disputed territory should not be under British jurisdiction. They do not ask that it should be placed under theirs, but propose its inhabitants should be under no rule at all till the arbitration is over that is, for the next two years.

The Duke said we could only give up the jurisdiction on one of two grounds either because we thought we had no right to it, or because we were afraid of the consequences. He was not afraid of the consequences, and thought we had the right.

Aberdeen had framed a despatch in conformity with what he thought would be the feeling of the Cabinet, but contrary to his own; that is, he had adhered to the line we had hitherto taken, that of maintaining our rights and making no concession. From the tone of Lawrence's note this line would lead to war.

It seems the State of Maine has declared it will not submit to the decision of the arbitrator should it be adverse, and the general Government urge the point because they are apprehensive of a quarrel with one of the States which might lead to separation.

The despatch or answer to Lawrence places very high our right to the territory and declares our continued jurisdiction. It says we shall maintain it, more especially as the plan proposed by Lawrence is one which is quite inadmissible, leaving the people in the disputed territory without any government at all.

I asked if this last sentence was inserted to leave an opening to further negotiation on the subject? If it was, it should be more clearly expressed. It should not be an opening of which the Americans might decline to take notice. If we got into a war our answer would be criticised. We should be asked whether we meant to leave the question open to further negotiation? If we did, it would be asked why we did not express ourselves so clearly as to force the Americans to make another proposal? If, on the other hand, we resolved to maintain the jurisdiction and run all the chances, we should diminish those chances by speaking very decidedly. The least appearance of wavering would lead to further bullying on their part. The impression is they only want a good opportunity of going to war.

I am convinced this opportunity is not a good one for us. We are not prepared for it, and the country would not stand by us if by leaving the question open we could by possibility have avoided war.

Aberdeen had understood a letter of Sir Howard Douglas as advising a provisional arrangement. On looking into the letter more closely it seemed his opinion was not that.

At last we adjourned the final decision till we had had time to look at the whole case.

Aberdeen, Peel, Lord Bathurst, and I are, I think, for allowing the thing to train on, leaving a clear opening for negotiation. But had it not been for me the letter Aberdeen read would have been approved and sent, and we should probably have had war.

Aberdeen is unfit for all the higher parts of his duty. All the ordinary work he does very well, but he cannot grasp the argument on a great question. He chose to assume that we had exercised exclusive jurisdiction. That point is by no means clear. We have consented not to cut wood on the disputed lands, and not to make grants. This is but reasonable that the property in dispute may not be deteriorated. We have engaged to leave everything as it is.

Peel read a letter from himself to Lord Anglesey, asking whether he wanted any further powers to maintain tranquillity during the Eecess. Lord Anglesey says decidedly not.

The Lord High Admiral had a most stormy conference with the Duke and Cockburn, and behaved very ill to

Cockburn. Cockburn is to express regret that he wrote i on some occasion instead of speaking to the Lord High

Admiral. So this matter ends for the present.

July 21.

At the Cabinet room read papers relating to the Boundary question. The Archbishop of Canterbury is dead. There was no House to-day, the Speaker being unable to attend. Palmella and the others are arrived at Plymouth in their crazy steamboat.

A second day of constant rain, and great fears entertained for the harvest.

July 22.

Cabinet. Arranged the Speech. It is very good. The Eussians are now said to have lost 7,000 men at Brailow. Wrote an answer to that fact of the American note which regards the suspension of our jurisdiction in the disputed territory during the arbitration. My object has been to state in strong terms the objections to the arrangement they propose of leaving the inhabitants of that territory without any government, to object to their proposal on the ground of its own demerits, and of its being contradictory to the ordinary principles by which the conduct of equal States has been regulated in similar cases, but to leave the door open to a fresh proposition on their parts.

As the United States Government are supposed to be much influenced by the fear of quarrelling with Maine, and Maine seems to apprehend that its acquiescence in the continuance of our jurisdiction might be held by the arbitrator to be an admission of our right, I have called that apprehension groundless, and I am in hopes that such a declaration on our part will go a great way towards quieting them.

The King says he took more pains to get on with Aberdeen than he ever did with any one (that was at Brighton), but all to no purpose. Aberdeen thinks the King hates him, but does not care about it. He has written to the King to tell him a Prince of Bavaria is desirous of paying his respects to him, that Polignac has a letter to deliver from the King of France, and that the Swedish Minister is desirous of presenting his credentials. To all these letters he has received no answer.

Lord Harrowby told Aberdeen he was the King's Minister eighteen years, and was never asked to the Cottage till the King sent for him to be Prime Minister.

July 23.

Council at Windsor for the King's Speech. The King objected to the paragraph which thanked the House of Commons for the Finance Committee instituted at his recommendation, and likewise to the pledge on his part that he would endeavour to reduce expenditure as far as was consistent with the dignity of his Crown and the interests of his people. However, he was prevailed upon to allow the latter part of the paragraph to stand, the former part being given up.

He was not well, having caught a bad cold, and was much affected by the death of the Archbishop of Canterbury.

The Bishop of London is to be Archbishop of Canterbury, and Chester London. I told the Duke I thought the last a dangerous appointment. The man Chester is a proud, overbearing Churchman. He will be a Thomas-a- Becket, and do infinite mischief in these times.

His appointment will create a great deal of hostile observation, and be considered as an indication of the Duke's feeling as to the Catholic question. He will be very troublesome. I told the Duke all this.

I told him, too, how important a diocese Chester was, and named Hodgson and J. B. Sumner as very fit men to be bishops, giving, however, the fair and true character of the men.

The Duke spoke of Addington as the man to whom Huskisson had intended to assign the task of bringing our case before the arbitrator as to the north-east boundary in America. I told him I knew Addington formerly, and I was sure he was not a fit man. I hope either Sir Howard Douglas or a lawyer man whose name I forget, resident at Fredericton, will be made our Commissioner. Hardinge should look into the case afterwards.

From what Sir George Murray said I am afraid the arbitrator must, under the words of the treaty, give the case against us. The Duke always said the King of the Netherlands was a bad man for us, and since he has been made arbitrator it seems he has been discovered to be in a flirtation with the Americans as to a canal between the Pacific and Atlantic.

The Duke of Cumberland was at Windsor; that is, at the Eoyal Lodge in the park. He is a Mephisto-pheles, and sure, wherever he can, to do any mischief. However, thank God, he leaves England next week, having not got his money.

The Cabinet dined with me at Koehampton. I asked Peel to drink a glass of wine, and showed him two or three pictures. The consequence was a cordiality of manner. I really believe he is only rather a proud, touchy man, and that the least attempt at management would make him very cordial.

July 24.

Wrote a paper, according to the Duke's suggestion, as an answer to the American demand that we should suspend our jurisdiction in the disputed territory pendente lite. All the reasoning had occurred to me before, but I had not put it together so well in the paper I read to the Duke yesterday as I did in the one I wrote this morning. Took the paper to Aberdeen. He had proposed nothing, giving up his own opinion to what he conceived to be that of the Duke, and waiting till the Cabinet had decided upon the substance of the answer before he put pen to the paper. It seems what he read the other day was chiefly Dudley's, and I dare say Huskisson's.

The Duke objected to the term c disputed territory' which I had used throughout, so I changed it to c undetermined line of frontier." I am inclined to think my paper will be substantially adopted.

Aberdeen told us to-day that Mr. Lawrence had told him in conversation that they must first have satisfaction for the injury done to an American citizen, and then they might perhaps propose a concurrent jurisdiction for the disputed territory. So we are to put forward our answer to the demand of satisfaction first, because that is our strongest point. That we cannot yield in honour.

The Consul at Odessa has sent the march route of the Eussian army. It marches in three columns. The left goes along the shore. The right marches on Shumla. The three columns are to unite at Arna Bourgas,[1] and thence march on Constantinople. They make twelve marches from Shumla to Constantinople. I see by the map that the centre and left must pass the Balkans before they can operate upon the communications of Shumla. Each column may consist of 30,000 men, besides the guards in reserve.

The command of the sea, of which we deprived the Turks at Navarino, would have made the Eussian enterprise abortive.

The Chancellor told me he had stated the same objections I did to the appointment of Blomfield; but he thought Blomfield would be manageable about the Catholics. I do not.

Eeceived a very civil letter from the Prince de Polignac. He has written for leave for both Henry and William to join the French army in the Morea. I asked Lord Hill to give Henry leave should the two Governments do so, which he promised to do. I wrote to Henry, and told him the arrangement I had made for him.

Had some conversation on the Catholic question with Sir G. Murray. He fears the measure will be delayed till the Catholics have gone so far as to make it impossible.

[1 Between Adrianople and Constantinople.]

July 26.

Cabinet room. Bead Zichy's account of his conversation with the Emperor Nicholas in April. The Emperor declared that he detested the Greeks, that he considered them rebels, that he was attached to the principles of the Holy Alliance, and should very unwillingly see the Greeks free. He desired that there should exist the Suzerainte of the Porte. He made war for the honour of Eussia, and to open the debouches of her southern provinces.

He declares the self-denying ordinance of the Protocol was introduced at his desire, and he thinks he did a great thing in getting England to adopt any measure by which she was to gain nothing. He considered the Protocol as leading to the treaty, but acknowledged the Duke of Wellington always spoke of war as a thing quite foreign to the object of the Protocol.

It appears by the Due de Mortemar's letters from Karson of July 5, that the Emperor was dead sick of the war, and would be delighted at receiving proposals he could accept.

Hardinge said Peel had a sad want of moral courage before the debate, but once in for it his physical courage carried him on.

I told Hardinge the Chancellor looked upon him as the future leader of the House of Commons.

Hardinge treated the idea as visionary; but I advised him to speak on matters of finance and of the subjects unconnected with his office, that the House ~~VOL. I. N~~ might know there was somebody en second in the event of Peel's failing them.

July 27.

Dined with the Duke of Wellington. After dinner there was some conversation respecting the Duke of Marlborough and the campaigns in Spain, c. The Duke of Wellington said the Duke of Marlborough first marched his army in columns in the manoeuvres which preceded the siege of Bouchain. The march to the Danube was la grande guerre, political rather than military, and not executed in as short a period as it would have been done in now.

The Duke seemed very much pleased at having taken Cambray one day, and Peronne la Pucelle the next, both by storm. In Peronne there were 600 or 700 regulars, and 2,500 or 3,000 National Guard. Its chief defence is water, but it could always be attacked as the Duke attacked it, and could only be taken in that way. He took a hornwork first, and then placed a battery of eighteen field-pieces which enfiladed a bastion, and drove the men away. The guards then stormed, and were much pleased at taking La Pucelle.

They spoke of Luxembourg, an impregnable fortress, with underground communications with distant outworks. The ground rocky, and the water bad; but it is placed in an impracticable country, leading to nothing, and is always neglected.

The Duke said he had advised the putting the fortresses of the Netherlands into such a state of defence that the French, who liked broken heads more than other people, might think twice before they attacked them. I observed that with so many fortresses the Netherlander might have no force left in the field. He said he thought that would be found. Coblentz was spoken of as the best fortified place, but very large.

The Duke said he thought Bonaparte's game was up from the retreat of the French from the lines of Torres Yedras. He subsisted by conquest; and the moment it was proved that the English could hold a point of the Continent against all his force the charm was at an end.

The news of the armistice was brought to the Duke just after the blowing up of Burgos. The people about him advised him not to pass the Ebro, but he said he would at least try and drive them out of Spain.

He passed the Ebro, and gained the battle of Vit-toria. The news of that battle led to the denouncing of the armistice. [1 This latter fact is mentioned in Savary's 'Memoirs." Stadion, having got the news, ran to the several doors of the Emperor of Eussia, c. (they were at a chateau in Silesia), and said, ' Levez vous, levez vous; on a gagne une grande bataille en Espagne!"

The Duke said he by instinct knew one marshal would not assist another, and often acted under that impression; but he did not know till afterwards that [1 Between the Emperor of Russia and the King of Prussia on one side and Napoleon I. on the other, signed at Pleschwitz June 4, 1813.]

180

Bonaparte really had not the power to make one marshal obey another. He had heard from the Archduke Charles (a much more acute observer, he said, than himself), or he had read or heard somewhere that the Archduke had said, that the Eepublican marshals quarrelled just like the Due de Burgogne and the other French princes in the time of Louis XIV. and XV.

Of Bonaparte he spoke with admiration.

There was some talk about Mallet's conspiracy, and the view Bonaparte took very early of the unstable character of his own power.

The Duke said the French had few glasses and did not use them much. All our officers had glasses continually at their eyes, and thus saw a great deal more than the French, who trusted to their patrols and reconnaissances.

The Duke told me he hoped he could diminish the charge of collecting the revenue, and also of the navy and army. He was very anxious for an efficient sinking fund.

He thought the Americans would do nothing till we were engaged with a foreign war.

I said, ' Or with a rebellion in Ireland."

July 31.

Council at St. James's. Met the Prince de Polignac, whom I thanked for a letter I had just received from him acquainting me with the permission of the French Government to Henry and William to join the French army in the Morea.

(81

The French send 18,000 men; 12,000 in one body first, and 6,000 afterwards. Count Maison commands them.

I had some conversation with Polignac as to the hospitals, provisions, quarantine, c., and I promised to mention these points again to the Cabinet. I did immediately to Aberdeen.

There was a Bavarian prince to be presented to the King Prince Maximilian, a cousin of the King of Bavaria. The young man has been waiting three weeks in London, keeping himself close, thinking he could not properly appear till he had seen the King.

The Bishop of London kissed hands for Canterbury, and Chester was sworn in a Privy Councillor, which the Bishop of London always is.

The Duke told me he wished to give the Bishop of Chester's living of Bishopsgate to Lord Grey's brother; but he had been Evangelical, and before he gave him a piece of preferment so conspicuous he wished to know what his opinions really were. It was for Lord Grey's credit as well as his own that there should be a professional fitness. I told him I thought Mr. Grey would communicate with Lord Grey, and not accept if his brother thought he should be embarrassed by the favour. The Duke said he abstained from communicating with Lord Grey; he made no conditions, he offered this as a mark of respect to Lord Grey. If Mr. Grey could not take the living of Bishopsgate that is, was not a fit person for it he might do something else for him, but nothing so good. He spoke of Mapledurham as vacant; that it belonged to Eton College, which would claim it; that he thought of giving it to Dr. Keate, the head master of Eton. If Grey could not have Bishopsgate, Keate might, and Grey Mapledurham.

I told him Keate could not properly hold Bishops-gate and continue head master of Eton, and it would be a great misfortune to deprive Eton of so good a master.

By the Duke's speaking of Mapledurham as vacant I hope my old tutor Sumner is the new bishop. I think he has the living of Mapledurham.

I told the Duke I had had no communication with Lord Grey; but my impression was that if the Government did anything for the Catholics he would support, in or out of office, and if they did not he would be in opposition. I understood the Duke to say he had already begun to take measures that is, to feel his way about the Catholics. The great difficulty there is with Peel not with Peel's real opinions, but with his position and reputation, which may throw great difficulties in the way. He is so embarrassed by his Oxford connections, and by being the head, in spite of himself, of the anti-Catholics.

The Duke wishes to have the East India Charter come on next year, to avoid all the meetings and pamphlets and speeches we should hear if people had a long time to prepare. He is against opening the China trade, of which the profits enable the Company to carry on the Government of India; but if it be necessary, which I doubt, to give the Company this pecuniary aid to enable them to carry on the Government of 50 millions of people, I think the money can hardly be raised in a worse manner than by a tax on tea, which the Company's monopoly really is.

Lord Melville seemed to think the clamour for opening the China trade would be irresistible. So I think, and that it ought to be opened.

The Bank Charter is to be renewed next year too, so we shall have enough to do.

August 1.

Lord Eosslyn saw Ellice, and cross-examined him, and he his wife. [1]

Mr. Grey, it seems, is learned, gentlemanlike, and rather high; has rather High Church dispositions, too, and has quarrelled with Sir George and Lady Grey for distributing tracts in his parish. He is a good parish priest and popular preacher. In short, he is really as good a man as can be found for the situation. He has 500. a year and twelve children.

I told all this to the Duke, who said he should be the man, and he would write to him to-night.

Eosslyn has not written to Lord Grey, neither will the Duke.

The Duke said he would do the thing handsomely and not ask him to resign anything he might have; but as the preferment was so good he thought he ought to do so.

This I told Lord Eosslyn. It seems he has a living from the Bishop of Durham, nominally 800. a year, but after paying a curate he receives not much above 500.

[1 i. e. about Mr. Grey, who was his brother-in-law.]

184   Cabinet. First, the Lord High Admiral, who is endeavouring to establish a claim to be obeyed without the intervention of his Council. He is gone to sea with two three-deckers and some small vessels, and is not to reappear till August 9. Nobody knows where he is gone. He has ordered pilots to be ready to take the to Copenhagen on the 10th from the Nore. She is to stay there twenty-four hours, and return by the Great and Little Belts. The orders are to be secret. This expression of his opinion is conveyed in a letter to the two naval lords, in which he tells them he may not have an opportunity of writing again till he returns to the Admiralty. The last order about the vessel going to Copenhagen looks like madness, but it seems it is to take G. Fitz-Clarence there for his pleasure. The letters will be laid before the King, but nothing done yet.

Then we had some talk about Lord Anglesey, who seems to be very imprudent. He has made almost public by a memorandum addressed to Sir J. Byng to be communicated to Lord Hill, and thus passing through many hands, his opinion that the Catholic soldiers are not to be trusted. He is out of humour.

Then came on the question of the East India Charter.

The Duke's chief reasons for urging it on seem to be that he thinks he could get the Company to take Ceylon off our hands, and thus save 100, OOO. a year; that by bringing it on at once we should avoid all the intrigues and talk and pamphlet-writing which would otherwise embarrass us; and that, come on when it may, the finances of the Company require the million they get by the China trade to enable them to carry on the Government of India.

The general feeling seemed to be in favour of delay, and of depriving the Company of the China trade, although by a paper drawn up by the accomptant of the Board of Commissioners it seems their finances are in a very bad state.

I said that if we meant to leave the China trade to the Company we might renew the Charter now; but that if we meant to throw it open, the Company, with five years of their Charter to run, would be intractable.

All, but the East India Company, were opposed to the China monopoly, because all suffered by it. It was in fact a mode of enabling the Company to govern India by a tax levied on a necessary of life in England.

I thought there would be great difficulty in carrying such a measure.

It would be said that the money obtained by the monopoly of the China trade made the Company extravagant. That the amount might be saved by economy.

It was then proposed that the Bank Charter should be renewed next year. Peel protested against having both in the same year. The Duke thought he could get some money from the Bank for the renewal of the Charter; perhaps get the management of the Debt done for nothing.

It seems to me he is sacrificing future advantage for present profit, and all to make a good financial show next year.

186   If the Bank is to be called upon to sacrifice its exclusive privilege within a certain distance of London, and to prevent the creation of other chartered banks, it will not be

much disposed to pay money for what is of no value. So, if the East India Company should be permitted to retain the monopoly of the China trade, it cannot be expected to take upon itself any additional charge that of Ceylon, for instance, the reason of its being allowed to retain the monopoly being its inability without that monopoly to pay its way.

On the subject of the Bank Charter I said that the subject of currency was one on which I always spoke with diffidence, but that it seemed to me that the solvency of a bank, and its trading upon good banking principles, as it is called that is, its lending its notes on short credits were no security against over-issue or against the calamities attending sudden and great variations in the amount of the circulating medium. That, on the contrary, a bank acting on the safest principles could and did contract the currency more rapidly than another, disregarding altogether the injury it inflicted by forcing the immediate payment of debts and by withdrawing the accustomed and expected accommodation. Hence the ruin of its customers. There has been more distress in Scotland than in England on this account.

In 1825 the Bank of England, seeing the exchanges were against this country, in a few months withdrew three millions of its notes. The country banks during the same period issued three millions more. The exchanges continued unfavourable. The crash came; and the Bank suffered, in spite of its own prudence, the penalty of the gambling and dishonesty of the country banks. So far from desiring that the circulation of the Bank should be diminished and that of country banks increased, I thought the contrary would be most for the benefit of the country.

Peel thought the withdrawing of the 1₤. notes secured us against any future redundancy of currency. I admitted it had a salutary effect, but observed that in 1825 only one-third of the excess was in 1₤. notes. The Bank is to be informed the subject may be brought before Parliament next Session.

The blockade of Madeira must be respected. It will be announced as that of Beleni was, not naming Miguel as king.

I met Lieven at dinner at Aberdeen's. He told me he expected the news of the attack on Schoumla between the 6th and the 8th. The whole army was to move from Karson on July 6, and to be before Schoumla on the 12th. They expected four days of fighting. Hassan Pasha was at Schoumla with 40,000 men on the 6th. By the 12th they thought he would have 50,000. The Eussians would have from 50,000 to 70,000, not more.

None of their best generals were there neither Langeron, Paulen, nor Woronzoff. Diebitch was quartermaster-general. He was quartermaster-general to Wittgenstein in the campaign of 1812.

All the fortresses had hitherto been found well garrisoned, and in every respect well provided.

The Sultan had set off for Adrianople. The day before lie left Constantinople he went to the mosque in a sort of foraging cap, having laid aside the turban for the campaign.

Hassan Pasha is the man who destroyed the janissaries.

Lieven did not speak with any great exultation.

Lawrence, the American Minister, had agreed with Aberdeen not to mention that the King of the Netherlands was the arbitrator chosen. (I suppose this silence was to last till he got an answer from Washington.) However, Lawrence wrote to Hughes, the American Minister at Brussels, telling him; and this he did not communicate to Aberdeen for more than a fortnight, nor until a gentleman had arrived from Brussels who knew the fact. Thus the King of the Netherlands will have been first informed by the American Minister, and been talked to by him three weeks before our Minister at Brussels knew officially anything about the matter. A very dirty American trick, which should be resented, and Lawrence shown up and treated as a man who has broken his word.

August 4.

Cabinet at 4. Aberdeen read the proposed instructions to Lord Strangford, who is going to the Brazils. The paper has rather the fault he used to attribute to Dudley, that of being more an essay than an instruction. However, substantially it is correct, and adduces good reasons why Pedro should, on the condition of his completing the marriage, acknowledge Miguel as king, all acts to be in the joint names of Miguel and Donna Maria da Gloria. The almost unanimous decision of the Portuguese in favour of Dom Miguel is insisted on. Pedro is told his abdication is complete. That he would have no assistance if he attempted to conquer Portugal, and that he could not do it. That he must not think of further dividing the monarchy; that is, by separating Madeira, c.

Lord Belmore is going out as Governor to Jamaica. I am astonished he should take such an appointment. He is a man of large fortune.

The Duke recommended strongly to Sir G. Murray the writing in very strong terms to the several governors of the West India Islands, and pressing them to urge the adoption by the local legislatures of the recommendations of Parliament.

Peel felt very strongly, and so did the Duke, that Parliament pressing the adoption of a measure in favour of the slaves, which the local legislatures rejected, would lead the slaves to a rebellion. The Duke referred to a book of a Mr. Franklin on the 'Rebellion in St. Domingo."

The idea of Peel was that the governors would do more by talking individually to the members of the Assemblies than by any speech.

Goulburn, who was for a long time Under-Secretary in the Colonial Department, said the members of the Assemblies were generally managers of estates, who had gone out as stable boys or in the lowest situations-men who wanted to purchase their masters' estates, and whose interests were opposed to those of the proprietors resident in this country.

I suggested that the governors should have hints for their speeches given to them.

The Duke recommended Fitzgerald to look into the timber question and that of gloves.

All have something to do but me. Aberdeen told me he was talking with Lord Wallace, who said no one had made more progress than I had this Session by knowing exactly when to speak and how much, and the merit was greater in me than in many others, as I liked speaking.

Aberdeen introduced the subject by saying,' I dare say you think this an unprofitable Session." I said I did. Then he told me what Lord Wallace had said. I said, 'Those only could have expected otherwise who did not know me. That I believed, if I had anything, I had Parliamentary tact, and I thought a good speech made when nothing ought to be said, crushed a man instead of making him."

Our consent to the French going to the Morea has been received as a personal favour by the King of France. He thinks it of great importance to his Government, the feeling was so strong in the country and in the Chambers in favour of it.

It seems the French army is by no means at the peace complement, nor are the fortresses well provided.

The King and the Government are very much in the hands of the Liberals.

The new Bishop of London has already begun to be troublesome. He has made objections to Mr. Grey's having the living of Bishopsgate, on the ground of his Evangelical opinions. The Duke told me he would satisfy him on that subject.

August 6.

The Emperor of Brazil has broken his word to our Minister at Eio, and will not now consent to negotiate at Monte Video. We must put an end to this war, which exists only for the plunder of neutrals.

Peel has asked Aberdeen to employ Cockburn, his brother-in-law. This is wrong of Peel, for Cockburn was most properly displaced by Dudley, and Aberdeen will not employ him. Cockburn expended 11,000. of the public money, and then declined going to Bogota.

August 7.

Met Polignac at dinner. He seemed very anxious to relieve Portugal from the state of Coventry in which it is now placed, and regretted the retirement of the ambassadors.

I told him the Emperor still intended to send his daughter to Europe, and would send her to Genoa about the end of July, on her way to Vienna. He did not know this, and was pleased to hear it.

How entirely morals and feeling are in this instance made to give way to political considerations. All Europe combines to force the marriage of a man of the worst character to an unhealthy child, nine years old, that man being the child's uncle, and both being descended from a madwoman. Miguel is very much in love with a Princess of Bavaria, and she with him, and for this reason she refused his brother. The Emperor will at last be married in all probability to a Princess of

Sardinia.

August 8.

Cabinet at half-past 3.

Eothschild has received a letter from Corfu stating that Ibrahim Pasha has evacuated the Morea.

The Eussian reserve not being yet in a condition to take the charge of the sieges on the Danube, General Eoth's corps has been ordered on that service, and is ascending the Danube from Hirschova. Had the reserve been in time, Eoth's corps would have observed Schoumla, while two other corps advanced by Yarna, and turned it. Now these two corps march to attack Schoumla. The Turks have not as yet done one foolish thing. They have only thrown forward a strong reconnaissance of 8,000 cavalry, which seems to have been well managed. I cannot help anticipating a snlash at Schoumla. I have from the first had a presentiment that this war would be terminated by some horrible catastrophe.

At the Cabinet first we had a letter from the Duke to the Lord High Admiral. He has behaved very ill to Cockburn since his return, and the King takes up the matter very warmly. He says, in speaking of the Duke of Clarence, ' He is a great disciplinarian, and ne must have discipline himself." The Duke of Wellington's letter begins by stating his regret at being obliged to advert to the same topics after what passed recently. It then states the charge: 4 That the command of a squadron of manoeuvre having been given by his Majesty to Sir, the — — , the

Duke of Clarence, with his military flag as Lord High Admiral flying on board the ' Royal Sovereign' yacht, took the command of a part of that squadron which had been assembled at Plymouth, before the arrival of the officer to whom it had been entrusted, and went to sea with it, the officer appointed to the command reaching Plymouth after his departure and remaining there some time' (it might have been added, ' by the Duke's orders'), ' to take in provisions, c."

The Duke then informs the Lord High Admiral that such conduct is contrary to the constitution of the country, and of the Board over which he presides, and entreats him in future to make his communications through the regular official channels.

He is again referred to his Patent. I cannot help thinking that now or very soon the Lord High Admiral-will resign. Spencer, his secretary, urges him forward. His family are afraid the fatigue will kill him. He is now and then mad or very nearly so. The King' would be glad to oust him, thus removing from a prominent situation a brother of whom he is jealous, and creating ill blood between the Heir Presumptive and his Ministers a thing all Kings like to do.

We read the Reis Effendi's letter to the Duke of Wellington and his answer. The letter is well written, and the expressions are well chosen. It holds out hopes that if we will send our Minister back to Constantinople they will arrange everything respecting-Greece to our satisfaction at the same time it says nothing specific. The Duke's answer states in sub-VOL. 1.

stance that we can only send back our Minister when the Sultan accedes to the armistice and to the preliminaries proposed to him by the Allies. In this answer our case is stated as well as it can be; but the Duke said, c It is all full of lies."

The Lord High Admiral wished to send the Procris," a ten-gun brig, to survey the Great and Little Belt. It seems the pilots have not been there lately, and forget the navigation. A month ago, on the same ground, the Trinity House wished to send a surveying vessel, and were told they must not, as the survey of the Belts at the present moment might excite suspicions on the part of Eussia. The Lord High Admiral is to be told the ' Procris' must not go, and the same reason is to be given.

Aberdeen read his answer to the American note, which I had already seen. The paragraph at the end, which I had inserted, admitting ' that, had a case of practical inconvenience arising out of the exercise of our exclusive jurisdiction been alleged, we should have been disposed to take into our mature consideration any reasonable plan for the removal of such inconvenience," was omitted. I saw the feeling of the Cabinet was so strongly in favour of a more decided negative that it was of no use for me to resist. I think the real strength of our case has induced the Cabinet to hold a more decided language than is prudent under all the circumstances of our relative positions. Our case is unanswerable.

We had some conversation about the war between Buenos Ayres and Brazil. The Americans and the

French make the Brazilians restore their ships. We alone are the sufferers. The Duke's feeling and that of the Cabinet seemed to be that we should insist upon the restoration of all our vessels, and blockade Eio if the Emperor would not yield. This blockade of the Eio de la Plata has been effective against English vessels only.

The question was raised whether vessels manned almost wholly by foreigners could be justly deemed nationalised by their flag. On this point the King's Advocate's opinion will be taken, and should he decide in favour of such a measure, all vessels of which three-fourths, or two-thirds, or some large portion of the crew are not natives, will be deemed pirates. This would be a most valuable clause in national law.

The Duke told me he had seen Mr. Grey, and told him he expected he would reside, and therefore he left him his living that ae might have something to fall back upon in the event of his residence in London being prejudicial to his health. The late and present Bishop of London both objected to him on the ground of his Evangelical opinions. The Duke desired them to make their own enquiries. The new Bishop of London did so, and was satisfied of Mr. Grey's fitness. He examined him twice. Having thus found him worthy, the Bishop behaved handsomely by him, put him au fait of his parish, and was liberal too about the house, and some purchase he had made of premises adjoining. Like a true parson, however, he advised Mr. Grey by no means to give up his living till after the harvest.

I called upon Lord Eosslyn, who was, I found, already acquainted with these circumstances, and had written last night to Lord Grey and Lady Jersey.

I told him he might tell Lord Grey that the Duke seemed as much pleased at the final arrangement of the thing as if it had been of some particular advantage to himself. After all, the only real pleasure of power is in obliging one's friends and in making people happy.

I told Lord Eosslyn the news from Bulgaria of the state of the Eussian army, c.

He said there was a report we meant to send French troops in English ships, and seemed to think it very shocking. I do not think it very shocking; but it may possibly be rather a delicate transaction. I a little distrust the prudence both of English seamen and French soldiers.

August 16.

Met Yesey Fitzgerald. He told me the Duke of Clarence was out. There was an interview at Windsor on Tuesday between the King and the Duke of Clarence, the Duke of Wellington being present. The Duke of Clarence was willing to act according to his patent; but he would not act with Sir G. Cockburn. He has an insane antipathy to Sir George. Of course it was impossible to sacrifice a meritorious public servant who had not been wanting in respect to the Duke of Clarence.

The Duke of Wellington is gone to Cheltenham for a fortnight. I dare say the place will not be filled up till his return. He would be unwilling to appear to be in a hurry to get rid of the Duke. In the mean- time the Duke of Clarence does the business as usual. Aberdeen told me he did not speak ill of the Duke of Wellington, but said he could not do otherwise as Prime Minister, nor he go on with Cockburn.

I think the place will be offered in the first instance to Lord Melville. Should he refuse it, and prefer remaining where he is, I should not be in the least surprised if Peel, wishing to have all the support he can get in the House of Commons, pressed the Duke to give the place to Cockburn, whose brother married Peel's sister.

He has already made an application to Aberdeen in favour of a Cockburn, the man who was in South America, but not where he ought to have been. Nor should I be surprised if the Duke yielded to Peel.

If Melville takes the Admiralty, to whom will they give the Board of Control? Will they give it to me, or offer it to Eosslyn? I think the latter; but in this manner I should be again passed by. As to the Foreign Office, which, from what fell from Aberdeen, I expected to have about the middle of October, I now think I shall not have it.

Eead all the papers at the Cabinet room. Our Consul at Bucharest says he finds the Eussian army on the right of the Danube is not more than 75,000 men There are 30,000 in Wallachia, 48,000 in the army of reserve, which is not corne up, and 30,000 Guards on their march. Total, 183,000 men.

The locusts have destroyed all vegetation along the Danube.

[198] The Pashas who surrendered Isatscha and some other place have been beheaded at Schumla by Hussein Pasha, The Pasha who defended Ibraila so well has been afraid to go into Turkey.

Twenty thousand of the garrison of Ibraila have entered Silistria.

The Turks mean to bring their flotilla as high as Silistria.

The Asiatic army united in the Troad is dissolved by desertion. Parties are placed at the mouths of the defiles of the Balkans to catch deserters from the grand army.

Paskewich has taken Kars in Armenia. He has only 15,000 men, and I do not think he can do much mischief. He can have no communications except by the Black Sea.

The Porte is sending all the money it can to Ibrahim Pasha. Of his agreement to evacuate the Morea nothing is certainly known. Whatever may happen the French army will go to the Morea, not to save Greece, but to save the French Government.

The Eussians are much alarmed by a report that Austria is arming, and that she will have 400,000 men soon. The Austrians have made weak efforts to recruit their army, but not to that extent.

Aberdeen is much annoyed at the appointments of Lord Stuart and Lord Strangford. Certainly both are very bad.

Lord Stuart says Villele, by the conduct he has pursued since his secession, has indisposed all parties, and shut himself out from office during this King's life. Villele [199] remained at Paris, and dared his enemies to accuse him. He was beat, and they did. He cannot defend himself without compromising the King's name.

August 19.

Lord Stuart says the instructions to Count Maison say nothing about his returning with the Turkish troops are driven out.

The French have as yet only withdrawn 3,000 men from Cadiz. I suggested to Aberdeen that we should see that the whole force is withdrawn immediately. It will never do to have a French garrison in Cadiz and in the Morea. It does not seem clear what passed in the conference between the admirals and Ibrahim. No account of it has yet been received.

August 21.

Dawson's speech at Derry fait epoque. It was rather incautious, I think; for he might have prepared the way for a change of vote without exhibiting Ireland as under the government of the Association, and declaring that either the Association must be put down or something done to settle the Catholic question. His picture of Ireland is, I believe, correct, but it was strongly drawn too strongly, considering his situation in the Government, and that he will be supposed to speak the sentiments of others. The Duke will be annoyed, but he cannot displace Dawson. His speech hastens the crisis. I think the question must be carried next year. His speech will hurry the Duke, will alarm the Protestants, and raise hopes, perhaps too sanguine, in the Catholics. I fear the Protestants may make the first hostile movement, and possibly bring on a civil contest, which will make concession impossible. This is what Lord Longford and many of the violent Orangemen wish.

I am not at all sure it may not be expedient to call Parliament together in November, to consider the Catholic question, and thus anticipate the violence of both factions.

I suppose the new First Lord of the Admiralty and President of the Board of Control will be sworn in at the Council held about the 26th or 27th for further proroguing Parliament.

If Melville goes back to the Admiralty, Eosslyn may have the offer of India; but if Melville retains India, Eosslyn will hardly be sent to the Admiralty.

Things are hardly enough advanced as regards the Catholic question for an offer to Lord Grey. If he came in, he would have the Foreign Office, and Aberdeen what? I should say the best arrangement would be

Grey, Foreign Office.

Eosslyn, India.

I, Admiralty.

Melville, Lord Lieutenant.

Aberdeen, Privy Seal.

The rest as they are.

Will Peel remain in office while the Catholic question is carried? He can hardly do so. Fitzgerald could lead the House of Commons for the Session; but if Peel goes out, he must appear at least to go out in reality ', and not have his office held for him for six months. If the latter course be adopted, it will not do much good to Peel's reputation.

August 21.

The second in command at Schumla is Halil Pacha, a man of five-and-twenty, but a brave officer whom Hussein had under him at the destruction of the Janissaries.

News of the llth has been received from Vienna, but none yet of the battle.

There are all sorts of stories of the Lord High Admiral, and the world says he is mad.

Ashley, who is under Lord Melville at the India Board, says he would not willingly return to the Admiralty.

The Chancellor said incidentally, in speaking of my office, that it certainly was not suited to me. I really am ashamed of it.

It is supposed that the Eussian admiral is gone down in an 80-gun ship. He was burning blue lights when the rest of the squadron left him. When they were met at sea by the Lord High Admiral they were endeavouring to work to windward, and missed stays every time.

August 22.

Should I not be placed on this occasion in any efficient office, and should I at the same time not receive any promise of an efficient office at an early period, what conduct shall I adopt? I shall certainly consult Hardinge before I take any decided step; but my own feeling is that I should resign. I will make a draft of a letter of resignation. The Chancellor, in the course of conversation this evening, said I ought to have some department. I made no reply.

[202] Eead a number of papers sent home by Codrington. Amongst them is a letter from De Eigny to him, in which De Eigny claims equal responsibility, and equal blame. He says he was left to watch the Morea in the 6 Trident' when Codrington's fleet was obliged to go to Malta to refit. He does not know apparently that the 'Warspite' arrived at Malta about November 8, and that Codrington had other ships at his disposal. I should doubt Codrington's having communicated the whole of Aberdeen's letter to De Eigny. I must look over the instructions and make a memorandum of M." de Eigny's letter.

There was a conference with Ibrahim Pasha on July 6, the result of which was that our Admiral and his colleagues were induced to think Ibrahim would evacuate the Morea as soon as ships came to take him away. Suleiman Bey (Colonel Siar) was present with other colonels, and declared he and the others would force Ibrahim on board, for they came to fight, not to starve. Six thousand Albanians have marched off to Patras, having revolted. It is said Ibrahim went after them with 12,000 men, but there is no clear information on this point.

Codrington speaks of an order from the Sultan for Ibrahim to march upon Eoumelia, but I cannot find his authority for this.

[203] The plan is for the blockading squadron to leave Alexandria when the Egyptian fleet is ready to sail, to meet it at sea, and force it to come to Navarin. Then to agree with Ibrahim that the two fleets shall enter the harbour at the same time. This seems a wild scheme, and I suspect some deception. I should not be surprised if Ibrahim marched to Eoumelia, and the Egyptian fleet sailed to the Dardanelles. It is what they ought to do. If the Porte brought the whole of its force to bear upon the Eussians, and agreed to the terms of the Treaty of London, I really believe it would be victorious.

The Egyptians have only three large frigates left, ready for sea, and in good condition; but they have in all six or eight corvettes, and fifteen or eighteen brigs.

A fever, as yet not declared to be infectious, has broke out on board the 'Warspite." On July 9 she had twenty-three men on the sick list, and on the 13th sixty-two. She lay four or five days off the low land of Poros, and to this the fever is attributed. She is gone to Malta.

I have had some conversation with the Chancellor and Vesey Fitzgerald respecting Dawson's speech. They are of the same opinion as myself. It hurries on the question too rapidly, and places the two parties in hostile positions.

The Chancellor and I am to look over the Bill I have drawn, and to see how the thing can be done.

The King has had a bad cold. He parted with the young Cumberland with great regret.

Dawkins is appointed our resident in Greece! All our appointments are bad. The French have sent Inchereau de St. Denis. The Russians a Count de Bulgari, said to be a clever man. We are worse represented, and the French better than any.

Lord Stuart, Paris.

Lord Strangford, Eio Janeiro.

Lord Belmore, Jamaica.

Mr. Dawkins, Greece.

Lord F. Leveson, Ireland.

S. Perceval, Clerk of the Ordnance.

Aberdeen, Secretary for Foreign Affairs.

Blomfield, Bishop of London.

All these appointments are doubtful.

Aberdeen will do nothing very glaringly wrong; but he will conduct foreign affairs without ability, and will commit a number of little errors which will let down the character of our diplomacy, and materially injure us.

August 25.

Council at Windsor Castle for proroguing Parliament to October 30. Present, Peel, Sir J. Murray, Chancellor, Aberdeen, V. Fitzgerald, and myself. The Archbishop of Canterbury, Bishop of London, and Bishop of Chichester. Why these last were there I do not know. The King looked very well indeed, and seemed quite gay. There is no news. The Duke returns on Saturday. I dare say he will be at Ciren-cester on Friday on his way.

Had some conversation with the Chancellor on the bad appointments of Lord F. Leveson, Strangford, c., and on the state of our diplomacy abroad.

August 27.

At the Foreign Office read a letter from Lord Cowley, announcing the Emperor of Eussia's return to Odessa. He arrived there on August 8. The Eussians have not force enough to attack Schumla, and while the reinforcements are coming up the Emperor goes to see the Empress. Lord Heytesbury, who had got within seventy miles of head-quarters, has been invited to go to Odessa. He complains of want of horses, of provender for them, and even of food for himself, and of bad water. He says all the officers he has met are tired of the war; that he sees no enthusiasm. The first of the Guards were to reach the Danube on the 10th. Even these could hardly be before Schumla before September 1. Other troops were coming up.

The Eussian steamboats were all out of order. The Turks certainly had some success before Varna.

If the Turks would order Ibrahim to march upon Adrianople, bring the Egyptian fleet to the Bosphorus, and accede to the Treaty of London, they might still succeed against the Eussians. Their success now would, I fear, induce them to be obstinate on the subject of Greece, and lead to continued complications and embarrassments.

Still their defence of the Balkans is an event for Europe of the highest importance. It assures us of the existence of one barrier to the Eussian arms.

August 28.

The Duke of Wellington still thinks the Eussians will succeed in the end. I confess I do not. I have a presentiment that they will fail. The army before Schumla ought to be destroyed.

August 30.

Saw Mr. Angerstein, the young man whom Dudley pointed out to me as a clever person. He told me De Kigny thought the French were sending more troops than were necessary.

The French intend to land at Arcadia and form a cordon across the country to Calamata, thus cutting off from provisions the three fortresses of Modon, Coron, and Navarin. They intend, too, to occupy the Island of Sphacteria, and another small island, not far from Navarin, called Prodano.

September 1.

The Plenipotentiaries were all going to Poros, to be near the Greek Government, and the Turks. The instructions to the ambassadors, written originally in English, have been ill-translated in some cases, so as to give a different meaning. The words a fair proportion (very ill-chosen words by-the-bye) have been translated la majeure partie, and the expression refers to the islands and territory on the continent of Greece to be made part of the new State.

Stratford Canning has the weakness of those who call themselves Liberals in favour of the Greeks, desiring to give the largest possible extent to the frontier to be assigned to them.

I had a little conversation with Yesey Fitzgerald at the Chancellor's, where I dined, on the subject of our diplomacy. He thinks it, as I do, miserable. In fact the Government is very ill served, and Aberdeen is not the man to make our Ministers do their duty, or to change them if they do not. The Duke can only have made him Foreign Minister under the idea that he might manage him as he pleased and so he does, giving all the appointments of a higher order as if they belonged to the Treasury. As far as patronage is concerned I should have no objection to this; but the Foreign Minister ought not to permit the appointment of a man he thinks unfit.

September 5.

On my return from Charlton I found a letter from the Duke of Wellington, offering me the Board of Control. Lord Melville has the Admiralty. I shall accept and go to Strathfieldsaye to see the Duke tomorrow. Under the circumstance of the approaching renewal of the Charter I ought to make up my mind to remain in the Board of Control and to endeavour to reduce the expenditure of the East India Company, so as to enable Parliament to renew the Charter and throw open the China trade.

The Duke tells me it is not yet decided who should succeed me as Privy Seal.

Upon the whole I am satisfied with this arrangement. Undoubtedly the Foreign Office is the object of my ambition, and had the late Administration been beaten down in the field I must have had that office. It is now placed in very weak hands; but I may overestimate my own powers, and I excite less envy and jealousy by taking at first the incognito office of President of the Board of Control.

Saturday, September 6.

Set off at a little before 9 for Strathfieldsaye. The Duke received me very cordially. I gave him a letter I had written, accepting the office, which he will send to the King.

We walked in the garden and he brought down the history of the Duke's resignation to the present time. It seems the Duke of Wellington had some discussion with Peel on the subject of the manner in which the office should be filled up, and did not write to the King till the 20th proposing any arrangement. This letter crossed on the road one from the King, expressing surprise at not having yet received any communication on the subject. The King, having had in the interval some reason to think the Duke of Clarence would remain, wrote to the Duke of Wellington begging him to do nothing further till he heard further from him. But the Duke of Clarence would only remain if Sir G. Cockburn was turned out, and the Duke of Wellington told the King that he would not do, and if he did, all the other members of the Board would resign. This latter part Cockburn told Spencer, and Spencer the Duke of Clarence, who thereupon, seeing the affair was more serious than he had imagined, sent for Cockburn and the others, shook hands with them, and asked them to dinner; but at the same time sent Spencer to the King to say he would not stay unless the powers given by his patent were enlarged. This was out of the question, so he resigns. The story is rather confused, but so his Eoyal Highness is. However, his retirement now stands on the ground of his asking fuller powers and being refused.

He was furious with the Duke of Wellington at first, but is reasonable now, and does him justice.

The Privy Seal remains in my hands for the present, as the Duke wishes to make his arrangements, and, as I understood him, other offices would become vacant from the state of the Catholic question that is, Peel's.

He complains very much of Dawson's speech, which has thrown him back with the King, and he is now no further advanced than he was a week after he first opened the subject to his Majesty.

The King now makes it a point of honour to resist.

The Duke thinks that with the Irish proprietors it is become a question of rents. He dreads the intemperance of the Orangemen, and believes the Catholics will be quiet.

He has represented to the King and others the different position of Ireland now and in '98. Then alii Protestant Ireland was united, and all England was with them. We had then a large army. Now we' have hardly any army, the Catholics are increased,, they are united, and half England think they ought to be emancipated.

The Duke begins to think the Eussians may fail.

Even their generals are dying, and he says things must be very bad when generals die. The Emperor is gone to avoid the sight of the horrors which surrounded him at Schumla. The Turks are in force in Lesser Wallachia, and surprise detached parties.

I do not think the Duke looking well; but here they say he is.

At six arrived despatches from Lords Cowley and Heytesbury. Lord Cowley's enclosed a report from Prince Philip of Hesse-Homburg, who joined the army before Schumla on July 31, and some observations of an Austrian officer upon it. The Prince's despatch is the 29th bulletin of the Eussian army. He represents its sufferings beyond those of the retreat from Moscow. He speaks with horror of what he has seen. The Emperor and all the army only desire to get out of this disastrous war. The 40,000 or 50,000 men they may bring up will only make things worse. They may take Varna and Schumla, though it is more probable they will not; but the army will perish.

The Eussians give up all idea of going beyond the Balkan this year. The Turks have 50,000 men in Schumla, more than 12,000 at Varna, all fresh and well. The Eussians have 40,000 before Schumla and 12,000 before Varna.

The Duke says they should have hugged the sea the whole way, and only masqued Schoumla. This was their first intention.

Lord Heytesbury seems captivated by the Emperor. He begins to take a Eussian view of things. The Emperor most improperly spoke of the Duke of Wellington 1 Alluding to the famous bulletin which first revealed the losses of the French army in Russia. Sir A. Alison observes that ' Wittgenstein experienced in his turn the disasters inflicted by him upon Napoleon in his retreat from Witebsk to the Beresina, in 1812."

RUSSIAN ENCROACHMENTS. 211 personally, as distinguished from the Government and the King. Said the Duke had misunderstood him. The King alone knew him and his loyalty. Lord Heytes-bury did not notice this impropriety, which, as the despatches are all sent to the King, was very artful.

Lord Heytesbury thinks the Eussians mean to keep Anapa and Poti. The latter town commands the entrance to the Phasis, and therefore its possession would facilitate the communication of the Russians with their new conquests. Yet Lord Heytesbury says ' it is of no importance to the Turks," whereas everything is of importance to them to keep, which, in the hands of the Eussians, would facilitate or disembarrass their operations in a future war. Poti is of importance to us, as we are interested in embarrassing the Russian communication with Persia.

Lord Heytesbury heard reflections on Metternich without defending him. On the contrary, he filled up a lacune in a sentence inculpatory of Metternich's general character.

He says the Emperor cannot in honour make the first proposals for peace. How much less can the Turk? Lord Heytesbury always forgets that the war on the part of the Russians is unnecessary and therefore unjust.

So desirous are they of peace that they no longer (many of them) consider the settlement of the Greek question essential as a part of any peace to be made.

The Emperor and his people are delighted with the French expedition to the Morea.

The Emperor talks of not continuing to denationalise his fleet should the war go on. He says he must bring it to blockade the Dardanelles. This would break the engagements he recently entered into.

Lord Heytesbury ought to have an admonitory letter, but Aberdeen is not the man to write one.

I had some conversation with the Duke on the subject of our diplomacy, and he agreed with me in thinking it a nullity. Why, then, did he make Aberdeen?

I am sorry to find the Duke still wishes to renew the Charter next year, with two or three objects, none of them of sufficient importance to justify such a measure. He wishes to get the City of London with the Government as Pitt had. This is more a private than a public object. He wishes to forestall discussion, which he sees beginning, as to the terms of the renewal, and he is more than all desirous of saving the 150,000. a year Ceylon costs us. He would transfer it to the East India Company, because they would govern it more cheaply. This is not a sufficient object for which to sacrifice the advantages of the China trade.

I must look thoroughly into all these subjects.

Lord Melville was written to on the 5th and desired to come up immediately. He will hardly be in town before the 14th or 15th, I think.

Sunday, September 7.

Had some conversation with Arbuthnot. Told him I was sure the Duke would not be able to keep Aberdeen. That he would find nothing was done very ill, but nothing well, and that our diplomacy was let down. Besides, Aberdeen told me if he had been Privy Seal he would not have taken the Foreign Office; and it seems when Arbuthnot lately asked him to lend him his gown as Chancellor of the Duchy, Aberdeen said he might have it, for he supposed he should not want it again unless he had the good fortune to return to that office. I told Arbuthnot I thought the Duke had better consider the Foreign Office at his disposal than the Privy Seal; that if the latter remained vacant a month or two I believed Aberdeen would ask for it.

I said at the same time I thought Aberdeen better than Dudley.

I said I feared the Duke might have embarrassed himself by giving me the India Board; that that office would have suited Eosslyn better than the Privy Seal.

Arbuthnot seemed to think some means might be taken for getting rid of Lord Beresford and putting Rosslyn there it was better not to bring military men into the Cabinet in civil offices unnecessarily. I told him people seemed to think Peel must go out if the Government took up the Catholic question, and that, if Lord Grey was to come in, the Home Office would suit him better than the Foreign. I expressed my doubts whether Lord Grey's accession to the Government would be an advantage. He was able, and would be accommodating and practicable; but now the Duke is sole Minister, and decidedly superior to all, a difference, should any occur, between him and Lord Grey, would be very serious. The accession of Eosslyn would conciliate Lord Grey, which is all we want.

I am inclined to think the Duke is as anxious as ever to bring in Eosslyn. This I gathered from Ar-buthnot. I had no conversation with the Duke on the subject. I never seek a confidence not freely given I imagine the Duke consults only Peel in making his arrangements.

Arbuthnot told me the King's unwillingness to lose the Duke of Clarence arose from his fear that Lord Grey would be proposed to him. Arbuthnot thought Lord Grey might possibly take the Privy Seal. I said it could not be offered to him in the first instance possibly he might prefer it to a more active office, but I hardly think he would.

The Duke will not have Lord Melbourne or any of the Canningites. I am glad of it. I do not like them, and I had rather be alone in the House of Lords. I gave the Duke my memorandum on the Oath oh c question, and drafts of replies to Lord Heytesbury.

I told Arbuthnot I always thought Aberdeen's appointment temporary; that it was otherwise inexplicable; that I the more thought it was so from some expressions of Aberdeen's, and from the circumstance of the Duke having first thought of having

Lord Stuart or Lord Heytesbury, both of which appointments could only have been provisional. Arbuthribt neither affirmed nor denied that it was so.

On my return to Koehampton I wrote notes to Lord Ashley, G. Barker, and Fitzgerald and Courtenay, informing all of the appointment, asking the two first[1 Alone, apparently, as an old advocate of Catholic Emancipation, which Lord Ellenborough had always advocated.]

215   when they came to town, and telling them the Duke seemed disposed to give us a good deal to do. The two last I want to have some conversation with.

Eead the evidence relative to East India trade before the Lords' Committee in 1820, both going to Strathfieldsaye and returning.

The Duke told me he should trouble me for some of my patronage, he was so pressed. I told him he might have all he wanted. I did not know that I had a single person I wished to give anything to. I mentioned the cadetships and writerships. He said the law appointments were what he wanted. He did not wish for the others; but he did not know how good they were. I had never thought of the law appointments. By-the-bye there is a bishoprick, c., besides.

September 8.

Eode to town. No further news. Palmella[1]was with Aberdeen, in the receipt of a lecture. These Pedroites seem disposed to levy war upon Miguel from this country, and have landed 2,000 men here. This is rather too bad. Last night I sent a note to Count Munster, apologising for not having called upon him, and telling him the accounts we received represented the sufferings of the Eussians as equal to those of the French in the retreat from Moscow.

He wrote to me this morning and told me his[1 The Marquis of Palmella was the minister accredited for Donna Maria and recognised as the Minister of Portugal. He was, however, as agent for the Pedroite or Constitutional party, in constant collision with the Ministry as to alleged violations of English neutrality in the internal struggle against Don Miguel.]

216   accounts from General Dornberg, a Hanoverian who lias entered the Eussian service, were silent as to distress and confident of ultimate success. These despatches are gone to the King, and Count Munster will show them to me.

I saw Wrangham. He had observed the various improprieties of Lord Heytesbury's despatch. It seems Aberdeen read it to Esterhazy in extenso, the part relating to Metternich included. He was very wrong in reading that passage, for now there is an end to all good understanding between Metternich and Lord Heytesbury.

It is thus, by little errors, that Aberdeen will let down the diplomacy of the country.

I wrote to Fitzgerald. He is going out of town. Courtenay is in Devonshire. Ashley is out of town, and Bankes. I read the debate in 1822 relative to the India Board on a motion of Courcy's. Canning's and Tierney's speeches give a clear account of the mode of doing business in the office.

I met Esterhazy quite delighted with the last news from Belgium. Wrote to the Duke, suggesting Captain Seymour as a Lord of the Admiralty in the room of Sir E. Owen, who retires to avoid a contest on his reelection.

The newspapers, think the Duke of Clarence is to remain.

September 11.

The ' Courier' announces the new arrangements. I hear Lord Melville was very unwilling to leave the India Board for the Admiralty, and only did so to accommodate the Duke of Wellington. I do not see why so great a point should have been made of it, for I might just as well have had the Admiralty.

Nothing new at the Foreign Office. Saw Aberdeen, who said he had kept the secret well, for he had known the intended arrangement when the Duke left town on the 12th.

I said I had not felt any great anxiety about it, for I must have resigned the Privy Seal in two months. It was a disparagement to me. He acknowledged I was placed in a false position as Privy Seal, being a working man. Thinking, as I do, that he is particularly well suited to the Privy Seal, I said there were persons, c., on whom it might be very properly conferred, but that my age, my rank, and my fortune disqualified me for it.

I find Aberdeen thinks there is much exaggeration in the report of Prince Philip of Hesse-Hombourg. He has the habit of denigreing everything. I am afraid that, although he sees the impropriety of Lord Heytes-bury's conduct at Odessa, he will not speak out enough to him, and, if he does not, he will do no good.

September 12.

Met Count Munster riding. He seems annoyed at General Dornberg's report from Belgium not being in unison with those we have received, and seems to believe Dornberg, who is his nephew and dear friend, and to think our informers exaggerate. In fact, I am inclined to think Dornberg is sold to the Eussians, and that he wilfully deceives Munster and the King.

The 'Times' makes a sally against Lord Melville on his appointment to the Admiralty. As yet it says nothing of me. I expect abuse as a dandy lord. It will be said the affairs of India are given up to those dandy lords, and a priggish lawyer.

September 13.

Eeceived at last a letter from Hardinge, in which he says he did not congratulate me, because he expected my move would have been to the Foreign Office. I have told him what I told Arbuthnot.

Had a note from Count Munster, with news from Odessa to the 28th. Madame de Lieven's brother, Count Constantine Benkendorff, is dead. So the war strikes its authors. Prince Menshikoff is dangerously wounded. M. Woronzoff has received the command of the corps before Varna. The Eussians have carried the sap to the Ditch, and expect to have Varna soon. Nous verrons! General Eudiger, who was at Eski Stamboul, on the road between Schumla and Constantinople, has been cut off, and escaped with some difficulty, having lost, as the Eussians allow, 300 or 400 men. Lord Heytesbury's despatches were brought by a Eussian courier, and contain no further intelligence.

Lord Melville came to town yesterday. He was with Aberdeen to-day. He said he could not let me in for a week or ten days. He does not like his change at all, nor does the navy.

News has been received that the transports have left Alexandria for the removal of Ibrahim Pasha from the Morea.

September 15.

Called on Lord Melville. Confirmed his promise of a cadetship in November to the eldest son of Mr. Allan Cunningham. By this I oblige Lord Melville, Mr. Chantrey, and Sir W. Scott, and prefer the son, who is, I hear, himself deserving, of a very worthy and respectable man.

I like the rooms of the India Board. They look on the Thames, and are very comfortable.

Lord Melville tells me I shall not find the business so very severe. It is less than it was twenty years ago that is, it is become so much greater that it is impossible for one man to do it, and consequently the clerks, divided into departments, report upon the vouchers sent with the different despatches, and upon the despatches. The President refers to the vouchers where he sees reason to doubt, and indeed he ought to do so in many cases to verify the correctness of the prices.

I spoke to Lord Melville on the subject of the renewal of the Charter. He seems to think the East India Company have not a sufficient case against opening the China trade on the ground of danger to the intercourse, or to their own trade. The fact is, the monopoly is necessary as a means of finance, to enable them to pay their debts.

I spoke to Lord Melville of the affairs of Persia, to which I must direct my immediate attention. We must bring our Persian diplomacy into a line with that we adopt elsewhere with regard to Eussia. I dare say I shall find our Eesident there is acting in the Eussian interests under instructions given as far back as 1813, or earlier.

A Mr. Alvey is secretary to Lord Melville, and was secretary to his father. He is a clerk in the office, and has been since 1795. He has just broke his leg in Edinburgh; but when he comes up I think I shall make him my secretary. He has 300Z. a year as secretary. I told Lord Melville if he would give me a list of promises I would, as far as I could, perform them. He did not seem to wish it.

He said he was much better off where he was than he should be at the Admiralty.

The Duke of Clarence is very anxious to be superseded as soon as possible. Lord Melville will do some unconcluded business before he leaves the office, and particularly arrange with the East India Company the new arrangements as to the rank to which their servants may rise in the army, and the reduction of their military force. I shall get in in about a week.

Saw Aberdeen. Lieven has announced the separation of the Eussian fleet, and seemed ashamed of himself. I left my memorandum with Wrangham to send to the Duke. Aberdeen does not know what to do. I do.

Codrington's arrangement with Ibrahim sounds better than it is. Ibrahim takes away men he cannot feed, and leaves 1,500 Egyptians and all the Turks in the fortresses.

September 17.

Eode to town to have some conversation with Lord Melville. I think I shall be a more active President than he would have been.

He advised me to see the Chairs every week.

Told me they did not like verbal criticisms.

There are several troublesome and disagreeable cases to be decided. It seems the chief labour of the office consists in reading and deciding claims and disputes.

The Treasury makes large demands on the patronage of the office. I shall be expected to perform all Lord Melville's promises, none of which he cares about. They are all Parliamentary jobs. I saw one letter from a Dutch Irishman, one Van Homrigh, member for Drogheda, which seemed to me very peremptory, and demanding that a promise of a cadetship made by Lord Melville to his son should be performed by me. It seems Planta came to Lord Melville one day, saying he must positively have two cadetships for Wood, patron of Gatton. One of these Lord Melville got from a director, and I have to repay.

I had a letter from Sir G. Clerk, begging a Mr. Simon Fraser, a friend of his, who had been long on Lord Melville's list, might be a candidate for a cadet-ship on mine. I answered I would place him on the list; but I heard there were such political demands that I feared it would not be soon that I should be able to do anything for him.

I called on the Duke of Wellington and told him I had decided on offering my private secretaryship to J. Bligh, Lord Darnley's son. He seemed much pleased, and said I could not have done better. That he was clever, wrote well and fast, and was very agreeable.

Donna Maria da Gloria is coming to England. She is to be received as well as Don Miguel was. She will go to Plymouth. What will be done with her is not decided. Whether she will stay here or go to Austria.

September 23.

A messenger from the Privy Seal Office brought my patent to Tunbridge Wells last night for the Privy Seal.

I went to the India Board at 2. Saw Lord Melville. The cases I have to decide first are those of Mr. Hill, removed from the office of chief secretary at Madras by Mr. Lushington, and whom the Directors wish to replace; a Sir something Claridge, Eecorder of Prince of Wales Island, whom they want to remove; and a Begum who has whipped her servant to death, and whom the authorities in India say must be pardoned.

The Duke of Wellington wishes to put an end to the practice of giving civil appointments to military officers in India. The regiments are left without a sufficient number of officers. The East India Company are unwilling to change the system, because they make the military pay go in part of the civil appointments, and thus save about 200,000. at the expense of making their army inefficient.

The clerks want me to receive the salary of both my offices and pay as much of the salary of the President as is equal to that of Privy Seal, towards the discharge of the official debt, which is about 800. The department is limited to 26,000. which they have exceeded. I must speak to Goulburn about this.

Lord Melville has appointed an eleventh clerk, leaving it to me to appoint the twelfth or not. I shall leave the situation vacant, for we have no money for it.

There is an application from Peel on behalf of a Mr. Thomas Whitmore for a cadetship. He is a member, and a good friend, and this his first ask.

September 24.

Found at the office Mr. Sullivan, our old retired Commissioner. I communicated to him and to Bankes the line I intended to advise the Chairs to adopt for the purpose of setting the Madras Government to rights. I propose that their despatch, ordering the reinstatement of Mr. Hill, the Chief Secretary, displaced by Lushington, should contain no expressions inculpatory of Lushington, or degrading to him, and I think I might write a private letter to Lushington, and one of the Directors or Chairs a private letter to Hill, giving them hints as to their conduct. If Lushington is to be retained, he must not be lowered in the eyes of his subordinate officer and with a view to the good conduct of the Madras Government it is essential that everything should be done to make the members of Council act cordially together.

Eeceived an application for a judgeship from a Mr. Langston, and for a cadetship from the Duke of Gordon. Told the Duke how I was situated, and said I should be on the look out for the first cadetship at my own disposal for him.

Saw Mr. Cabell, the chief clerk in the Secret and Political Department. He has not been there long, and could not give me much information.

Got the papers relative to Persia, and took them to

Eoehampton.

September 25.

Eode to London. In the morning read a very curious paper from Major Taylor, the Eesident at Bassora, and a minute of Sir John Malcolm's, upon the policy to be pursued with regard to Persia and the Pasha of Bagdad. I am sure we have too much sacrificed our interests on the side of India to a weakness in favour of Eussia. All our exertions at Teheran have been for Eussian interests. The possession of Erivan gives them now the command of an entrance into both Persia and Armenia. In the latter country they have many Christian adherents on the road to Erzerum, by which they are now advancing. They have by intimidation, physical and moral, the latter through the Bishop of Etzmiadzin, induced 70,000 Christians to emigrate from the Persian frontier into Eussian Georgia.

Sir J. Malcolm fears they will be compelled, as we were in India, to make new conquests to secure those they have already made. They have already been within 300 miles of Mosul, where the Tigris becomes navigable to the Persian Gulf, and there seeems to be nothing to oppose him.

Eead the case of a Begum, daughter of the late Nabob of the Carnatic, who pleaded guilty to a charge of manslaughter rather than appear in public, which to her would have been the extreme of degradation. The charge was that she, together with three slaves, whipped a female slave to death.

It seemed very doubtful whether the slave died of the chastisement inflicted. The judges thought she did not. The operators were young girls, the eldest not above thirteen, the youngest eight.

I am to write to the King for her pardon.

Went to the office. Sir J. Murray and I were sworn in, the patent being there.

At the Cabinet room read a long letter from Lord Anglesey, who begins to think the crisis is approaching, and seems inclined to issue a proclamation against the meetings in Ireland, which take place nominally for the purpose of reconciling factions. The people come in great numbers, regimented, with officers, dresses, and bands.

I would not thus precipitate a crisis which may yet be averted; but concession alone can avert it. We are to have a Cabinet to-morrow on the subject.

At night received a box with another defence of Codrington, which I suppose I must answer.

Aberdeen puts it all upon me fairly enough, as I wrote the letter of recall.

Mr. Bligh declines being private secretary. I had a letter from Lord Darnley, very civil, gratified, c., but circumstances prevent it. As he still looks forward to employment at home for Mr. Bligh, it is evident he thinks the private secretaryship not good enough. ~~VOL. i. Q~~

226

September 26.

Saw Lord F. Somerset at the India Board about the King's troops in India. The company, with four regiments sent for the war in Ava, to be withdrawn.

Cabinet at 3. A proclamation decided upon declaring the illegality of the meetings lately held in Ireland. They are to be prevented and dispersed. Lord Anglesey is to be empowered to send at once for the troops on the west coast without waiting for orders from the Horse Guards.

The Chancellor of Ireland, who is in Kent, is ordered to go back to Dublin immediately. The Attorney-General is abroad. We had the Attorney-and Solicitor-Generals of England and the Chancellor to word the proclamation.

It was thought that those who are well-disposed would be induced to join the agitators from fear, if Government showed no disposition to act in preservation of the public peace, that the Protestants would act for themselves.

That these meetings would derive strength, and the attendants at them confidence from impunity and from witnessing their own numbers and array.

That it would be more easy to put them down now than hereafter. These reasons prevailed. Still it is a fearful step and may precipitate the crisis. I suggested it would be better to send at once the troops which are ready. They and the proclamation should appear at the same time.

The Queen of Portugal is at Falmouth.

227

The Duke of Wellington thinks Varna will be taken. I betted Lord Bathurst a crown it would not be. This bet we made at dinner at the Duke's.

I spoke to the Duke on the subject of Lushington's case, and Persia. He thinks it better to have the Eesi-dent in Persia dependent on the East India Company. He leaves him a freer scope as the representative of a great Asiatic Power, and relieves our Indian policy from the embarrassment to which our European connections with Eussia may give rise. Indeed, now our policy in Europe and in Asia ought to be the same to pull down the Eussian power.

September 27.

Went to town at half-past 10 to receive the Chairs. They came at 11. I laid myself out to combler them. I hope I partly succeeded.

We talked of Persia. They seemed to be aware of the danger to them on that side, but felt they could meet it. They had no objection to instructions being given to Macdonald to obtain all possible information on the subject of the countries lately subjected to the Eussians, and on the neighbouring frontier of Turkey and Persia.

They acknowledged the ability of Sir J. Malcolm, expected him home in 1831, to assist them on the renewal of the Charter; attributed to him the wish of being appointed provisionally Governor-General, and rejected altogether his idea of the expediency of having always provisional successors, in whom the country might have confidence, to the Governors, c. They said the law pointed out the provisional successors, and if a man was unfit to succeed he should not be placed in the Council weak reasoning. I promised to take into immediate consideration two questions they are anxious about, one relative to the assimilation of the currency, the other to the promotions, c., in the Bengal army.

I told them I agreed to replace Mr. Hill as Secretary to the Government at Madras; but as Lushington was to be retained, they must not lower him in the eyes of those who were to serve under him. This must prepare them for alterations of their draft. On the subject of the King's troops to be kept in India I had some difficulty in managing them. They yielded rather to force than to reason, and I understood them to accede to the arrangement proposed by the Horse Guards, with the reservation that until the supernumerary officers were absorbed no remplacans were to be sent from England at their expense. I have to write a letter in answer to theirs to Lord Melville on the subject. I told the Duke I should show it him on Monday.

We had some conversation as to their finance.

The Begum's petition for pardon I have forwarded through Peel to the King. We parted very civilly, with mutual professions of goodwill. They went afterwards to Lord Melville. I should like to know what they said of me. I asked them to dinner on Thursday next, and have asked Bankes and his wife, Ashley, and all the members of the Cabinet who will be in town to meet them. If this does not do, I do not know what will.

Cabinet at 2. Considered what should be done.

229 The Russians having declared that, leaving a portion of their fleet to act with us under the treaty, they will employ another portion in the blockade of Constantinople.

This is contrary to the recent stipulation of neutrality in the Mediterranean. We have told the Turks this neutrality will be preserved, and on the faith of it they have sent ships for corn to Egypt, and drawn their troops from the Dardanelles. "What will become of Christian honour if after this declaration on our part their ships drawn out by the promise of neutrality are captured by the Russians on their return? I do not think anything very specific was determined by the Cabinet, but the feeling was very strong against the Russians. The French seem to entertain the same feelings of indignation at their breach of faith. I begin to see daylight in this unfortunate Greek Treaty. I now think we shall get out of it. I expect that this jealousy of the Russians will soon supersede with the French all romantic absurdity in the cause of the struggling Greeks.

The Queen of Portugal, so Palmella calls her the Duchess of Oporto, so Itabayana styles her is coming to London, or at least very near it. We are to hire a whole hotel for her. I said all I could in favour of her remaining at some villa twelve miles off, as her people wished. I fear her arrival in London will create rows, and crowds.

It is only by a lucky accident that collision has twice been prevented in Ireland 230 between the Protestants and Catholics. The last occasion was at Ballybay, where the Protestants had assembled in arms to resist the entrance of Lawless and his Catholic cortege. General Thornton persuaded Lawless to change his route.

The Duke thinks Lawless's progress should be prevented by holding him to bail, which will probably be done.

I fear we are approaching the crisis. Fitzgerald thinks the Orangemen of the North would drive the Catholics of the South into the sea.

The King is not much better. He is still desirous of losing more blood, and his right hand is swelled by the gout to twice its natural size. He cannot sign his initials.

The Conference on the Eussian question takes place to-morrow. It seems Lieven has nothing to say, and is thoroughly ashamed.

Lord Jersey tells me Stanley is very desirous of leading the House of Commons, and wants Lord Lans-downe to lead the House of Lords.

They are very bitter against the Duke. I must confess the decisions taken by the Cabinet of late, though contrary to my first impressions, are what my better judgment has approved. I feel the advantage of being brought into contact with able men. I am sure nothing has so strong a tendency to produce wrongheadedness and erroneous views as living alone. A man never knows his own just value till he measures himself with able men.

Took my letter to the Chairs to the Duke. He approved of it.

The King is better.

The Conference was to be renewed to-day. It separated without doing anything the other day.

September 30.

Kode to the office. Signed despatch relative to Madras promotions, the draft privately communicated relative to the brevet rank of officers in the East India Service, and the reductions proposed in the Indian army.

Had a long conversation with Mr. Leach, the chief clerk in the Department of Accounts, relative to the question of making the currency of the Company's dominions uniform.

Wrangham, whom I saw at the Foreign Office, told me Lieven could not change the orders given to the Russian Admiral.

In walking up from the office met E. Clive, who is now very eager for Catholic emancipation. I have asked him to meet the Chairs on Thursday.

October 1.

The Eussians are to blockade the Dardanelles. We are to take care our own vessels, which have sailed under the idea they would be neutral, should not suffer; but to the Turks we only make a declaration! We do not co-operate with the Eussians, but we are to consult! All this cannot stand discussion. There is a feebleness in our foreign policy which surprises me. Indecisive as Aberdeen is, I thought the Duke would have been more decided. It seems they were afraid of breaking with France. I believe they would have run no danger of that. The French are more jealous of the Eussians than they are desirous of vain-glory in Greece; besides, they are more afraid of breaking with us than we of breaking with them.

I desired Aberdeen would give a hint to Lord Hey-tesbury not to throw Poti, which is at the mouth of the Phasis, into the lap of the Emperor, and tell him we attached much importance to it. The possession of it would give immediate communication with the new conquests in Persia.

In the evening I read Colonel Macdonald's accounts from Persia, going back to the beginning of the war.

The Shah has destroyed the ancient aristocracy which had influence with the people, and has placed his numerous sons and grandsons in the command of the different provinces. These are all jealous of and hostile to each other, and he foments their jealousy that he may reign securely for his life. He could bring more than 100,000 cavalry into the field; but parsimony made him refuse all supplies to his son, who was thus obliged to make war with the strength of Azer-bijan alone. The Eussians are odious to their Mahometan subjects. When the Persians advanced into Georgia the people rose upon the Eussians. They have made themselves detested in Persia too. The Armenian and other Christians may just now prefer the Eussian to the Persian yoke, as the former are conquerors; but there are evidently the means of doing much against Eussia in that quarter. Georgia is poor, and the frontier unhealthy. The cost ⌊ 233 of bringing artillery and provisions is enormous. In Persia, if it was really defended by the people, a large army would starve and a small army be beaten. The possession of Erivan lies upon the frontiers of Turkey and of Persia. Our influence in Persia has been much weakened by our vacillating conduct. I must endeavour to retrieve our affairs there.

October 2.

The Duke of Wellington dined at Eoehampton. After dinner he told me how we stood with Eussia. We are to send out two line-of-battle ships to reinforce our fleet in the Levant (this will give us six, and we have as many large frigates there), and to order our admiral to give protection to all British vessels which may have cleared out from England before the notification of the blockade. This is to be done by force if necessary.

So far this is well; but we should provide that no vessel of whatever nation should incur capture or detention which may have cleared out on her voyage on the faith of our declaration in the King's Speech, and to Turkey that Eussia had deposed her belligerent rights in the Levant. I have written the sketch of a paper to this effect.

Nothing more has been done. The Duke seems to doubt what France will do. We say we can no longer co-operate with Eussia. If France says the same Eussia is Voted out, and France goes on with us. If France co-operates with Eussia, we are voted out, and free. In one way or the other the Duke thinks we shall get rid of Eussia.

234   The French begin to be tired of their campaign in the Morea.

The Duke thinks with me that public feeling is turning against the Eussians, and that the feeling in France will be one of jealousy of Eussia, rather than of foolish vanity respecting Greece. Whatever the feeling is there, the Government must follow it. I am convinced that if we speak and act friendly, France will be with us.

The Duke fears Lord Anglesey will not issue the proclamation when he finds it must have the signatures of Lord Norbury, Saurin, c.

They really mean to have one regiment sent to Ireland to relieve troops sent from thence. They say they do not want more. However, the Guards march from London. It is better to show there is a determination to have force ready.

The Duke has had a conversation with Barbacena, and gave him a good rowing for bringing the Queen of Portugal here without previous communication. She is to stay here till they hear from Eio.

The Duke is very angry with Itabayana and Pal-mella for newspapering, as he calls it, and will hold no communication with them except officially. This he told Barbacena, and the cause of it. [1] I had the Chairs to dinner, and the late Governor-General, E. Clive, Ashley, Graham, Bankes, the Duke, Lord Melville, and Sir G. Murray to meet them. Lady Amherst and Mrs. Bankes dined with us too.

[1 ' Barbacena is not more exempt than the others from the practice of appealing to the newspapers." Letter of the Duke of Wellington, October 28, 1828, in Wellington Correspondence, v, 178.]

235

October 3.

Eode to town. Went to the Foreign Office. Saw Aberdeen. In the letter to ' Lloyd's' announcing the blockade, Aberdeen uses the expression ' in the opinion of his Majesty's Government, vessels of his Majesty's subjects which have cleared out on the faith of his Majesty's declaration to Parliament will not be liable to it." I told him I disapproved of the weakness of these expressions. At least he should have said, his Majesty will take measures, c., which would have applied to measures of negotiation as well as measures of force. To my surprise he said he thought so too, but he could not induce the Duke to use any other expressions than those inserted in the letter. This I do not understand. To Lieven and to Lord Heytesbury all is said that should be said, and Lord Heytesbury is directed, in a secret despatch, to declare to the Emperor, should reasoning fail, that the additional force we are sending to the Mediterranean has orders to protect all our vessels cleared from hence by October 1, and from any Mediterranean port by October 30.

In a quiet way, and not knowing the strength of his expressions, Aberdeen now and then uses words which go far beyond what would be used by a man of more passionate feeling. Some of the observations Lord Heytesbury is desired to make to the Emperor of Eussia will make him jump six feet high. He can never have heard such language before.

236 The mischief is, that the meek expressions used in the letter disparage us in public opinion, while if we at once said what we really do, tlie country would be with us.

The French had by September 5 landed 11,000 men in the Morea. More were in sight.

The Sultan has declared Ibrahim an infidel for his treaty.

Ibrahim, too much pressed by the French, declared if they moved a step further he would not go. He would go by the treaty, but not by force.

At Constantinople the arrival of the French expedition has made them furious, and the Sultan has ordered troops to the Morea. Eeally the spirit with which he faces every new danger is magnificent.

The Catholic Association seems to have had the power to prevent any more large meetings. I am in hopes Ireland will be quiet still.

October 4.

Had a long letter from Lady Jersey. They are endeavouring to organise an Opposition, and are angry about Ireland and Foreign Affairs. I do not wonder at it.

October 5.

Wrote a letter to the Duke of Wellington, to whom I shall send Lady Jersey's letter.

October 6.

Sent the letter to the Duke, such papers as bear upon the subject of our policy in Persia, and my two drafts of despatches to Colonel Macdonald.

237 Saw Mr. Leach relative to East Indian Finance. He has got together perfect accounts, which will give me all the information I can desire; but I must finish

one thing before I begin another, and act on the principle my father was always recommending, Hoc age.

Eead again with attention Lord Combermere's memorandum on the Bengal army.

The Prussians have entered into an engagement with Eussia to prevent the Austrians from acting. Nostiz, a Prussian general with the Emperor, let it out incautiously to Dornberg, who told Lord Heytes-bury. I receive with doubt all Dornberg says.

The Eussians have retreated from before Schumla. The Turks are taking the offensive, and scour the country in all directions. The Eussians are said to have lost the heights at Silistria. At Varna they have their guards, and expect to take it. It is feared they will. The Turks have attacked the Eussians at Prasadi. If Varna should be taken, the Eussians cannot now advance with the Turks in force on their right flank and even in the rear.

General Paskewitsh advances, but as there is no one to deny what he says he may tell great lies; and it is clear he does tell some.

Henry has joined the French army.

October 7.

Ireland seems quieter. The proclamation, of which Lord Anglesey gets all the credit, has been well received.

The ambiguity of our conduct respecting the blockade of the Dardanelles does us harm.

238   October 10.

Looked over a number of despatches. Wrote a memorandum for Bankes, laying down some general principles to govern the alterations of the Privy Council sent up.

The first is, never to make verbal alterations where the words originally used express a meaning to which we agree.

The second, to soften all expressions of censure, in which the Court is too apt to indulge, where there is no intention of punishing; indiscriminate censure makes men callous.

The third, to strike out altogether paragraphs which are merely conversational, neither expressing censure, nor approbation, nor giving any direction.

The Court evidently has its favourites, and the men of whom it is composed, once servants of the Company, are very ready to exercise their power of answering men who are in the situation they once held themselves.

Eeceived two letters from the Duke. One as to the separation of the civil from the military staff; the other as to Persian politics. He is for the more pacific line, and would have the Persians give their great neighbour no justifiable ground for interference with them. I would, in Persia and everywhere, endeavour to create the means of throwing the whole world in arms upon Eussia at the first convenient time.

An application for a writership for a nephew from Lady M. Eoss, and from the everlasting Sir Compton

239   Domville for a writership, because he cannot have a cadetship. I could hardly answer the man with civility.

October 13,

Saw Aberdeen. He is quite enchanted with the situation into which he thinks he has brought us. The French act with us, and no longer co-operate with Eussia under the Treaty of London. But, what I cannot understand, Eussia not co-operating, is still to have her voice in the settlement of the Greek question. This is as if a man should be allowed to have a voice in the conduct in the affairs of a partnership, after he had withdrawn his money. To be sure, the French and we outvote the Eussians in the Conference.

It seems Metternich has communicated some overture from the Turks which nearly amounts to a recognition of the principle of the Treaty of London. Nothing is done till we have our Ministers again at Constantinople.

The Eussians bluster and say they will take Varna and advance, making a winter campaign. In the meantime Moldavia and Wallachia are exhausted, and the peasants are flying to Transylvania.

October 16.

The Chairs have written an ill-tempered letter on the subject of the King's troops. They do not acquiesce.

It appears by the financial despatch I read last night that there has been a great increase in the civil expenditure of India since 1817. The expense of collecting the revenue has increased very largely in proportion to the revenue,

Madras is the best regulated settlement. This it owed to Sir Thomas Munro.

Although the trade to India has increased, the return to England has decreased. It is now less than a million a year clear profit including everything. It has fallen off since 1813-14 about 210,000.

It appears to me that the directors will not make their servants in India reduce the expenditure by merely talking to them. They must punish those who are extravagant, refuse to sanction increase of salary and creation of office. I believe they must send out commissioners with full powers. I doubt their doing all that may be done otherwise.

Saw the last despatches from Lord Cowley with the enclosures.

The army before Schumla, or rather at Jeni Bazar, is reduced to 20,000. That before Silistria to 8,000. There are 50,000 sick, and 20,000 have fallen by the sword. The original army was not above 120,000. The guards are 18,000 or 20,000. The army now to the south of the Danube is nominally 110,000, but not much more than 70,000. The Cossacks have disappeared. The cavalry is ruined. The country produces nothing. The commissariat is miserably conducted. They sent lately from Odessa to Yarna fifty vessels laden with hay. It was not pressed, but tied up in bundles. The whole only fed the cavalry one day. Diebitch is out of favour. Woronzoff is most trusted.

A General de Witt is the only man who talks of moving on to Aidos should they take Varna.

In the meantime the Turks improve, and in the last sortie from Yarna fought well with the bayonet, charging like regular troops.

This war checks the progress of Eussian power, and makes the Turks a military people again. One great man has restored them.

October 18.

Wrote to Lord Camden, expressing my satisfaction at hearing he intended to go to the great meeting, telling him. Lord Jersey, Baring, c., would be there, suggesting to him the proposing a resolution himself to this effect: ' That this meeting earnestly desires the settlement of the Catholic question on conditions consistent with the security of the Protestant Establishment." Wrote to tell Lady Jersey I had done so, and to Lady Londonderry, that she may write to Lord Camden and put him up to it.

Hardinge is making considerable reductions, and will do a great deal of good.

Saw the Duke. He came to town last night. It seems he had written to me about Mr. Hill's being restored, in consequence of some letter he had received on the subject. He recommended great caution in so delicate a proceeding. I satisfied him nothing had been done wrong. I am to write a private letter to Lush-ington, softening it. This was my own first idea.

I told the Duke of the great increase of establishment and expenditure in India, and said I feared the VOL. i. E reductions the directors had ordered would not take place without sending a commission out. He did not like a commission, as it superseded the Governor-General; but he thought the Court might order reductions of officers and salaries, and tell the Governor-General he should be recalled if he did not obey. I have sent for returns which will bring the whole subject before me.

The Duke approves entirely of the despatch to Persia as now written. He thinks Persia might be induced to pay for the officers. We can tell Colonel Macdonald to try what he can do, but the officers must be kept at all events.

He had not yet read the letter respecting the Indian army. He thinks the longer the Eussians stay in Bulgaria the worse it will be for them, and they will at last lose their artillery, and waggons, and sick.

October 21.

Finished my letter to the Chairs in answer to theirs. I put an end to the discussion. Sent the letter to the Duke.

The Turks have advanced to relieve Varna with an army of 30,000 men, placing the corps the Eussians had thrown on the south of Varna (which is separated from the main army by a lake and mountain almost impassable) between two fires. There have been several actions. The Eussians were driven back on the 30th, when they attacked the Turkish redoubts raised by the relieving army. They allow a great loss of officers, four generals, c. The loss has fallen principally on the guards, which will make the war more unpopular than ever at Petersburg.

Aberdeen has written a despatch to Lord Stuart for communication to M. de la Ferronays. It contains our views with regard to what should be done in the Turkish and Greek business. It is not a despatch, but an essay, long, and with very little in it. It ends with a hope the Eussians will let us off from the Greek Treaty and permit France and England to settle the matter as they can with the Turks. The Eussians can hardly be such fools; but we shall be still greater fools if we do not let ourselves off.

Saw Mr. Leach and arranged what financial accounts should be prepared.

In their letter to me the Chairs bring forward a pretension which struck me as new, and Mr. Leach says he never heard of it before, namely, that the total number of troops payable by the Company, whether in India, here in depot, or on the sea, going and returning, is 20,000 by the Act. This would give only 17,000 effective in India. I have said it is an interpretation which I apprehend to be now given to the Act for the first time, and in which it is not probable that Parliament will be disposed to concur.

October 24.

The Duke has written a memorandum on my letter to the Chairs respecting the King's army in India. He suggests many things I did not and could not know, and seems indisposed to put an end in so peremptory a manner to the discussion. I must work his suggestions into my letter. I found Druminond copying the Duke's memorandum, and had to wait till it was finished. The Duke is satisfied with the draft I sent him of that part of the despatch to Macdonald which relates to the payment by Persia of the British officers. Saw Aberdeen. He is mightily well satisfied with his own diplomacy. He thinks France will act with us, and enable us to settle the Greek question in spite of Eussia. He must measure better than he has hitherto if this is to be accomplished. He is dissatisfied with S. Canning for having agreed with the other ambassadors in rejecting altogether the overture in the Vizier's letter, which, in fact, offered us what we wanted substantially; and still more, for having, in conjunction with the others, given orders to the admirals to continue the blockade of Candia, and to effect an armistice there. By their instructions, the ambassadors had no power to give orders to the admirals, and every consideration of policy should have deterred Canning from agreeing with them in opening a Candian question when we have enough to do with a Greek one in the Morea.

Aberdeen says the King is more wrongheaded than ever about the Catholics.

There is a beautiful account in the newspapers of the Sultan leaving Constantinople with the standard of Mahomet. It must have been a splendid and heart-stirring spectacle.

October 25.

Employed all the morning in arranging the Duke's memorandum on the King's army in India, and in working the facts and reasonings it contains into such part of my original letter as it seems desirable to retain. The meeting at Penenden Heath seems to have ended with some confusion, occasioned by the intervention of Hunt, Cobbett, and Shiel. However, the Anti-Catholics had a force of two to one. Lord Camden did not propose any amendment, and made a weak speech about himself, reading a letter, c. There appears to have been no previous concert on the part of the friends of the Catholics. The petition voted was very moderate. Cobbett could not obtain a hearing.

October 26.

Last night and to-day I read an interesting minute of the late Sir Thomas Munro on the policy to be adopted with regard to the Hindoos. The minute enters at some length into the state of the revenue derived from land, and the ancient tenures. It advocates the Eyotwari system that is, the system of taking the land tax at once from the actual proprietor and occupier of the soil, in preference to the Bengal system of creating, where they are not found, middlemen under the name of Zemindars. He is in favour of a permanent settlement of revenue, but says that there must be a previous survey. He argues that the land revenue being once fixed, and at a moderate rate, landed property will be created by the cultivation encouraged. This is already the case in some districts where the Eyotwari system has been established. Where the Zemindari system is established, it is the interest of the Zemindar to make the Ryot pay as much as he can beyond the sum fixed for the tax, and the Ryot has no sufficient protection against extortion. He says that what is in fact made over to the Zemindar, where once Zemindar is created, is a portion of the revenue of the State.

Sir T. Munro says we know very little indeed of the laws and customs of the Hindoos.

He thinks our judicial arrangements better than those we have established for the collection of the revenue, because we have established native judges for causes to the amount of 500 rupees.

He advocates the employment of the natives in all situations in which they can be employed consistently with the preservation of our supremacy. It is an able, eloquent, and statesmanlike paper. No man knew so much of the real state of India.

October 27.

Went to a Council at Windsor. The Duke, the Chancellor, Aberdeen, Sir G. Murray, and Yesey Fitzgerald were there, and Croker had been sent for to make up the number six. He was not wanted.

Esterhazy was there with Lebzelteru, who is come for the Queen of Portugal, and Itabayana, [1] who presented to the King the Order of Brazil.

I saw my old tutor, the Bishop of Chester, [2] and had some conversation with him. He is rather altered. I have not seen him since 1810.

[1 Minister Plenipotentiary of the Emperor of Brazil, father of the Queen of Portugal.
2 Sumner, afterwards Archbishop of Canterbury.]

The Duke thought my letter to the Chairs, as it stands now, perfect. He thought too that we had done quite right in restoring Mr. Hill, but had some doubts as to the law. That, however, is clear.

I read Lord Heytesbury's despatches of the 2nd and 10th. On the 10th there was no news at Odessa of a later date than the 1st, though the bulletin of the 1st reached Odessa by the steamboat on the 2nd.

The loss of the Russians on the 30th had been most severe, when Prince Eugene of Wurtemburg was driven back.

There was a report at Belgrade on the loth that the Eussians had stormed Varna and had actually entered the town when the Turks from Schoumla attacked their reserves and rear and ruined them utterly. There is some doubt as to this, in consequence of some confusion of dates, but the Duke believes it.

Lord Heytesbury takes very well the censure he received for his conversation with the Emperor, which I must have mentioned about the 6th or 7th of September.

In the first reconnaissance of the Guards on the 20th the regiment of the Chasseurs was quite destroyed. In the action of the 30th the Guards lost one of the celebrated standards of St. George.

I cannot help thinking there is no easy communication, except by sea, between the Russian grand army and the 8,000 Guards on the south of Yarna. The Duke seems to think there is a passage between Varna and the Lake.

October 28.

The Company wish to dispose of Mergui and Tenasserim, keeping Arracan. I wish they could sell the countries to the King of Ava. Unfortunately they have received refugees from the Burman territories whom they must protect or carry away.

I am to dine with them on November 12.

They have consented to make several regulations which will have the effect of keeping their native regiments more efficient in East Africa; but they decline separating the civil staff on the ground of the expense. I shall answer their letter, but I have little hope of succeeding with them.

They make no further fight about the King's army, having vented their ill-humour in their last letter. They rather wished to avoid my reply, and thus to have the last word. However, I sent my letter.

A Mr. Kennedy, who is come from Petersburg by the steamer from Hamburg, has written to the Foreign Office to say that, after he was on board, a supplement to the c Berlin Gazette' was brought, in which there was an account of the capture of Varna by the Eussians on the llth. The account is so circumstantial that I fear it may be true. It mentions incidentally that the Eussian troops had been in the town on the 7th, which is in unison with part of the report from Belgrade, but it gives no details of the storm of the 7th. It says the Turks were so much alarmed by what took place on the 7th that Jussef Pasha on the llth came out and laid down his arms. The Capitan Pasha threw himself into the citadel, but had surrendered. There had been 22,000 men in the place at the commencement of the siege, including the armed inhabitants. Only 6,000 men remained. The Kussians marched in at the breach. I dare say the place had long been nothing more than a position. The fortifications were never good, and they had been knocked to pieces long ago.

The war is more than ever unpopular at Petersburg, and the losses of the Guards will make it more so. I should not be in the least surprised by a revolution.

October 29.

It seems the account of the capture of Varna is not in the ' Berlin Gazette," but only in two German newspapers. We have no other account of it.

November 1.

Varna is certainly taken. The Capitan Pasha seems to have thrown himself into the citadel and to have had leave to retire with 300 men.

Sent my letter to the Chairs. The Duke is not in town, and it was not worth while to send it to him.

Eeceived a letter from Henry, [1] dated Navarino, October 3 and 4. He seems to be established in the family of General Maison. He had gone with the General over the works of Navarin, though it is yet uncertain whether Navarin will defend itself or not. All the Egyptians have embarked. The Greek women [1 The Hon. Henry Spencer Law, brother of Lord Ellenborough, who was then with General Maison's staff.] and children preferred going with them to staying in the Morea. Ibrahim had gone incognito to a review of the French army, but his curiosity was such that he went very near, at last accepted a horse, and rode with the General and the Admirals. He was very attentive and very inquisitive. After the review there was a breakfast at General Maison's, and Ibrahim drank too much wine and became very entertaining. He asked whether some of the French regiments had not come from Spain, and on being told that the greatest part of the army had been in that country, he said the French were a curious people, to send the same army to establish slavery in Spain and liberty in the Morea.

I shall send a copy of Henry's letter to the Duke and Lord Hill, not for its importance, but to keep him in their minds.

November 4.

The French Minister of War-has given orders to General Maison to march to Athens and Negropont. Sir Pulteney Malcolm has sent a copy of the orders home. He declared them to be contrary to the express stipulation of the French Government.

Aberdeen sent for Polignac, who denied all knowledge of these orders, and allowed they were contrary to the declarations of the French Government and to its intentions. Aberdeen has sent for the Duke, who is at Strathfieldsaye.

The French have taken Navarino, Coron, Modon and Patras without resistance. They, however, went through all the formalities of a regular storm, and Henry and William have seen war without fighting.

251   Read the last three days accounts of Mergui, Tavay, and Mar tab an, which the Directors wish to get rid of. My first impression is that it would be wise to do so; but the subject must be very well considered.

Eeceived a letter from Sir E. Farquhar desiring to see me on the subject of his claims. I declined seeing him. I said that I must decide judicially upon all claims against the Company. That I could not give a full and correct report of a conversation, and yet ought to make the Directors acquainted with all that was urged in support of a claim. that they might offer observations and reply. I must therefore have written communications on all subjects of that nature, which I should transmit to the Directors.

Letter from W. Wynne, enclosing one from the Bishop of Calcutta, deprecating a reported intention of sending a Scotch clergyman to Malacca.

Letter from Lord Camden, enclosing an authentic report of his speech at the Kent meeting.

November 5.

Met Prince Polignac at the Foreign Office. The French will not go beyond the Morea. I fear, however, Maison will have got to Athens before the orders reach him.

La Ferronays wants to get the army back again.

The Ambassadors at Poros have ordered the blockade of Candia because the Turks of the island, whd had lost their leader in an ambuscade, rose headed by his son, a boy of fourteen, and massacred the Greeks.

252   The only account of this comes through Capo dtstria, and is probably much exaggerated. How a blockade is to put an end to hostilities I cannot see.

The Eussian army is to go into winter quarters, and the Emperor is gone off to Petersburg. The capture of Varna has not turned their heads, and has made them more disposed to accede to terms than they might have been before. What they call Russian honour is safe. I am convinced the thing which would lead most directly to peace would be the return of our Minister to Constantinople. The moment France and England have their hands free, Eussia will see the time is not favourable for war. Eussia will never set us loose. We must extricate ourselves.

The apparent objects of the Treaty of London are obtained. The Turks are out of the Morea, and piracy-is put down. It would be too foolish, when we have got our object practically, to go on quarrelling with Turkey about forms.

November 6.

They will allow Lord Combermere to buy the King of Oude's picture at 5,000 rupees.

Enclose to the Governor of Bengal a copy of Sir Thomas Munro's opinion in favour of continuing under proper regulations the custom of giving presents.

We had some conversation on the subject of Mergui and Tavay. I told them I had already begun to read papers on the subject, and that my first impression was in favour of their suggestion, that it would be advisable to get rid of the territory to avoid the occurrence of conflict with the Burmese and Siamese, and to save 160, OOOZ. a year.

I have desired to see two gentlemen who are supposed to know most of the country.

Bankes told me he had read Prendergast's case, and thought the point upon which he laid most stress, namely, that the East India Company so entirely directed the affairs of Oude at the time the debts were incurred as to be responsible for the payment of them, was untenable.

The doubtful point is whether the debt is chargeable upon the King or upon the kingdom of Oude. If on the territory, the Company, having taken half, would be liable to one half of the debt; but this Prendergast does not urge, because on his first point he thinks he should get the whole repaid, and on the second point he could only get half.

I must look into the case at Brighton.

The Directors like their patronage too well to be disposed to take the King's assistant surgeons. They might leave sixteen of them now in India, and save the expense of sending them home.

The proposal of having stations for invalid soldiers instead of sending them home, they seem disposed to entertain. I may make something of this.

Upon the whole the Chairs seem to be in good humour, at least with me.

At the Foreign Office I saw Lord Heytesbury's despatch of the 17th from Odessa.

The only thing really well done by the Eussians seems to have been the night attack of General Grismar upon the Turkish army which advanced from Widdin upon Crajova.

The Eussians seems to have got possession of Varna only by bribery, and the Emperor very appropriately gives Count Woronzoff a golden sword.

They have actually lost from 70,000 to 80,000 men in the campaign. They have neither commissariat, hospital staff, nor engineers.

It appears that even Admiral de Eigny told General Maison he could have no authority to advance upon Athens. The French expedition was strictly confined to the Morea. Maison was going to act on a private letter of the Minister of War, written before the protocols were settled. It is to be hoped he may have been arrested by the representations of the Ambassadors and of his Admiral, but otherwise he may have got to Athens before the first orders can have reached him. He intended to employ on the expedition General Schneider's corps which was at Patras, and about 2,500 men besides.

The French seem to have behaved very well about it. Stratford Canning wrote directly to M. de la Ferronays, and he immediately, before any communication had been had with England, sent a telegraphic message to Toulon, ordering out a fast sailing vessel with instructions to Maison.

November 8.

Saw Aberdeen. His private letter to Stratford Canning was just in time to prevent him from agreeing to the blockade of Candia by British ships, and to

255 General Maison's march upon Athens, which has been arrested.

November 10.

The Duke and the Ministers very well received at the dinner at Guildhall.

Sat by the Duke at dinner. He told me he had written a memorandum on the subject of Greece, and had proposed a way out of the treaty.

He said he knew that three weeks ago the Opposition had not been able to form themselves. They want to rally under Lord Grey.

I talked to him on matters connected with the office, and gave Falmouth's almost forgotten message, that he was friendly to Government.

November 11.

Eead Stratford Canning's last despatches dated October 13, 14, and 16. He should be told that, whatever his opinions may be, it is his duty undoubtedly to make them known to his Government; but as an Ambassador he should always make it appear that his personal opinions coincide with those of his Government. He otherwise, as far as in him lies, nullifies by his private conversation the effect of the arguments he uses as a Minister, and subjects his country to disadvantage while he disparages himself.

The Duke's memorandum is in answer to reasoning of Canning's on the future limits of Greece, and on the meaning of the Treaty of London, which is throwing away a great deal of good powder. In conclusion he suggests that we should in conference

256 point out the many incon-[veniences which result from the suspicion of diplomatic communication with the Porte say, that the Porte has practically acquiesced in the evacuation of the Morea; that after our declaration that the French troops should not go beyond the Isthmus, to do so would be a breach of faith, and without that the Greeks can do nothing; that the liberation of the Morea accomplishes the object of the treaty; that the armistice exists de facto; that the Turks seem disposed practically to acquiesce; that therefore our Ambassador, who should never have left Constantinople, should now return there.

In this measure he hopes to carry the French along with him.

I agree entirely in all this. It is what I should myself have suggested, and did, a day or two ago, in conversation with Aberdeen. But I go further, and so I told him. I would, being once with the French at Constantinople, resolve that peace should be made on the basis of the Treaty of Akerman; or, that if they chose to pursue the war, the Eussians should not pass the Balkan. This they cannot do if we prevent them from navigating the Black Sea. By sending ten sail of the line into that sea with as many frigates and steamboats, each armed with eight 68-pounders, we should shut up the Russian squadron and enable the Turks to act. We should likewise convey Ibrahim with 25,000 men to Constantinople. This would be giving the Eussians a Treaty of London. It would be war, if they pleased to make it so; but war at sea with Eussia,

257 and France on our side, would be nothing. The question is, how/far the French will go on along with us? Will they adopt the proposal to be made to them at the next Conference? I think they would if we would consent to add Attica to the Morea; but to this there are great objections. The Turks would not give up Athens as they did Modon, c. As the Duke expresses it, they would make a Varna of it. This would lead to war between them and the French, into which we might be dragged. Besides, if the Greeks have Attica, it is argued they must have Negropont, which is Turkish, and has

never been Greek. If we once pass the Isthmus we embark in a war unjust and without object.

The memorandum observes the Greeks want no frontier. Against the Turks they will be protected by guarantee, and by the Turks against all others. The Turks are still to have the Suzerainete.

November 12.

The Duke told me that the King was every day urging him to recall Lord Anglesey. He read to me a letter he had written to Lord Anglesey expressing his disappointment at his not having had O'Gorman Mahon, and Steele, removed from Commission of the Peace for attending a meeting of an illegal character, and telling him very seriously that his conduct in visiting and treating equally well persons attached to the Association, and those who were quiet subjects, placed him in a situation of the greatest embarrassment with the King. [1] See Wellington Correspondence, vol. v. 240; O'Gorman Mahon's name is not given at length. The visit alluded to was to Lord Cloncurry. Lord Anglesey's defence may be found, ibid., p. 255, and seq.]

VOL. I S

The letter was admirably written.

Dined with the Directors, the dinner being given to me. Ninety were asked, and eighty-five were there. Of official men, the Duke, Peel, Sir G. Murray, Goulbiirn, Vesey Fitzgerald, Lord Bathurst, Hardinge, Planta, Holmes, Arbuthnot, Lord Grenville, Somerset, Ashley, Graham, and Bankes. Besides these, Lord Tenterden, the Yice-Chancellor, the Chief Baron of Scotland, Serjeant Bosanquet, the late and the present Lord Mayor. All the rest, except Mr. Eobarts, I did not know. There were most of the Directors, and I believe the rest were principally servants of the Company. I was introduced to Smith, Toone, Lindsay, Clarke, Lushington, Alexander, and Farquhar, of the Directors, and to Serjeant Bosanquet. I was glad to meet Captain Woolmer of the Trinity House.

In returning thanks when his health was drunk the Duke spoke in very high terms of me. When my health was given I made a speech, in which I endeavoured to please all and to make all pleased with me. I succeeded, at least with Astell, for he thanked me when I sat down, and came up again to thank me when I was coming away. Yesey Fitzgerald congratulated me very cordially on having so spoken, and on having been so spoken of. Hardinge told me too that I had done admirably, and I believe I did just what I intended. I did not say all I intended because I found the meeting was not in the state of excitement which could alone have enabled me to say eloquently and impressively part of what I wished to say. Peel said he was surprised, and made a set speech.

I sat between the Chairman and the Duke, and had a good deal of conversation with the latter. His idea is that the best way to bring the Eussians and Turks to reason and to peace will be to say nothing to either. I said that if we were satisfied the Turks could stand their ground in another campaign that plan might be very well; but if a smash came we should not forgive ourselves for our inactivity. He seems to underrate their numerical force of regular troops, not placing it higher than 30,000 men. I suggested that the moment we got our Minister back to Constantinople we should take measures for obtaining information. I told him I thought, if his memorandum was acted upon, Canning would resign.

Canning wished lately to be allowed to go to Naples, and Mrs. Canning was to join him there. He asked this on the plea that he had nothing more to do at Poros, and in the present state of things could get no further. His request has been refused.

Brighton, November 14.

Eeceived a letter from Aberdeen, The Cabinet was nearly unanimous as to the limits of Greece, and the return of the Ambassadors; but some difficulty arose from our previous admissions and declarations. These, however, will not signify if France goes with us.

Aberdeen says the accounts from Paris are still more satisfactory, and they now only throw out an idea that a part of Attica should be annexed to the Morea.

November 15.

Eeceived from the Chairs a memorandum of the nominations they wish to make this year 28 writers, 112 cadets, 56 medical.

Eeceived a letter from Mr. Jackson, enclosing one from Mr. Wyatt, begging to have a clerical error corrected in Mr. Lush's patent. The Signet Bills are at Koehampton, and it is very inconvenient to me to send the key of my blue box.

I have cautioned Mr. Jackson to see that it is only a clerical error. This is, I suspect, the patent which Wyatt hurried through to anticipate some other man who wanted a patent for the same thing. I have told Mr. Jackson to be careful.

November 18.

Eeceived a letter from Aberdeen. He says, 'We had one Conference yesterday (the 16th). All went off well." The French troops are to be withdrawn immediately, and we are to guarantee the Morea and the islands against the invasion of the Turks. Lieven took the proposal ad referendum; but I suppose he will agree.

Nothing final was settled about the return of the Ambassadors. The French wish that it should be to some place near Constantinople, but are evidently prepared to go to Constantinople if the Turks insist.

Although the guarantee does not necessarily comprise what may ultimately be Greece, by means of negotiation I think the question of limits may be considered as settled. The French made a fight for Attica; but we were Go thick and prevailed.

I wrote to Aberdeen to offer him my congratulations on the fair prospect before him.

Undoubtedly the Duke has managed very well to keep the French constantly with us.

I told Aberdeen that if, as the Duke seems to think advisable, we are to leave the Turks and Eussians to do what they like, saying nothing to either, under the idea that when left to themselves they will sooner see the folly of their going on, we ought to have full information as to the probability of the Turks being able to hold out for another campaign. We should have information not only as to their armies on the Balkans, but in the neighbourhood of Erzeroum. We should never forgive ourselves or be forgiven or deserve to be forgiven if a smash should take place and the Eussians get to Constantinople.

Lord Essex told W. Ashley yesterday he thought the Government could not last. It seems he thinks the Catholic question will ruin us. It will bother us; but we shall stand.

W. Ashley met Ward, the member for the city, at dinner there. He said we had the elite of the city at the Directors' dinner. It seems Ward spoke in very high terms of me. So much the better. He is a great citizen.

November 19.

Eead the remainder of the papers relative to the uniform currency of India.

I concur in Mr. Leach's opinion that the best thing that can be done is to do nothing.

November 21.

Went to the office. A letter from the Prince Eegent of the Carnatic to the King, containing nothing but praises of Lushington, and evidently obtained by him through his son, who is a Government agent at the court of the Nawab.

The Duke thinks the last letter of the Chairs in reply to mine on the subject of the King's army is very unfair, and must be answered if it is not withdrawn. [1] I shall get the facts contradicting it from Lord F. Somerset, and endeavour to make them withdraw it; but I do not think I shall succeed.

November 22.

Saw Aberdeen. Lord Bingham describes the Turkish army as miserable in equipment; some with bayonets, some without; the muskets of all calibres. However, they fight, which the Russians do not! I suppose the want of food and eau de vie had taken away their spirit; but in the last engagement with Prince Eugene of "Wurtemburg the men lay down. The Chasseurs of the Guard were destroyed, all but 180, in a wood. The Turkish cavalry killed them man by man, the Eussians making no resistance. Lord Bingham says they lost 15,000 men before Yarna. The Capitan Pasha would not surrender on the conditions offered, or at all, as Youssouf Pasha did on worse conditions than the [1 See Wellington Correspondence,, vol. v. p. 269.]

Capitan Pasha might have obtained, for Youssoufts people became prisoners and the Eussians would have allowed them all to join the Grand Vizier. The loss sustained by Prince Eugene was not avowed; but it was very great. The non-commissioned officers in the Chasseurs of the Guard are gentlemen. Lord Bingham says there is no. t a man in the Russian army who does not desire peace as much as we can. If the Turks can make a good fight, I do not desire peace.

Beresford seems to be extremely unpopular with the artillery.

November 24.

Went to a Recorder's report at Windsor Castle. The Duke, Peel, Aberdeen, Sir G. Murray, Goulburn, and the Chancellor were there. Aberdeen had the new Spanish Minister, Leo, to present, and Mr. Barbour, the American Minister. The latter seems a very gentlemanlike, well-conditioned man. We all walked over the Castle. The King's apartments are finished. Fires were lighted, and the carpets put down. The corridor is beautiful. The American was enchanted.

The Duke showed me the opinion of the law officers in Ireland, which is, that the Catholic Association will come under the enacting part of the Convention Act, though not described in the preamble that is, as assuming to represent though not elected. They likewise think indictments might be laid for conspiracy. The latter, I think, will not do. The former may; but it seems not to be enough that men should claim to represent unless that claim is acquiesced in. Perhaps it may be shown that it is. The opinion of the Irish law officers is now before the Attorney- and Solicitor-General here, and if they concur in the opinion, proceedings will be instituted.

The King is very desirous of recalling Lord Anglesey. No progress has been made with him on the Catholic question.

The Duke told me he would send me his correspondence with Lord Anglesey. His letter I have seen.

The Duke thinks he shall get out of the Greek Treaty by the meeting of Parliament, and he hopes to get out of the Portuguese business too.

Saw Hardinge. He has in contemplation a plan for giving men their discharge before their pension becomes due, by which he hopes to get a man's service for eighteen of the best years of his life for very little, and to make a good settler at Van Dieman's Land or in Canada of him afterwards. I have no doubt Hardinge will do great things at the War Office, and some day or other he will be Chancellor of the Exchequer, and a very good one.

Don Miguel has fractured and splintered his leg severely. Bad surgeons may bother him very much, and he may be more amenable to reason.

I sent to the Duke my memorandum on Tenasserim with the Chairs' letter, and the necessary maps, as well as the letter from Moulmein received to-day.

No news at the Foreign Office. Aberdeen gone to the Antiquarian Society.

I told the Duke of Montrose yesterday that I had a letter from the Nabob of the Carnatic to forward as, I was told, through his office, that of the Lord Cham-berlain. To-day Sir W. Knighton called when I was with the Chairs, and left a verbal message that I was to send the letter to, I forget what number, in Pall Mall. Courtenay told Waterfield the President communicated directly with the King, and that I should send the Nabob's letter and the suggested answer, which I shall do.

November 26.

Sent my letter to the King, the draft of the King's answer, and the translation of the Nabob's letter, together with the original letter in its large tin box.

Heard from Mary 1 that in consequence of a general order of Lord Beresford's, censuring the horse artillery in very severe terms, four lieutenant-colonels had resigned. I thought it right the Duke should know this.

Eead and made amendments in the ' Civil Despatch' to Bengal. It is a collection of very indifferent essays. I have added a paragraph which in effect tells the Governor-General if he will not make the reductions some one else shall.

Looked over the despatch with Bankes at the office.

Saw Aberdeen. Eead his late despatches to S. Canning. I told him I thought they would bring Canning home. The language is very civil; but it practically tells him what he suggested was dishonest These despatches are better written than those Aberdeen wrote at first. The Duke, however, gives the substance.

There is a report that Lord Sidmouth is to have the 1 His sister, the Hon. Mrs. Dynely, R. A., wife of Major Dynely, afterwards Lieut-General Dyneley, C. B.

Privy Seal. I hope not. It would show the Duke despaired of bringing the King round upon the Catholic question.

November 28.

Wrote a despatch to Bengal, entering into the question of the policy to be pursued with regard to Turkey and Persia.

Eeceived a letter from the Duke. He has enquired into the Woolwich case and finds that Lord Beresford was in the right. I think, however, that his enquiries have only extended to the complaint respecting ' the range firing' and not to the letter in orders reflecting generally on the horse artillery.

I was occupied with business to-day for ten hours.

I have a good account of Captain Eathborne's services, and shall give him the cadetship he asks.

November 29.

Wrote to Captain Eathborne to tell him so. I said I had much satisfaction in placing in the service of the East India Company a gentleman who, I had no doubt, would imitate the conduct of his gallant and respected father. I hope I have made the old man happy.

Called on Lady Jersey. By her account Lord Eosslyn has taken a correct view of Dawson's conduct and Lord Anglesey's. The absurd thing is that Lord Anglesey thinks he alone can pacify Ireland, and that if it was not for his influence with the King all sorts of mischievous things would be done in Ireland. 'It seems Lord John Eussell wished Lord Grey to countenance Catholic clubs, which he prudently declined. He said he had just the same constitutional objection to Catholic clubs which he had to Brunswick clubs, and that they would only embarrass the Government. Lord John wants sadly to hook him in to Opposition.

Lord Melbourne is very eager in Opposition.

The Duke manages to get from Lady all the secrets of the Opposition, and while he does all his own business, all Aberdeen's, and overlooks the business of all the departments, he finds time to call upon ladies and to secure them to his party.

December 1.

Went to Windsor. Eecorder's report. Two men to be executed for burglary; one for endeavouring to cut his wife's throat, a case of jealousy, and jealousy not without reason; but the man had continued to live with his wife some months, indeed, I think, more than a year after she had admitted her infidelity. Still it is a melancholy case, for the poor man had been very happy, and the wife's conduct seems to have changed his character altogether long before he attempted her life. The woman seems to have had no compunction in giving her evidence against her husband. The fourth person ordered for execution was Munton for forgery. A strong case.

The thing that distresses me in all these cases, however, is that men are punished not with reference to the extent of their own crimes, unless they be very great, but with reference to the number and circumstances of similar crimes committed by others at the same time. Our laws are so framed that all cannot be executed who incur the penalty of death and wisely and humanely so framed, I think; but still the consequence is that in every case it is not the law but individuals who decide whether a man shall suffer or not, a very difficult and painful duty, executed, I believe, most conscientiously; but I wish it did not fall to the King's Ministers to execute it.

The Eussians have acceded to our proposed modification of the blockade as regards English vessels, which may have left England before the 1st, or any Mediterranean port before October 30.

The sickness increases in the Eussian army. The troops are moving towards Silistria. Youssouff Pasha attacked them, and according to the Eussian account was repulsed.

The despatches from Lord Heytesbury are dated November 14.

By the newspapers it seems that the Capitan Pasha has been made Grand Vizier, the former Grand Vizier, who never was a soldier, having been supposed not to have made sufficient efforts to relieve Varna.

Heard from Henry. He says the French are for the Turks but not much disposed to quarrel with Eussia. He has had fourteen days of dysentery and is now at Zante that is, on November 13.

Eeceived a letter from Planta enclosing one from Mr. Mckinnon, who wishes to be an East India Director. Told him I did not know wherein the influence of the India Board consisted, that I was the only man in England who could not ask a favour of the Directors. That all I wished was that the best and most capable man should be elected. Of Mr. M. I knew nothing, and I could not know him to be the fittest till I knew all the candidates.

At the Eecorder's report to-day the King walked well and seemed well, but rather in a hurry. I should say, as regards the head, not so well as last Monday.

Lieven had an audience. The Russians are in a great fright lest we and the French should go back to Constantinople alone.

December 5.

I told the Chairman we were precluded from reducing the Persian mission to its former standard by Canning's understanding with the Persian Government. The Persians were assured when we transferred the mission from the King to the Governor-General that the mission should be maintained on a scale of increased splendour.

December 8.

Foreign Office. Eead Lord Cowley's despatches. The Russians have raised the siege of Silistria. They had brought up their whole army except about 8,000 men left at Yarna; but they had no provisions. The rain had made the country nearly impracticable, and a storm of hail and snow came on, with the glass at 8°. They marched off and passed the Danube at Hirsova. This was on the 12th. There is some account of their having experienced a serious attack on the 8th. Hussein Pasha had ordered the Turks at Kalafat to countermarch by the right bank of the Danube upon Silistria, upon which place he marched from Schumla. This fine movement seems to have had deserved success. The Eussians have left behind them their heavy guns. The few remaining horses were harnessed to the baggage. The lighter guns were buried. They expect to dig them up in the spring!

At Bucharest the Eussians have what they call a hospital that is, thousands of men lying on hay, without medicine or a surgeon, and ill-supplied with provisions. The two Bucharest apothecaries who were ordered to attend the hospital are dead. The only medicines are procured from the chemist's shops of Bucharest. "Witgenstein is gone to his estates. Die-bitch to Yassy, where the head-quarters will be established. There are not less than five or six generals at Odessa. Langeron is at Bucharest. They all seem to have deserted the army. In Wallachia they speculate upon the evacuation of Varna and even of the Principalities. The Eussians, who at the Treaty of Akerman obtained for the Principalities the remission of two years' contributions, now say the Treaty of Akerman is at an end and the arrears must be paid up to them! The country, however, is exhausted.

The Prussians have urged the Sultan to make proposals to Eussia. The Eeis Effendi charges the Prussian Minister with overlooking the interests of his own country and acting in a sense purely Eussian. Truly enough. The conduct of the Eussian Cabinet is disgusting.

Zuylen de Nyvett, the Netherland Minister at the Porte, has been guilty of an impudent gaucherie which has made the Sultan indignant, and will occasion his recall.

The Sultan is more magnificent and the Turks more sturdy than ever. I fear we shall not act boldly enough, and so lose the opportunity of getting our Minister back to Constantinople. The Sultan will make no concession in favour of the Greeks by treaty; but he will yield practically what he will not yield in words, and we should be insane if we did not look to what is practically a fulfilment of the unfortunate Treaty of London.

In the meantime 10,000 Asiatic cavalry have passed the Bosphorus. My hope is that the Eussians in Varna will be taken prisoners.

Munster has, at the instigation of Lieven, whose tool he is, been setting the King against Metternich on account of the affair of the Duke of Brunswick, in which it is quite impossible that Metternich should not have acted for the best for us, for he can have no interest or feeling the other way.

The Austrians have been playing too fine a game. They have made both Eussians and French most hostile to them, and they may suffer for it.

I called at Hardinge's to tell him all I had just heard about the Eussian army; but I did not see him. I told Emily [1] to repeat my news to him.

[1 Lady Emily (afterwards Viscountess) Hardinge. She was sister of Lady Victoria Stewart, Lord Ellenborough's first wife, and of the second Marquis of Londonderry, better known as Lord Castlereagh.]

December 8.

Saw Aberdeen. The French seem backward in bringing Church and Ipsilanti back into Greece. Capo d'Istria wanted Maison to lend him some light troops; but Maison would not. They go on blockading Candia, although the orders not to do so must have been received long ago. Miguel is getting better.

Saw Lord Darnley. He wants the Duke to frighten the King about Ireland. There is to be a grand Liberal dinner at Maidstone on the 21st, Lord Darnley in the chair.

Received back from the King the letter to the Nabob of the Carnatic, approved. I began to think his Majesty meant to keep my box and take no notice of my letter.

December 10.

Despatches as late as October 5 from Colonel Macdonald (in Persia). The Shah seems much alarmed at the dissolution of our treaty with him, to which the Prince Abbas Mirza was pledged the East India Company paying a sum of money to get rid of the obligation imposed upon us. The Shah thinks he is abandoned by his only ally. The Prince seems determined to go to Petersburg. He will throw himself into the hands of the Eussians. He wrote to get Bagdad, Bassorah, c., from the Turks.

There is a rebellion in Khorasan and in Kerman. In the former the Persian Government seems to be very weak. The Eussians are going to send a splendid mission to Teheran, with fifty Cossacks of the Guard, while, under the directions of the miserable Government of Bengal during the interregnum, our guard of Poonah Horse has been withdrawn and the Envoy severely censured for his extravagance. His allowances for the gentlemen of his mission and everything have been reduced to 10,000 rupees a month.

The rebellion in Kerman seems to have been put down to a certain extent by one of the King's sons, but with infinite cruelty.

Paskewitch has 30,000 men effective out of 110,000 men under his orders. He has 100 light guns. He lost a great many men at Akiska. He seems to have the talent of concealing his movements. The Eussians wish to keep all they have conquered or may conquer on that side.

With 200,000. I could stop General Paskewitch,

December 11.

Saw the Chairs. They seem not to like some of the alterations in the joint letter to Bengal. Perhaps the last may be premature and too strong. It tells the Governor-General practically that, if he should not be economical, one will be found who is.

I talked a great deal to them about Persia. Afterwards saw the Duke upon the subject. He sees the importance of preventing the Persians from moving against the Turks, and I have this evening written a despatch to Macdonald, explaining our reasons for wishing to be released from the 3rd and 4th articles of our treaty, but declaring that our friendship for Persia is unchanged, adding, however, that we can do nothing VOL. I. T for her if she quarrels with her neighbours and engages in European contests.

December 13.

Found at the office a letter to the Envoy in Persia, unaltered and approved. Accordingly I sent it to the India House for immediate transmission.

Yesterday the Chairman told me it was reported Sir John Malcolm had fallen asleep at church, and waked, having lost his memory. The non-arrival of my despatches by the last ships gives some credit to the report. I mentioned it to the Duke, who was much shocked. It was what he expected. He had told Malcolm he would die if he returned to India. He had had a paralytic attack once when he was on service with him, and I hear too that some tendency of that sort had been perceived before he left England. He will be a great loss to the Company.

December 15.

Went to Windsor to a Council. Parliament to meet on February 5. Had some conversation with the Duke.

The Duke has sent me memoranda on the question of giving up Tenasserim and on that of maintaining Hill. He is for giving up Tenasserim, as the retention of it would lead to a new system,

I told him I should ask his opinion about Cutch. He inquired if I had a good map. I told him that was exactly one of the things I had in my memorandum [I He lived till 1832]

275   suggested the expediency of obtaining. We have not information enough.

Present at the Council, Aberdeen, V. Fitzgerald, Goulburn, the Duke, Sir G. Cockburn, and myself. I asked Sir G. Cockburn if he knew Captain Eathborne. He did not; but he said he was a very old officer, very respectable, and torn to pieces by wounds. He seemed very glad to hear I had given his son a cadetship.

Aberdeen told me Canning was worse than ever, and that the Ambassadors had bothered the Admiral, and led him, in spite of his instructions, to continue the blockade of Candia.

Aberdeen had a long audience of the King, who, he told me, was quite with us on the Greek question, though I have no doubt Munster, instigated by Lieven, has been doing all the mischief he can.

Goulburn promised that if he found the Government had ever paid for presents to Indian princes, he would buy six black dray horses for Eunjeet Singh if we could not get the Company to pay for them. The Duke saw no objection to it.

At 9 o'clock received a letter from the Chairman saying he had no messenger, and begging me to ask Aberdeen to lend them one.

I wrote to him, to Aberdeen, and to Lord Cowley, to whom the despatch should go under flying seal.

December 17.

The despatch to Colonel Macdonald goes by a Foreign Office messenger to Lord
276   Cowley to-day. He will forward it to Constantinople [I have no doubt that the Court of Directors and the Board have the power of Parliament in all revenue matters within the Presidency. However, Mr. Groom and Mr. Bankes seem a little to doubt whether, the tax having once been discontinued, though not in consequence of any doubt as to its legality, it can be legally re-enacted. I believe the only person who would entertain any doubts upon this point is the Eecorder. However, it will be submitted to the Counsel to the East India Company, Serjeant Bosanquet.

December 18.

Eead at the Foreign Office Canning's despatches and protocols. He is hostile to the views of his Government; but being so, he behaves more like a gentleman than Lamb did.

Asked Backhouse to let me know on what grounds Sir J. Malcolm and Sir H. Willock were permitted to wear the order of the Lion and Sun given to them by the Shah of Persia. Colonel Macdonald is very desirous of being allowed to wear not only the order, but that given to him by the Emperor of Eussia. The rule in the King's service is that no foreign order shall be permitted to be worn except for military services; and I think it a very good one. I fear, however, that if Colonel Macdonald is not 'allowed to have these orders I can get no other honour for him, as he is not in a situation to deserve the Grand Cross of the Bath.

Saw the Chancellor at the House of Lords, where I sat as a Commissioner for the
277   prorogation. He promised he would write to Lord Bathurst about the course to be adopted in Sir Claridge's case. It seems the Privy Council had at first desired him

to send his answer to the charges. They thought that to order him home would be productive of great inconvenience.

Sir Gwyllym, a Welsh puisne judge at Madras, was ordered home, but there were other judges left. The Eecorder is alone. I told the Chancellor we thought we could do without a Eecorder there, and rather wished to try the experiment quietly. He saw the use of this, and promised to write to Lord Bathurst about it.

Met Lord Melville at the House. The Chairs went to him to-day after they had seen me. I asked if they were in good humour. He said Yes. I am sure they ought to be.

There is a report of Dudley's being the intended Privy Seal. I told W. Ashley, who mentioned it to me, I did not believe it. I did not believe any of the Canningites would ever be admitted, although to Dudley personally there was no objection, and the King liked him.

The Chairs wish me to write to the Chief Justice of Bengal upon the subject of his very indiscriminate admission of persons resident in India as barristers and attorneys. I desired to have the opinions of the two late Chief Justices on the subject. It will not do for me to interfere upon this matter unless I have very strong ground, and can do it with effect.

278   December 20.

Office. Found my letter to the Madras Government returned by the Duke, unaltered and concurred in.

Foreign Office. A letter from Lord Stuart, by which it appears that of 157,000 men who passed the Danube there are but 54,000 in existence, and the Russians have besides lost all their material and 47,000 horses. The Emperor is ready to agree to any terms, and asks no money. At first the money payment was to cover the expenses of the war. The Turks, on the other hand, say they will hear of no treaty not made in Congress, that so long as treaties exist between them only and the Eussians, the latter will always be picking quarrels. They require the guarantee and intervention of other Powers. Further, they say they will make no peace till the Eussians have passed the Pruth.

Saw Lord Melville. Lushington, who in April was writing to Wynne, and declaring that he could not express his anxiety for the success of the Goderich Government, now writes to Lord Melville,[1] rejoicing in the retreat of the Whigs, and in the establishment of a Protestant Government, which he hopes will last for ever. This to Lord Melville, who has always voted for the Catholics! Can anything be at once more stupid!

Lord W. Bentinck seems to have thought Lushington did wrong about Hill.

Eeceived back from Lord Graham the memorandum on Cutch without any observations.

[1 Lord Melville, when a member of the Liverpool Cabinet, was a supporter of ' Catholic Emancipation while in everything else acting with the ultra section of his colleagues. He was thus, as Stapleton describes him, the exact reverse of Lord Liverpool (' Life of Canning," i. 127).]

279   December 21.

Eead the papers relating to the question of admitting barristers and attorneys at Calcutta. It seems to me that the judges wish to keep the patronage all in their own hands. This must be guarded against. I think the barristers should be appointed from hence by the Directors with the approbation of the Board; the certificate of two judges and some years' practice at the bar being required to make a man eligible. I am sure the judges should have nothing to do with it. One judge appointed his own son a barrister. They have, by the regulation of 1799, retained the power of making their own clerks. This is unseemly. I perfectly recollect my father's being very angry with a judge at Calcutta for having nominated his son as a barrister.

December 22.

Eeceived the despatch relative to Tenasserim from the Duke. He thinks the retaining of the islands and the arrangement of the exchange should be left to the Local Government. I have altered the despatch accordingly, giving a strong opinion at the same time as to keeping the islands. The Duke not having read the papers does not know their value, and that the farm of the edible birds' nests will pay any expense the retention of these may occasion.

Lushington quite disgusts me. Having in his letter to Wynne expressed the deepest anxiety for the success of the Government, of which he was a member, in his letter to
⌊ 280
Lord Melville he congratulates him on again belonging to a Tory and PEOTESTANT Administration, and hopes the Whigs are out for ever.

Eeceived a letter from Lord Londonderry requesting rather drily to have his papers back. I have sent them. He wants them that he may determine what line he shall take about the Catholic question. I have told him in reply that of course he will take what line he thinks best, but that as the question is in the only hands which can do it any good I think the best course for its friends is to be quiet. He will not be quiet, because he is vain.

Talked over with Bankes the admission of attorneys at Calcutta. He agreed with me in thinking an Act of Parliament should settle it.

Went to the Foreign Office. Eead Lord Cowley's last despatches. It seems that two-thirds of the Eussian army have been employed in Bulgaria and Georgia. Of this force they have lost two-thirds, and it does not appear probable that the recruits will fill up the vacancies. At Yarna there is one brigade. At Pravadi another. The works of Varna are put into repair. The troops have bread and meat enough, but no forage. However, they have no horses. Varna is represented as being quite ruined. The houses are none of them water-tight. The number of dead bodies embarrassed the Eussians very much. Half the Turkish prisoners taken there died on their march. Even the Eussians thought this looked ill and had an inquiry; but the result was that they died of distress which could not be avoided. The people are all leaving Varna and dying
⌊ 281
on the road. The situation of the troops before Silistria must have been dreadful. The cold was premature and violent. It snowed for three days, and the troops had no cover. Numbers died. On the two last days of their retreat they were hard pressed by the Turks. They had but 15,000 men at Silistria, the worst of their army. There is some idea of Paskewitch's being brought from Georgia to conduct the next campaign.

December 24.

Cabinet. The Duke read the correspondence between him and Lord Anglesey. It is evident from the tone the correspondence had assumed on Lord Anglesey's part that it would be impossible to look for any future cordial co-operation between him and the Government, and therefore he will be recalled.

Lord Anglesey's conduct has long been particularly obnoxious to the King, and his Majesty has repeatedly urged the Duke to recall him. This the Duke objected to, even after the very improper step Lord Anglesey took in issuing the proclamation[1] without the concurrence of his council. There is a letter from the Duke to the King, written from Sudbourne,[2] on that subject. The Duke, however, wrote a strong letter to Lord Anglesey (which I have in its place mentioned, I think, as being read by the Duke to me), to which he received a justificatory reply, well written. The Duke answered, Lord Anglesey replied, and since that time he has hardly [1 A proclamation against illegal meetings. The objection was to its being found without the Irish Privy Council by the Lord Lieutenant singly. See Wellington Correspondence, vol. v. 105-7.

2 Wellington Correspondence, v. 133, where this letter is given in ex-tenso.]

written at all to Peel, never to the Duke. The removal from the magistracy of O'Gorman Mahon, in part the subject of discussion, he never mentioned to Peel when he had adopted the measure. I think the dates of the last letters are November 11th, 14th, and 18th.

We had much discussion as to Lord Anglesey's successor. The Duke proposed Lord Grantham, saying that the fittest man would have been Lord Melville, but that could not be. I cannot make out why. There seems to be some odd sort of mystery about it. The objection to Lord Grantham is that he would ask Lord Goderich's opinion, that he is not friendly to the Government, and would require explanations it would be very difficult to give as to the situation of the Government with respect to the Catholic question, and very hazardous to give where there would be a certainty of their being communicated to the most hostile faction, that of Huskisson, c. 1 thought of Lord Bristol and Lord Eosslyn. The Duke mentioned Lord Verulam; Peel, Lord Amherst. The Duke and Peel both said Lord Tweeddale would have been the best, but he is at Eome. The general feeling seemed to be that the successor should be a Catholic,[1] and that it was highly expedient to select a man with whom Lord F. Leveson will remain. I care little about Lord

Francis's remaining. I believe Lord Amherst would be the best. I look with much apprehension to the explanations the offer to Lord Grantham might bring on. I think he would decline after all. The Duke said: ' I will oppose the question till it can be brought on by a [1 That is, as supporter of ' Catholic Emancipation."]

Government, and, as a Minister, I must bring it on without the King." The Cabinet is divided upon it, but it is evident that those who oppose do not object to the Duke's doing all he can with the King. Unfortunately, the conduct of Lord Anglesey has made the King more hostile than he ever was.

It seemed to be admitted that the Cabinet must in the course of the next three weeks determine upon its line. Vesey Fitzgerald expresses himself well. He takes a good deal of part, and does everything in a very gentlemanlike and unassuming manner.

Sir Edward Codrington has written to the Admiralty to inquire whether, after the explanations given by him, the Government disapproves of his conduct as a naval officer. It is very difficult to know what answer to give, as it is desirable to avoid the necessity of a court-martial. I am to look through all the papers and report upon the case on Sunday at three.

December 25.

Wrote a note to the Duke, suggesting that he might gain time to choose a successor to Lord Anglesey more deliberately by allowing the Government to remain for a few weeks in the hands of Lords Justices. I renewed my objections to Lord Grantham, and said something in favour of Lord Amherst and Lord Verulam.

December 26.

Beading Codrington papers all day.

284

December 27.

Saw the Chancellor. He suggested that the Admiralty should merely say, in reply to Sir E. Codrington's letter, that he was recalled in consequence of the receipt of a letter from Sir J. Murray, of which the substance may be stated. He will then ask Aberdeen whether his explanations have been satisfactory, and Aberdeen will say No. There may be a question in the House of Commons, which does not much signify.

I had some serious conversation with the Chancellor about the Catholic question. He says the Duke must see the King soon, and tell him what he wishes to do. The King's Speech must be considered in a fortnight. The Chancellor expects the King will send for him and Peel.

The Chancellor will tell his Majesty it is much better to concede quietly and with good terms what cannot be prevented. That if the Ministers meet the question and are beat, as they would be, they must go out, and His Majesty would only be able to find Ministers resolved to carry the measure in any manner.

The Chancellor thinks Peel will not be a member of the Government which brings forward the question.

In the meantime the Catholics have got hold of a letter written on December 11 by the Duke to Dr. Curtis, the Catholic primate. In reality the letter says no more than the Duke said last session in the House, but they make much of it.

The Chancellor says the Master of the Eolls cannot live. He deprecates having

285

Wetherall there, who would ruin the Court of Chancery and be a most mischievous man in the House of Commons, a great Tory, and bigoted Protestant. He proposes to make Alexander Master of the Eolls, and Wetherall Chief Baron. Then he would try to get Scarlett as Attorney-general. The Chancellor approves of my notion of governing Ireland by Lords Justices till the Duke can fix upon a good Lord Lieutenant.

December 28.

Went to town to the Cabinet at three. I had written nothing I could do more than refer to, so I told in conversation all I had observed in reading the papers. The Chancellor's idea was not approved, and it was determined a letter should be written from Aberdeen to the Admiralty, stating that his Majesty's Government did not feel themselves called upon to pronounce an opinion upon the professional character of Sir E. Cod-rington. That, observing in the explanations required from Sir E. Codrington, and in the communications made by him, that his conception of the instructions under which he was acting was erroneous, they had decided he might be relieved in his command.

We expect a question in the House of Commons upon this subject.

There is a letter from the Duke of Cumberland to the Orange lodges, in which he declares the King's opinion upon the Catholic question. This will be a most awkward thing to fight when it is brought forward. The Duke is clearly wrong, but I suppose it

286 is the duty of a Minister to defend all the Eoyal family. It seemed to be the general opinion that there ought to be some precis of the Codrington correspondence, or some memorandum. I suppose I must write one.

December 29.

At Brighton dined with Lord Shaftesbury. Met the Lord Chancellor and Lords Granville and Dudley. Had some conversation with the Chancellor. He is, I see, seriously alarmed about the effect the Catholic question may have upon the Government.

December 30.

Occupied all the evening in writing a memorandum on Codrington's case. I thought it over in my own mind first, and then wrote it currente calamo ten sheets. I am sure that is the best way of writing a reasoned paper.

January 2.

Eeceived a letter from a Mr. Eowe applying for a judicial situation at Bombay. He tells me Sir Edward West is dead. I shall not be sorry if he is, for he has been a most mischievous judge.

I have written to the Duke, stating the circumstance, and my opinion of the extreme importance of selecting a fit man.

January 3.

Eeceived a letter from the Duke, who is very hostile to giving Macdonald permission to wear the Eussian and Persian orders. He thinks, as I do, that the rule against the King's subjects looking to any sovereign but their own for their reward is one which ought to be adhered to. It is only in the case of military service performed in the field that it is allowable for a man to receive an order from a foreign Sovereign, and then he must have his own Sovereign's permission. The Duke says he has fought many a battle upon this point; and, in spite of the rule, the King has recently allowed Lord Mountcharles to receive an order from Miguel!

The Duke says he thinks Macdonald ought to be rewarded, and he has thought of a way of doing it, which he will talk over with me when he sees me.

January 5.

Lord Anglesey has published an answer to Dr. Curtis's communication to him of the Duke's letter. The answer is dated the 23rd. It justifies his removal.

I hear the Bishop of Calcutta has resigned. Wrote to the Duke to tell him. I said the only persons who occurred to me were Calvert, Warden of Manchester, and Turner, Castlereagh's tutor. That the latter was the fittest of the two. I mentioned all the particulars respecting both, and that I did not think Calvert would take it. By giving the bishopric to Calvert the warden-ship of Manchester would be placed at the Duke's disposal, and by giving it to Turner Lord Londonderry would be obliged. Turner is a very fit man.

The Emperor of Brazil wishes to leave the settlement of the Portuguese question to the Emperor of Austria, having the wish thereby to save his dignity should concessions be required, and desiring more than anything else to obtain a Royal wife through the Emperor of Austria's means. Barbacena seems to have Pedro's entire confidence.[1]

The Greek Plenipotentiaries, Canning, Eibeaupierre, and Guilleminot, are gone to Naples, having recommended the most extended delimitation of Greece.

Eussia has not yet answered our suggestion that the conduct of the negotiation relative to Greece should be left to England and France.

There seems to be no doubt that, in the event of a conflict between Eussia and Austria, the Prussians would take the side of the Eussians, although the King of Prussia wishes for peace.

M. de la Ferronays, who was once ambassador at Petersburg, is very much afraid of displeasing Nicholas. J3e therefore seems to insist on a recognition of the armistice required by the treaty before we sent our Ambassadors to Constantinople, but he wishes to get them there.

The Emperor Nicholas is said to be bloody-minded and very obstinate. The Turks seem to be full of enthusiasm, and the Asiatics are coming forward en masse since the Sandjaksherif has been taken from Constantinople.

There is a sort of opening offered directly with the Porte through the Pasha of Eoumelia. Hitherto we have only communicated through the Internuncio, the Prussian, and the Netherlands Ministers, who are all quarrelling.

[1 The Marquis de Barbacena was commissioned by the Emperor of Brazil to accompany his daughter Donna Maria to Europe.]

Polignac seems disposed to take advantage of the opening, but he has written to his Court for instructions.

Had some talk with Aberdeen about the Catholic question. He seems very much out of humour, and not to care a fig about it.

Codrington has replied upon Lord Melville, and well. I do not think we shall get rid of him. However, I believe our case to be a good one.

My idea as to the Catholic question is that we might have a committee in the Lords, composed of all the influential peers twenty-one and in that endeavour to come to an understanding. I do not think the King could resist or would wish to resist the opinion of such a committee, which would save him harmless, and there is no longer time for the Duke to prepare any measure of his own with the King's concurrence. If the King would consent to a committee, all the rest would follow. I think these peers would do for the committee:

Archbishop of Canterbury, Lord Chancellor,
Bishop of London, Lord President,
Bishop of Durham, Duke of Wellington,
Bishop of Lincoln, Melville,
Archbishop of York, (?) Ellenborough,
Eldon, Lansdowne,
Colchester, Grey,
Holland, Lauderdale,
Rosslyn, Goderich,
Wellesley, Camden, Harrowby.
Suppuant. *Suppléant*
Londonderry, Charlemont (if he was in England)
Clare, England),
Gosford, Anglesey.
VOL. I. U.

These names are arranged in two columns

290   An Irish bishop of the session, instead of the Archbishop of York, for five bishops would be enough.

Called by appointment on Mr. Bebb, an old India Director. He is blind and deaf. He seems, however, to be an able man, and to have much information. I heard him talk for an hour. His conversation seemed to be the substance of a paper he gave me, which he said he had transmitted to the Court of Directors. His object is to have the duties taken off raw cotton on its introduction into our territories in India, and generally to facilitate the transfer to England of fortunes made in the East Indies by increasing the number of articles of commerce in which the transmission can take place.

As to cotton, he says he believes the long confinement of the cotton during the passage must necessarily diminish its value in comparison with the American cotton, which has a shorter transit. It seems, too, that the clouds of dust which cover the country in which the cotton plant grows in India injure it very much. A great deal of mischief is done, too, by careless cleaning. Besides, the cotton of India, coming from the northern provinces, is a year old before it is shipped. I fear there are natural difficulties it will be impossible to overcome.

January 7.

Called at the Treasury. The Duke is at Gorhambury. He is expected to-morrow or next day. He had written to me, saying he entirely concurred in my views as to the sort of person who should be placed on the judicial bench in India, but the Privy

291   Seal did not forward the letter, as he had imagined Sir E. West returned, whereas he is dead. There was aii inclosure to tell me Sir J. Malcolm was well at Ahmednuggar on the day on which he was said to have been taken ill at Poonah.

Aberdeen is at Gorhambury. I am rather disposed to think that Lord Verulam's going to Ireland as Lord Lieutenant may be settled there. The Times talks of the Duke of Northumberland in most respects a very good man.

January 8.

Saw Hardinge. He has made great reductions in the staff of the militia, and saves this year 40, 000*l*., and in subsequent years 75,000. The frauds he has discovered in the pension list are enormous. He saves 18,000. this year, and in the course of five or six years the savings will amount to 200,000. a year. He means to place floggable men in a different class in the army. It seems about thirty have been punished in each regiment.

Eeceived a letter from, the Duke. He has no objection to either of the clergymen I had mentioned for the Bishopric of Calcutta, but recommends my seeing the Archbishop of Canterbury and the Bishop of London on the subject, either with him or by myself.

He likewise recommends my seeing the Chancellor and the Chief Justice about the judges' appointments. This I had intended to do, but not the other, thinking that bishops have not such means of knowing parsons as judges have of knowing lawyers. However, I have no objection.

292   It seems the late Lord Londonderry had made a point with Lord Liverpool of Turner's being provided for, and the living he has, which was given to him by Government, is claimed by the Catholic patron. I have thought of Everard if Turner should not do. In the meantime I find the Bishop of Calcutta's resignation is not perfect. It must

be by writing, under hand and seal, delivered to the King's Commissioner Delegate, and by him accepted and registered. However, the poor bishop will, I think, die.

January 9.

Office. Eeceived from W. Ashley the paper I desired him to make out, containing a list of the lawyers who have applied for Indian judgeships. He has done it well, giving the dates of the applications, the persons referred to, c.

Mr. Backhouse is to answer about the 2,000. belonging to the Shah of Persia.

Cabinet. The question whether Lord Anglesey should be recalled immediately for his letter to Dr. Curtis. Decided he should be, and Lords Justices appointed. He is told in Peel's letter that 'Her Majesty's Government have had under their consideration a letter published in the newspapers, and purporting to have been written by Governor-General [1] to the Eev. Dr. Curtis, and of which the authenticity has not to this day been denied. Her Majesty's Government cannot think that it was consistent with the Governor-General's [2] duty as her Majesty's representative to write such a letter, and therefore," c.

1 Obviously should be Lord Lieutenant.

2 I. e. Lord Lieutenant.

Nothing determined or to be determined yet as to his successor.

The Slave Bill Huskisson rejected two years ago has now been read a first time in the Assembly of Jamaica, by a majority of one only. I congratulated Sir George Murray on his strength in the Assembly.

Aberdeen gave me a letter of his to read addressed to Barbacena, in reply to a demand made by him for effectual succours to place Donna Maria on the throne of Portugal. I corrected the style for him, and in one or two instances made the argument more clear and forcible.

January 10.

Aberdeen told me he had adopted almost all my alterations, and that I had improved his style.

There is a letter to Peel in the Times, very wicked, and very well written. It asks him how he reconciles his remaining a member of the Duke's Government after his letter to Dr. Curtis with his declaration in 1827 that he could not remain a member of Canning's Government, when he entertained as Minister a similar design of carrying the Catholic question whenever he could. Aberdeen tells me he knows Peel has used language similar to that in the letters to his confidential friends.

January 12.

Office. Bankes not there. Saw Mr. Leach. He is to make out a statement of the exact terms under which every portion of the Indian debt has been contracted.

Wrote a rough memorandum, which Bankes will convert into a letter, requiring information from the

Consuls in all countries having commercial intercourse with India and China.

Foreign Office. Eead the protocol of the three Ambassadors relative to the limits of Greece, and all the other points left to them, indemnity, c. The whole proceeding is Russian. There is a want of common justice throughout which is disgusting. I do not think the protocol or any of the papers have been written by him. I think Guilleminot wrote the protocol, at least as far as it regards the future limits of Greece. There ought to be a memorandum on these documents forming the basis of a reply.

We should really determine as soon as possible upon the language to be held upon all points, the Catholics, Greece, and Portugal. It is so much better to know long beforehand what is to be the line taken. Then one may consider at leisure all that may be said, and, what is more important, all that should not be said, for I am convinced it is of much more importance to learn what it is expedient not to say than what should be said.

I wrote to the Eecorder, reminding him that several members of the Cabinet had expressed a wish to have printed copies of the evidence on the trial of the person whose cases were to be decided upon at the Council sent to them some days before. Eeceived an answer that he had, in consequence of my note, given directions accordingly.

January 14.

Finished the alterations to the new part of the protocol to Lushington. I hope it will recall him. Bankes has put into very good language the hints I gave him yesterday, but he has added nothing. What he has done could not have been done better.

Met the Duke of Wellington. Told him I had written a sketch paragraph for the Speech respecting Ireland. He said he had done so too, and he should be much obliged to me to show him mine. The first thing was to get the King's consent. I told him I had written my paragraph with that view. So had the Duke.

January 15.

On my way to Windsor read the sessions paper and the greatest part of the paper relative to the higher salaries granted to some persons in the Mint at Madras.

The rooms were cruelly cold at Windsor. All the Cabinet there but Sir J. Murray and Vesey Fitzgerald. Sir George is, I believe, not well. I am not sure whether Goulburn and Harris dined and slept at the Castle. All the others did. The King has literally not spoken to me since I received the Privy Seal from him. The Conynghames never forgive. However, it is of no great consequence, since it does not prevent, or has not prevented, my political advancement. Whether the King would consent to my holding an office which brought me of necessity into personal communication with him I do not know.

He seemed very well.

I thought Aberdeen seemed afraid of carrying the Catholic question, under the idea that we should then have nothing to keep together a Protestant party. The Chancellor seemed, to my surprise, to entertain for the first time similar apdrehensions Aberdeen thinks of nothing but of keeping his place, and is terribly afraid of every wind that blows.

The Duke is staunch, and, Hardinge tells me, and I believe, more desirous of carrying the question than any one. The Duke told me he did not like the allusion to the coronation oath in the sketch paragraph I sent him. He had written something avoiding that subject. He and the Chancellor were to see the King that evening. He seemed to speak as if he thought he should bring the King round.

I do not think he had read attentively the sketch I sent him. It was written on the assumption that the King had mis en avant his coronation oath, and wished to throw upon Parliament the onus of his departing from the interpretation he had given to it.

I believe this to be a true view. However, I told the Duke I merely mentioned the coronation oath because I thought the King would require it. If he could get him to agree to anything without the mention of it so much the better.

Lord Liverpool was at the Council to deliver the garter of the late lord, his brother.

This new Lord Liverpool has no son and three girls, the prettiest and the best educated in London, and great fortunes.

Two men will be executed, one for having in his possession the implements of coining, the other for robbery with violence. One other was to have been executed, but on further consideration we thought his was not a sufficiently bad case.

297   January 16.

All the Ministers, except myself, dined with the Kins. Lord Tenterden too. This is rather a marked slight on his Majesty's part, but he is at liberty to choose his own private society. It would be hard to deprive him of the privilege of every gentleman.

Saw the Duke. We are to have a Cabinet to-morrow. He will then state all he has been about. The bishops at one time seemed satisfied with what he proposed, but they are off. They are afraid of doing anything, because they have been abused for their conduct respecting the Dissenters. They brought contempt upon themselves by their weak and vacillating conduct. They promised to support the Government. Eldon frightened them. They lost their heads one day voted one way, and the next day another. If they promised to support the Duke now, they would desert him.

Eead Codrington's memorandum, dated January 2, 1829. I think he means to publish. He is still in the same error, imagining that the instructions of October 16 only confirmed and explained those of July 12.

A note from Hardinge suggesting some arrangement for mutual saving between the company and the Crown as to invaliding.

A letter from Lord Cowley acknowledging mine, and telling me he has sent on the despatch to Macdonald.

January 17, 1829.

Cabinet. The Duke gave a detail of all he had been doing during the summer on the subject of the Catholic question. On Thursday last, the 15th, the

298   King relieved the Government from the sort of understanding which prevailed when it was formed, and the Catholic question may now be considered as a Government question, the King only desiring that he may know what is the opinion of the Cabinet as to the details of the intended measure, and be enabled to exercise his judgment upon them.

It seems the Duke has been in communication with the Archbishop of Canterbury, and the Bishops of London, Durham, Winchester, Lincoln, Chester, and Oxford, and has communicated to them his plan, which they admitted was more satisfactory than any they had yet seen. At first they seemed disposed to acquiesce, but latterly they have been induced by apprehensions as to the opinion of their clergy to refuse their support. Therefore the Duke said we must consider that we approach the subject without the support of the bishops.

The Duke's idea is that we should begin by endeavouring to put down the Catholic Association that that should be the preliminary. He thinks the measure should either be a final settlement, or one leading to it. A suspension of the oaths would lead to it.

The permission of any sort of intercourse with the See of Borne, futile in itself, would be contrary to the whole tenor of our legislation for the English Church, which prohibits such intercourse.

A State provision may be an ultimate arrangement; but could not succeed now.

[299 To require more than the taking of the oath of allegiance from existing Catholic clergymen would be a measure of persecution, but all future Catholic priests might be required to take out a license.

Such is the practice in Sweden, and in all those parts of Germany which were not Catholic at the Treaty of Munster.

Bishops of the Catholic church might be prohibited from assuming any title in Ireland. They might be bishops in Ireland, Bishop Doyle, Bishop Carter, and so on, but not titular bishops.

The King is very desirous of putting down the 40s. freeholders.

The Duke too. He thinks some further qualification besides the freehold might be required, such as payment of cess, c.

Catholics to be admitted to Parliament and great offices, with the exception of those connected with the patronage of the English Church.

I think this was all. Much of it was in the memorandum I gave the Duke in September.

The Duke proposed we should not discuss it to-day.

Peel then stated that he had, since the carrying of the question by a new Parliament, been of opinion that the wise course was to prevent the recurrence of collision on so important a subject between the two Houses. He had opposed the question as long as there was a chance of opposing it, on principle. It was now a question of detail. Considering his peculiar situation, he had intended to resign; but resigning, he should still have supported the measure.

Now the bishops had refused their concurrence and Lord Anglesey had been re-
[300 called, he felt the difficulties of the Government were increased, and he had put himself in the Duke's hands.

The Duke said that not only did he think the difficulties of the Government would be increased tenfold by Peel's resigning, but their means of meeting those difficulties diminished in an equal degree. He had therefore, from a sense of duty, and equally from inclination, requested Mr. Peel to remain and conduct the measure, which he had consented to do.

Goulburn begged it might be understood that he reserved himself for the details, before he divided in favour of the measure.

I then suggested that we might at once look into the means of effecting the preliminary object, that of putting down the Association. This, the Chancellor said, had been to a degree done.

Vesey Fitzgerald seemed to misunderstand me, and to suppose I thought it possible the preliminary question alone might be proposed.

I said I understood the principle was admitted, that we were now to discuss the details. This was the second reading. To-morrow we should be in committee.

It was proposed by Peel that we should to-morrow consider in what terms the two questions should be mentioned together in the King's speech, and the new position of the Government revealed to the public. This will be done. We meet at four, and shall sit de die in diem.

All this is much better than I expected. The great difficulty will be about the 40s. freeholders. Many of the Whigs are against that measure, and I fear those who are against the measure of emancipation will join the Whigs in endeavouring to defeat the whole Bill by attacking that detail which many will think indispensable as a security.

I do not fear much opposition from the bishops. The mention of the subject in the King's speech, and the intimation of the intention of Government to bring forward a measure, will soon make them reasonable. They have now refused their sanction solely on extraneous grounds.

Peel has acted nobly as well as wisely, and I wrote a note to tell him I thought so. He was much pleased.

January 18.

In the morning wrote sketch paragraphs for the King's speech relative to Ireland; two memoranda, one on the 40s. freeholds, the other on the mode of suppressing the Catholic Association, and a sketch of a Bill for the latter purpose.

Sent the sketch paragraphs to the Duke.

Cabinet. It was decided that the King's speech should mention Ireland, recommend the suppression of the Catholic Association, and the consideration of the law affecting the Eoman Catholics. In some respects I think the Duke's sketch and Peel's, which were not substantially different, were better than mine.

We then considered the mode of putting down the Association. Peel read his sketch Bill, which gave to the Lord Lieutenant the power of issuing a proclamation declaring any association unlawful. I read mine, which gave to the Secretaries of State, the Lord Lieutenant, the Lords Justices, and the Chief Secretary to the Lord Lieutenant, the power of issuing warrants to dissolve and disperse any meeting they might, or any of them, consider as tending to create disaffection or disquietude in the mind of the King's liege subjects. Persons not separating within fifteen minutes after the reading of such warrant to be liable, on proof of the fact before a magistrate, to be imprisoned for three months. The issuing of the warrant and the names of the persons arrested to be communicated to Parliament, if sitting, in fourteen days; if not, in fourteen days from its next meeting.

Lord Melville thought the old Act for the suppression of the Association might do with amendments. I and others were against this. The old Act has been evaded, it has been slurred, and has never been executed. It would be better to take the amendment and not the Bill. It seems two clauses, which it was intended to insert in the old Bill, were omitted on the suggestion of Lord Wellesley. The Chancellor seemed to think any Bill might be evaded.

It seemed decided that no recourse should be had to a jury. It was doubted whether any discretion should be left to magistrates. I was for leaving none to them throwing everything on the Government, and making the magistrates mere instruments of execution on the proof of a simple fact.

I think the result was that the Lord-Lieutenant should have the power of issuing a proclamation, declaring any meeting to be illegal. That persons subsequently attending such a meeting should be liable to punishment for a misdemeanour. That the Secretary, c., might issue a warrant for the dispersion of any meeting, not previously declared to be illegal. Persons not dispersing in fifteen minutes to be imprisoned on summary process.

I am sure we must, in order to carry the measure, really put down the Association, and instanter, and we must, besides, make the King speak very decidedly in his speech, both against the Association and for a final settlement.

The matter, with Peel's instructions, will be referred to the law officers.

We then considered the question of abolishing the 40s. freeholders. I was in favour of meeting the evil rather by precautions and safeguards. I rather object to disfranchisement now, though I should have voted for it in 1825, and have no indisposition to effect the objects of the measure now; but there has been such a clamour against it, and the 40s. freeholders have come forward in such a new character of late, that the whole question has changed its aspect. I am in favour of ascertaining a man's right to vote before his vote should be admitted. This I would effect by requiring a year's notice of the intention to register, and having sworn officers to ascertain during that year the real value of a man's freehold. By allowing the freeholder to vote immediately on registration, he would stand in point of time as he does now. Now he cannot vote till a year after registration. I see no objection to demanding proof of the payment of cess, or of land tax, if it should be established in Ireland; nor do I see any objection to requiring proof of the payment of the last half year's rate, for the object of the law in permitting freeholders to vote is to secure an independent constituency. I thought that by multiplying the votes of the 40s. freeholders, by giving up to 50. a vote for every 40s., we should avoid the constitutional objection to disqualifying the freeholder. However, there seemed to be objections stated to the mode of doing it. Peel advised us all to read a letter he has received from Leslie Foster on the subject.

I have sent for my evidence before the Irish Committees in both Houses in 1825, for the purpose of looking into this particular subject. We are to meet again upon it on Tuesday.

As really fictitious freeholds have been created by recent statute, there seems to be no objection to dealing with such.

In England proof of payment of the land tax is required; but the imposition of the land tax was subsequent to the existence of freehold qualifications. In boroughs those only can vote who have paid their poor rates. A pauper cannot vote, but poor laws are subsequent to the existence of freehold qualifications. The law only looks to the freehold as the proof that its possessor is an independent man.

We had some talk after the Cabinet respecting the movers and seconders.

The Duke mentioned Lord Salisbury, who would do very well.

There is an idea of having the Duke of Northumberland, and if the Bill should be carried, we all agreed that a great Protestant Peer voting for the Bill would be the fittest Lord-Lieutenant, and the Duke of Northumberland might be the best man. Goulburn talked of the advantage of doing away with the Lord Lieutenant at some not distant time.

Lord Farnham, it appears, is favourable to the settlement. He is an able man, and Peel is to consult with him respecting the 40s. freeholders. Aberdeen proposed

Wicklow as seconder. He has always voted for the Catholics, and Lord Farnham would be much better.

Peel thought of Castlereagh for the Commons, but he is not to be trusted. He could not make a decent speech, and that is what we want. Otherwise it would be a fit compliment to his name. I think Lord Clive would be better.

It really is like a dream. How beyond hope it is that this question should be taken up by a Government in this King's life!

January 20.

Went to London from Hatfield expecting a Cabinet, There was none. Found at the Cabinet-room Sir G. Murray, and Herries. Sir G. Murray seemed to me to put several points on the Catholic question extremely well. Aberdeen showed me his sketch of that part of the King's speech which must refer to foreign affairs. The idea was not bad, but it was too long a performance, and he had omitted several things; for instance, to state the reasons for our departing, in consenting to the French expedition to the Morea, from the pacific line we had hitherto followed. VOL. i. X

At Hatfield in the evening H. de Ros told me Lord Holland had got hold of the idea that the sealed orders given to the captain of the ship which accompanied the Portuguese when they left Plymouth, were to the effect that he should prevent their going to Terceira,[1] and that he intended to inveigh against this as a breach of neutrality.

January 21.

Came to town. Before the Cabinet saw the Duke, and arranged with him that Dr. Barnes, formerly Archdeacon of Bombay, should have the first offer of the bishopric of Calcutta. The Duke has no objection to Turner, if Dr. Barnes should refuse the situation.

Goulburn, whom I saw at the Cabinet-room, asked me about the bishopric, and spoke against a Mr. Mill, who is a very clever man and a good man, but a controversialist. He highly approved of Barnes, but he told me Lord Liverpool had offered the bishopric to Barnes on Heber's death, and that Barnes had then refused it. I should not be very sorry if Barnes refused it again.

I told the Duke Mr. Mackinnon had desired to see me, and it was about the Directorship. I said I had given the same reply to him and Sir W. Young, that I knew not what the influence of the Board of Control would be; that I could not act in favour of a Director, as I was bound to control them; that I only wished the best man should be chosen a Director, and for that purpose, as I could not know who would be candidates,

[1 Terceira was holding out for Donna Maria against Don Miguel, now in possession of Portugal.]

desired to reserve myself till the last moment. He said I had better continue to do the same. He would ask Planta about it. He had heard something against Sir W. Young.

I told the Duke I had heard Mr. Mackinnon had induced people at Ipswich to vote for him by telling them he was a candidate for the Directorship, and should come in as a friend of Government; that then he should distribute his patronage amongst them. I said I did not think this looked well, and the Duke agreed with me.

Cabinet. First we considered the question of the disfranchisement of the 40s. freeholders. It was agreed that Lord Farnham, Leslie Foster, and Yesey Fitzgerald should be a committee to report. A fourth from the southern counties was wanted; but the name was not decided upon.

The ideas thrown out were that there should be no disfranchisement because it would be violently opposed as un-constitutional, and because, there being no dependence upon either, it was really delusive. The man who really had not a 40s. freehold would swear to one of 20. as easily as to one of 40s.

There must be some other security than that of the man's oath for his having a 40s. freehold. It was consistent with the practice of England to attach some further condition to the right of voting than mere possession. In towns paying scot and lot in counties assessment to the land tax, the pauper would not vote, nor the exciseman, c.

Thus the law endeavours to find an independent man. In England the 40s. freeholder usually is so; in Ireland he is not, and collateral securities must be found.

By some it has been suggested that a receipt for the last half year's rent should be required.

In removing one grievance affecting the higher orders we must take care not to inflict another, more real, perhaps, which affects the great mass of the people.

The measure of disfranchisement, or of dealing with the 40s. freeholder, has two objects, not only the reduction of Catholic influence, but the diminution of the present inducement to make small freeholders.

Peel thinks the Catholic influence would not be diminished. That the only thing done would be the placing a landlord-ridden man in the place of the priest-ridden tenant.

This being referred, we considered the question which some think most difficult and most important; that of the connection which is to exist between the Catholic Church and the State.

The Duke adheres to his original idea of licenses, which was mine. The Chancellor modifies that, and I think, beneficially, by requiring registration, not licenses, and by giving the Crown the power of striking a priest's name off the Kegister. The penalty to be imprisonment on summary process before two magistrates.

Peel suggested the putting down of Jesuitical and other colleges; a very good thing, which will carry many votes.

He likewise threw out the giving a power to the Crown of requiring the disclosure of all communications from the Pope, whether on spiritual or other matters. This was objected to.

Peel said he did not value the licensing, and would be rather without it. It was for others not for himself. He spoke of the thunderclap the announcement in the King's speech would be, and the very doubtful effect of it on public opinion. I believe we are treading on very dangerous ground. However, Forward!

The Duke spoke again of all the enactments of English law to prevent all communication with the See of Eome, and thought that permitting it in any case would break in upon, rather than add to, the security of the Church.

The general feeling was against subjecting the intercourse with the See of Eome to inspection.

An important question is, what the new oath shall be? Peel has had a memorandum made on all the oaths now in force, which will be on the Cabinet table to-morrow.

There was some conversation respecting the Oath of Supremacy. Some Catholics have declared their readiness to take it. The Chancellor thought the word Jurisdiction meant Legal Jurisdiction, and that any Catholic might take it, and it seemed allowed that it originally intended that Catholics should take it. [1] It would be a great convenience if we could have it.

We meet again to-morrow and next day.

[1 It may be remembered that after the ' Papal Aggression ' of 1851, one or two Protestant peers objected to the oath on the ground that the Pope now ' had," though he ' ought not to have jurisdiction in this realm of England."]

310

It was fully understood that the outlines of the measure must be communicated to the King before he could be called upon to consent to the words of his speech announcing it.

The Duke said the King might be brought to hear it, but that was all.

I thought Fitzgerald seemed rather Irish to-day. He hates the 40 s. freeholders, who ousted him.

He is very desirous of giving a pecuniary provision to the clergy. This we cannot do now; but the registration will lay the foundation of it.

Aberdeen was not present.

The Duke of Northumberland goes to Ireland as Lord Lieutenant. He takes our view of the Catholic question. He reported himself ready to set out in a fortnight, and in no time had arranged his household. He carries to Dublin all his splendid outfit as Ambassador at Paris, and means to assume the state of a Sovereign, keeping himself aloof from politics and parties. He is the beau ideal of a Lord Lieutenant. He will be very popular too.

Peel has, without telling everything to Lord F. Leveson, made known to him that the King has permitted his Government to consider the whole question of Ireland.

Lord Francis is all joy.

January 22.

Lord Anglesey's procession to Kingstown was a failure. He was attended by a rabble, and O'Connell shared his triumph. There was no riot.

311

Cabinet. Bead a memorandum of Peel's upon the subject of the oaths to be required.

He is for repealing the Declaration against Transub-stantiation, for retaining the Oath of Supremacy if the Catholics will take it, and for requiring a long oath compounded of others, and amended to meet objections that have been raised, and flaws that have been discovered.

My idea is that we should do away with all distinction between Protestant and Catholic by requiring the same oath from both.

It was apparently decided to adopt Peel's proposition. We then considered the exceptions of offices to be made. The only question was as to the office of First Lord of the Treasury and Home Secretary. At first the feeling was not to except either, but to require the placing of the Church patronage in the disposal of the persons holding these offices in other hands, when the offices should be held by Catholics. Not only was this overruled, but the exception was extended to the two other Secretaries of State, on the ground that the three secretaries formed but one, and that there would be an idea of security attached to such exceptions.

the second

The Duke of Cumberland has written to the King requesting to be permitted to come over for the 5th. The King referred his letter to the Duke of Wellington, who informed his Majesty that the Cabinet were employed every day in considering the question his Majesty had permitted them to consider, but that he was not yet able to submit anything specific and definite for his Majesty's approval.

Wo entered but little into the MVOIU! question, of the relation in which the Church of Rome should here-after stand to the Government. It seemed, however, to be decided that registration should be required of all existing ecclesiastics of the lioinmi Catholic Church in Ireland, and an oath. They now take oaths, and register the taking of the oath.

I do not see that much would be added to the security by this enactment. As to those hereafter to be ordained, their registration, or taking an oath, will be a matter of course, and the Crown have the power of removing them for cause. The penalty, is not fixed upon.

While we are thus working every day at the work of emancipation, the high Protestants, misled by the recall of Lord Anglesey, imagine the Government is Protestant, and Sir Thomas Lethbridge has offered himself to Peel to second the address! There is a difficulty about the movers and seconders. It is desirable to get Protestants who wish for a settlement. In the House of Commons Lord Clive would do perfectly. Peel thinks of Ward, the member for the City, as seconder. The awkwardness is, that it is necessary to let the mover and seconder a little into the secret.

In our House Lord Thomond and Lord Salisbury are thought of; both very good, particularly the latter.

It is certainly quite impossible to calculate the effect that will be produced when it is known that the Government have resolved to bring forward the question. There may be a violent reaction which will make it almost impossible to carry the measure. The King,

POSITION or sn; KOIIKKT ri: i; i,.

with the Duke of Cumberland at his back, would perhaps turn us to the right, il)otil, He could hardly, however, form another Government on opposite principles, ami the union of the Duke, Peel, c., in favour of the measure, would, I hope, deaden opposition. IY I must expect to have strong things said against him. He should rise as soon as he can and speak very boldly. He may thus put the Protestants down by a single speech.

The Chancellor seems to think our idea of licenses hardly enough to meet the public eye in the way of securities, and asked me to try if I could not find some other, I am for adding to the oath proposed by Peel words to this effect: 'I do sincerely promise and swear that I will not disturb the Protestant bishops and clergy of this realm, or the churches committed to their charges in the possession of any rights and privileges as by law, c., c., as shall appertain to them or any of them."

They are nearly the words of the Coronation oath, and the King should be satisfied if the Catholics will swear not to disturb that which he swears to preserve.

Read a letter of Nesselrode to Lieven. It is the best written of Russian papers; very cunning. The Russians are in a great fright at the idea of our sending our ambassador to Constantinople before theirs. Their alarm shows the advantage the treaty gives them, and its wickedness.

January 23.

Saw the Chairs. They promise me a very satisfactory draft on the subject of cotton. The letter to Dr. Barnes was sent, offering him the Bishopric of Calcutta. He lives at Sowton Eectory, near Exeter. Sent the Eecorder of Prince of Wales' Island letter to the Privy Council.

Told Mr. Alves I was disposed to say as little as possible on the subject of the judicial system at Madras till I had considered the whole subject. The paragraph suggested by him in the P. C. ties up Lushington's hands and so far does good; but in writing to such a man we must be very careful not to lead him to imagine we disapprove of any part of the existing system, for the least hint would induce him to overturn it all.

Cabinet-room. There was a curious paper there, procured by Lord Heytesbury from a Eussian employe giving an account of their financial state. The war is represented as having cost them in all ten millions of our money, and the next campaign will be more expensive. They got sixty millions of roubles from the assignees of different establishments last year, and thirty-six millions from a loan raised in Holland. They will have to pay back the sixty millions this year, and I should think they must raise a loan of 200 millions of roubles.

I wrote last night sketch paragraphs imposing an oath upon every Privy Councillor of the Eoman Catholic religion not to offer any advice to His Majesty touching the government or discipline of the Church of England, and not to use directly or indirectly the patronage or influence of his office to nominate to benefices in the Church of England. I think a provision of this sort would supersede the necessity of excluding the Eoman Catholics from the offices of First Lord of the Treasury, c. In the event of these offices being held by a Eoman Catholic the patronage would be placed in the hands of a Protestant Commission. I merely loosely allude to the substance of any papers I write, because I preserve them all.

I likewise threw into the form of a Bill the provision suggested by the Duke for striking names out of the register.

Fitzgerald and Peel, and indeed the Chancellor, were hostile to the proposed form of making the registration.

It appears to be a power never yet exercised in this country, that of punishing a Eoman Catholic priest for the exercise of his spiritual function. [1] It is feared there would be general resistance to the enactment that those punished would be martyrs that if you imprisoned or punished severely by fine, the whole measure, instead of being one of peace, would be one of persecution. That it would be discussed every year on petitions praying the removal of a spiritual grievance. That the priest left at large must exercise his [1] Except, of course, when the anti-popery laws were in full vigour. Under Elizabeth many persons suffered death for exercising priestly functions, though the capital sentence was usually reserved for those suspected of participation in treasonable plots. But these laws had probably been hardly ever put in force in Ireland.]

316

spiritual functions; must administer the sacrament when called upon. Would you punish a man for doing that which he is bound to do by his conscience?

Should the power of removal be absolute or limited by words? If absolute, there would be the appearance of endeavouring to assume arbitrary power; and if limited, you must go before some tribunal to have proof that the offence for which the priest was removed came within the limiting words.

It was said the power would be seldom, if ever, exercised. That there was the greatest difficulty in exercising that of the Alien Bill You might, if you legislated in this manner, take away one grievance, but you would create a greater.

On the other hand it was said, this is a new security and effectual. It does not apply to the existing mass, bat to those who are annually ordained. The Government would therefore have to contend, not against the *who performs spiritual functions without having taken*

The law now punishes the Eoman Catholic priest a certain oath. The priest not taking the oath is not deprived of his spiritual functions, and therefore the same difficulty may occur now, as it has been argued would occur under the proposed regulation, that of a *priest bound by his conscience to do one thing, and by the law*

~~": :: J'. MH. IT lis:; f: if: v:; I;;-:":! :-~~ the law to abstain from doing it.

[317] licenses are required previous to tke performing of spiritual functions, in afl Protestant countries on the Continent, but are they revocable? The Duke says so. I see no traces of any provision to that effect, although I have no doubt they would be revoked if they were abused. [1] It is clearly consistent with the ordinary practice of nations to require such securities as may satisfy the governing power that the spiritual functions of priests not professing the religion of the State shall not be abused.

I suggested the placing of the power of revocation in the hands of a Commission, or the limiting the power by words such as these: ' Who shall have abused his spiritual functions for political or civil purposes

On the giving to the Government the power of inflicting deprivation on such priests only as should have been guilty of a civil offence, and convicted thereof in the ordinary manner, Fitzgerald was strongly for a pecuniary provision.

The Chancellor, Peel, and I think all thought this, if advisable, could not be carried that greater opposition would be made to it in the country than in Parliament. That hereafter it might be; but that the late Lord Liverpool and others had thought a State provision for the Eoman Catholic clergy inconsistent with the Coronation oath.

Finally the general opinion seemed to be against the giving to Government the power of striking the names of priests from the register. The Duke yielded very reluctantly. So did I. I think it is the best security. The Duke seems to think it the only one.

Peel suggested a number of little securities. The [1 See Wellington Correspondence, v. 496, for account, by Baron de Fahnenberg, of the laws of the Grand Duchy of Baden on this subject. They included the right of appointing or confirming the ministers of any Church, but not, apparently, of deposing or removing them]

318 permitting no bishop to officiate without license. The penalty, banishment. (This was in Grattan's Bill.) The suppression of monks, Jesuits, monastic houses, of religious habits worn in public, of religious processions, of the use of steeple and bell!

of the use of titles of dioceses and parishes, the taking of the whole question of the Irish clergy into our own hands.

It was thought the licensing of bishops would gradually lead to an understanding with the Pope, who would only name those who were likely to be approved, and ultimately to a pecuniary provision.

Peel read a memorandum he had written on the laws as they affect differently English and Irish Eoman Catholic priests. He had looked through all the Acts of Parliament.

It is remarkable how little we all know of what Parliament has already done.

Before the Cabinet began, the Chancellor said he had seen Sir W. Knighton, and that he understood the King had expressed some surprise he had not yet received a memorandum promised to him of what passed on Thursday week.

The Chancellor and Peel had some recollection of the King's having mentioned this; but the Duke said he had not mentioned it to him. Peel's idea was that the memorandum was to state that the King, acting under the advice of his Protestant Ministers, had permitted his Cabinet to take the subject into consideration.

I drew their attention to the words Protestant Ministers and permitted, and I suggested the Protestant Ministers should be described (others said named), and that the King had, under their advice, acquiesced in the subject being taken into consideration.

Directed would have been a better word; but it seems that it would go beyond what was the fact.

The word permitted implies that we were before precluded; which by our oath we could not be. We might, as I understood, advise the King if we pleased individually at any time, or propose the subject in the Cabinet; but the King's opinion being known, and the divided state of the Cabinet, it became a question of expediency whether the proposal should be made or not.

The word acquiesced will be used, and the Ministers advising the King will be named.

We meet again to-morrow.

January 24.

The Chancellor wrote the memorandum for the King; it was approved by the Duke and Peel, and sent. The terms were unexceptionable.

Cabinet at half-past 3. In the morning I had sent to the Duke sketch clauses which I thought might be inserted if his suggestion of the revocable license was not adopted. These clauses made the abuse of spiritual functions for election purposes, and the occasioning any civil injury or damage by means of such functions, a misdemeanour; and then interdicted the exercise of any such functions during the King's pleasure, on the conviction of any Koman Catholic priest of any misdemeanour created by the Act, or any other misdemeanour.

We had a great deal of conversation which ended in nothing. The conclusion seemed to be that any Eoman Catholic Bishop hereafter consecrated, should give notice of his intention to exercise episcopal functions, and during two months from the receipt of such notice the King should have the power of interdicting such exercise.

Peel proposed the taking away of the Charter of Maynooth, and bringing the education of the priests under the influence of Government. I said, ' You have provided masters, but where would you get your scholars? If you evince a design to draw into your hands the whole education of the Catholic priesthood, no scholars will be sent there. You must in that case interdict in future the exercise of spiritual functions by any priest not educated at Maynooth, and if you do that you will meet with general resistance. Besides, it is a strong thing to repeal a Charter. It would be better to withdraw the grant, and to constitute a new college. Your arrangements relative to Maynooth should not favour a part of the general measure."

Difficulties were started as to preventing the regular clergy from performing spiritual functions, and it was thought that regulations enacted for the suppression of Jesuitical establishments, and of future convents, might be evaded.

The Duke is to-morrow to bring a resume of all that has been decided to the Cabinet, and I should think that on Monday he would go to the King.

It seems that as soon as the King has approved of what is proposed, we may allow the world to know the change that has been effected in the principle of the Government.

January 25. Sunday.

Cabinet. Peel told us he had seen Leslie Foster, who was for a settlement; but strongly against paying the Eoman Catholic clergy. He will therefore support the Biu.

Leslie Foster is to be introduced privately to-morrow by the Park into the Foreign Office, and thence into the Cabinet-room, where he is to be examined! Leslie Foster consulting with the Cabinet how Catholic emancipation may best be brought about!

Peel, after the Cabinet, spoke of the probable resignations. He thought Wetherell might resign. I hope he will.

He is a discredit to the Government; but Peel thought the weak state of the Master of the Eolls' health might possibly induce honest Wetherell to protest his Protestantism. He had some doubts as to Tindal. I have none. The fact is, the old Protestants think the Government will take that line, and begin to talk foolishly. Peel thought Lord Lowther would not resign that the Duke of Montrose would vote against it. I dare say he will and not resign. Sir G. Hill will not. I fear Bankes will; but I can go on without him for three months very easily.

What will Lord Shaftesbury do? I think Lord Beresford will remain; but if he goes, there is a place for Lord Eosslyn.

It is due to Sir C. Wetherell to observe that, as the sequel will show, he stuck doggedly to the convictions which he professed. VOL. I. Y

After all, we cannot tell what the King will say. We all speak as if he would agree to our proposals, and probably he may; but this is not certain.

The Colpo, when the denouement takes place, will be curious. To-morrow the Duke brings forward his memorandum to be submitted to the King, and the words of the proposed speech upon the Catholic question.

The memorandum must be worded with great precision.

On Tuesday the Duke goes to "Windsor, and on Wednesday we dine with Lord Melville, when we shall know how the King received the first overture.

If the King accedes, on Thursday communications will be made privately to the members of Government.

The Duke is annoyed, I think, at his first security not being adopted. I fear we may have run the securities too close, and that there may not be enough to satisfy the King and the Protestants.

January 26.

Office. Saw Bankes. The Government of Bombay has sent overland representations against the conduct of the Chief Justice.

The Chancellor tells me this Chief Justice did very ill once before, and that the best thing is to recall him. I shall read the papers as I go to Brighton to-morrow.

Eeceived a visit from Mr. Fergusson. He came, I believe, to speak about his election to the Directorship; but I had some conversation on the subject of the admission of attornies, c., in Calcutta. I gave him the same answer I had given the others, as to the Directorship. In fact he is, I believe, the best man, and as we could not reject him, we had better elect him, and make a favour of what we cannot prevent. In future cases we may adopt a general principle.

Cabinet. Leslie Foster was brought through the Park to the Foreign Office by Yesey Fitzgerald, and thence through all the dark passages to the Cabinet-room, where we examined him as to the expediency of giving to the Crown a power of prohibiting the exercise of the spiritual functions of any priest. Such power to be exercised within two months of his ordination.

I think his evidence showed the inutility of the exercise of such a power. The priest's character is not formed when he is ordained. Such a power is only important in connection with the plan of educating all the priests. If we show the disposition to educate all the priests, and to provide that they shall all have a good education by appointing, and by retaining the power of displacing, their instructors, and have no power of interdicting the exercise of spiritual functions by priests not educated at our college, we shall have masters, but no scholars. Leslie Foster thinks if we can secure the bishops, the priests will follow; and that the attempt to influence the appointment of priests in this manner is not worth the excitement and opposition it would occasion.

The Duke will only state to the King in conversation the points upon which the Cabinet is agreed, and give him no copy. He will only make pencil memoranda of the several heads for his own convenience.

We divided upon the general tone of the King's speech, relative to the Catholic question. Peel's first idea was better than the Duke's, but the Duke was very fond of his own. They are to settle it together.

The King returned the memorandum written by the Chancellor, and desired it might be sent back to him when it had been read to the Cabinet.

January 27.

On my way to Brighton read the American pamphlet which gives a history of the several negotiations between the United States and England, relative to the trade with the West Indian Islands. It is ably written, and oversets Mr. Adams.

Eead again the papers from Bombay, relative to the conduct of Sir Charles Chambers and Sir John Grant. It seems that they issued writs of habeas corpus to bring up the persons of chiefs to whom privileges had been guaranteed, and when the Governor in Council addressed a letter to them representing the public mischief which would result from the measure, they libelled the Government from the Bench, and published their speeches executed by themselves these speeches being calculated to bring the Government into contempt.

January 28.

Office. Sir Charles Chambers, one of the puisne Judges at Bombay, is dead. It seems probable that Sir Edward West is dead too. Archdeacon Barnes declines going to India as bishop.

[325

The King agrees to the words proposed for his speech; but he seemed very reluctant when the Duke mentioned that the Catholics were to be excluded from judicial offices connected with the Church. The King said, ' What, do you mean a Catholic to hold any judicial office? To be a Judge of the King's Bench?"

When seats in Parliament were mentioned, he said, ' Damn it, c., you mean to let them into Parliament? ' If he should be able he will take an opportunity of turning us out; but I do not think he will have the opportunity. The Duke thinks he can make the King prevent the Duke of Cumberland from coming over.

At the Cabinet dinner (at Lord Melville's), we had the several parts of the speech considered, and were occupied a long time in altering them. Aberdeen's part was very bad.

Peel has asked Lord Clive and Lord Corry to move and second in the Commons. The Duke will ask Lord Salisbury and probably Lord O'Neil in the Lords. If Lord Corry refuses, Castlereagh will be asked.

Peel and the Duke will see individually the Protestant members of the Administration.

I advised Peel to speak as early as he could, and to make a great speech at once, taking a very high tone, not at all apologetic.

January 29.

Saw Bankes. Had some conversation with him respecting the dispute at Bombay. It seems to me on reading the papers, which I did this evening, that the whole question is one of jurisdiction over natives not in the service of the Company, nor in the

[326

employment of Europeans, nor within the recognised limits of the Presidency. The power now claimed by the Court has never been exercised before. That its exercise would be inconsistent with the maintenance of our authority in India I firmly believe for it would supersede the power of the provincial courts, and expose the Government to contempt it would violate all the prejudices of the natives, and our pledges to them that they should be governed according to their usages it would hold up our Government as divided. The more I think upon the subject, the more satisfied I am that on the renewal of the Charter we must make all the Company's officers King's officers, and govern India in the King's name, retaining all the machinery of the present system.

Sir Charles Chambers seems to have acted with great intemperance; Sir J. Grant more moderately and in a more dignified manner. I am not sure that there will be found anything in his conduct that will require exemplary punishment; but it may be necessary to remove him to Madras or Calcutta. Sir J. Malcolm has shown great firmness.

Besides this question of jurisdiction, which we must settle by Act of Parliament, there has arisen another question, very inconvenient under present circumstances that of the press.

There does not seem to be as yet any idea of the course we intend to pursue on the Catholic question. Peel had not spoken to Bankes when I saw him to-day.

The King of France's Speech to the Chambers is much better than the one we were concocting yesterday. Indeed we must alter ours now. I sketched some paragraphs to-day relative to the Greek question.

327   January 30.

Three new applications for judgeships in India. Saw the Duke. He agrees with me in thinking that the Government should support Fergusson for the Directorship. I hope to manage to conciliate Fergusson, and to bring him into our views as to the judicial administration of India. At any rate as a member of the Court of Directors, he is much more likely to take moderate and reasonable views than he is if excluded from the Court by our means. I do not believe we could exclude him, and we should only show our teeth without biting, and convert an independent man into an enemy.

I found the Duke agreed with me, too, in thinking the best man for the Chief-Justiceship at Bombay is Dewar, the Advocate-General. He seems to be an able man, and a discreet man. He is personally a friend of Sir J. Malcolm's, and has apparently been really of opinion that the view he took professionally of the jurisdiction of the Supreme Court was correct. His appointment, and the placing him over the head of Sir J. P. Grant, will do more to re-establish the Government in public opinion than any measure we could adopt.

He has taken the right view of the jurisdiction of the Court.

I desired Bankes to send Dewar's questions to the law officers of the Crown, with a request that an immediate answer might be given.

Dewar's argument will be sent to them at the same time.

328   The Duke perfectly concurs in the Bishopric of Calcutta being offered to Turner. Accordingly I wrote to him, and to Lord Londonderry, and to old Lady Londonderry. Lord Londonderry is much out of humour I believe because he has not been made Lord Lieutenant of Ireland. He received very coldly, and even grumpily r, the offer of the Down Militia which was made to Castlereagh. He is not, or was not, coming up till March.

Lord Beresford is pleased with the prospect of a settlement. The Attorney and Solicitor-General are delighted, and think that the coercive measure for putting down the Association could not well be carried without the measures of relief.

The only thing communicated has been the speech. No details of the plan have been given.

I am to see Peel before I communicate to Fergusson that the Government takes him up.

The Duke said he was quite prepared upon the subject of Portugal.

I told him I thought the speech of the King of France made some change expedient in ours. The Times fires a good random shot to-day, but I do not think it has any information as to the course Government will pursue on the Catholic question.

January 31.

Cabinet. We went through the King's speech and licked it into form. The part relating to foreign policy is the. worst. That relating to Ireland is well done now.

A question as to the vacating of the seats of the

329   Lords of the Admiralty was considered. In law their seats are vacated by their transfer from the situation of Counsellors to the Lord High Admiral, to that of Lords Commissioners, and I think it would be very foolish to try to pass a Bill which would be much opposed for the sole purpose of saving the Commissioners some money.

Told Lord Melville what I had thought of for Bombay the making Dewar Chief Justice. When I told the Chancellor I thought he seemed not to like it; but he only said he did not know anything of him, and begged to be informed in what year he went out. If his character here answered to his character in India there could be no objection. I must write to Astell for the vouchers he has.

Lord Clive has written an excellent letter to Peel accepting the offer of moving the address. Lord Corry came up thinking the speech was to be anti-Catholic, and was a little taken aback on finding it recommended a review of the laws affecting the Koman Catholics with civil disabilities. However, he acknowledged he thought a settlement desirable, and agreed to second, reserving his judgment as to the details.

Lord Salisbury has not yet answered the Duke's letter, and will not see him till Tuesday. The Duke decides upon Lord Wallace as the seconder if he can get him, which is doubtful.

Dined at Lord Beresford's. Sir Alexander Grant was there, and evidently knew nothing, He made a desperate fish by saying Sir F. Lamb had offered to bet him 100 guineas that a Bill for emancipation was already prepared. This he said to Lord

(330   Beresford and me. I said it was wonderful how much people knew. O'Con-nell said the same thing six months ago. I think Grant acquired no new light.

The Times having felt its way yesterday, and none of the newspapers having positively denied its statement, to-day grows bolder and speaks of the thing as certain, and as announced by itself yesterday. It evidently knows nothing.

Sir A. Grant said Lord Grey and Lord Lauderdale were not coming up till March.

Arranged with Peel that Fergusson should be supported by the Government, and that Mackinnon should have a civil letter. In all future cases we are to make head and name the Directors.

The Chairs are well satisfied with the proposed arrangement for sending our assessor to Prince of Wales' Island as soon as Sir J. Claridge comes away.

Astell told me that Sir John Malcolm represented himself to have had three warnings, and to be very anxious to return to Lady Malcolm and his daughter who has been obliged to return to England for her health. He proposed that Sir Charles Metcalfe should be made provisional successor to Sir J. Malcolm.

Saw Colonel Salmond, who is a claimant, in the name of his nephews, on the Bencoolen Compensation Fund. It seems that British subjects were encouraged to cultivate the nutmeg, c. On the cession of Bencoolen to the Dutch the value of the property of these persons was not only in all cases much deteriorated, but in some lost.

It was agreed that 22,500. should be given by the

¼   ¼

Company, and the same sum by Government. The sum of 45,000. being the estimated value of ⅓ of the property, and it being thought that the property would be depreciated; but it has in many cases been altogether lost.

February 1.

Called on Lord Camden. Found Lord Bathurst there. Lord Camden seems in very good humour, and evidently knows a good deal, but I think not all. I consider myself bound to secrecy, and therefore said nothing. Hardinge came in, knowing, I suppose, something. It is a bad arrangement this, or rather a bad want of arrangement which leaves none at liberty to speak, even to their most confidential friends, who keep the agreement, while those who do not keep it acquire the reputation of frankness.

Adm. Digby, who dined with us, had heard something at the clubs. I did not add to his knowledge.

February 2.

I had not intended to go to the Council to-day, for I thought the King would be just as well pleased if he saw none but his Protestant 1 Ministers; but in the morning I got a note from the Duke begging me to turn the speech into an address as I went, and to take the Privy Seal with me, as he might probably ask me to resign it.

I found all the Ministers at the Council. We made before the Council a good many verbal alterations in the speech, and as the King's copy had not been altered[1 I. e. those who had hitherto opposed the ' Catholic question."]

he was rather annoyed. When we came to the passage he had himself inserted, in which the Association was represented as ' having assumed functions which the Constitution had reserved to Parliament alone," and found it omitted, he made a little fight for it; however, as the words ' inconsistent with the spirit of the Constitution ' were applied to the Association before, and expressed the King's meaning, he was satisfied.

He made a much more mischievous proposal afterwards.

The speech, after expressing the confidence of the King that Parliament would give him power to put down the Association, proceeded thus: ' His Majesty recommends that when this essential object shall have been accomplished, you should take into your deliberate consideration the whole condition of Ireland, and that you should review the laws which impose civil disabilities on His Majesty's Eoman Catholic subjects."

The King said: 'The whole condition of Ireland includes the Catholic question, and I see no reason why that part of the paragraph should not be omitted." The Duke said: 'Your Majesty has Eoman Catholic subjects in other parts of your dominions besides Ireland." The King acquiesced, and at the end of the speech he expressed himself quite satisfied with it.

An order in Council was made for the return of Sir J. T. Claridge from Prince of Wales' Island.

I found the Privy Seal had been offered to old Westmoreland; 1 but he could not quite make up his mind to 1 He had originally been left out of the Cabinet on account of his ultra-opinions on all questions.

vote for the Catholics. Poor man, it must have been a cruel contest! So I brought the Seal back again. It is not yet quite certain that Lord Westmoreland will not take it.

Lord Salisbury moves in the Lords, Lord Wicklow seconds. Lord Wallace broke down as a mover or seconder in his youth, and has such a horror of the thing that he said at once, ' If you mean to speak to me about moving or seconding I cannot do it."

Peel saw Lord Lowther to-day, who is quiet, but not favourable. He was pleased at being sent for, and said that on hearing the reports he had written to his father to know his opinion. It was a matter of much delicacy to take a different line from that upon which his family and himself had acted so long, and on which their interest was supported.

Finding Peel had not yet seen Bankes I wrote to him on my return to town, and told him I thought he would have seen Peel before; that I thought a communication with Peel would be made satisfactory to him; that he would probably see Peel to-morrow; but if he wished to know to-night the line we meant to take, if he would come up to me I would tell him.

Bankes came a little before 11. I gave him a full detail of all the steps which have been taken, and read to him that part of the speech which relates to Ireland. He seemed much affected, breathed hard, and was very nearly in tears. At last he told me that he was perfectly free to act as he pleased, his father having imposed no restrictions upon him, but that he feared he should be obliged to leave us. He thought he should not be able to approve of the Bill, and that we should find it impossible to arrange it satisfactorily. To the speech he had no objection. In any case he should retire if he found it necessary, quietly, and in such a manner as to do no injury to the Government. He was very much obliged to me for the confidence I had placed in him, and said he would rather communicate confidentially with me upon the subject than with any one. He seemed very cordial indeed.

February 3.

Saw the Chairs, at the Treasury, with the Duke of Wellington. The Duke assured them he thought a declaratory Bill necessary, and that the existence of the authority desired by the Judges would ruin India.

Eead the speech to Hardinge. Ashley and Win. Ashley are delighted with it. H. Corry, too. The Ashleys do not know what line their father will take they think he will not be very hostile. He has separated himself from Eldon since the latter has been out.

Lord Anglesey saw the King on Sunday. The King says Lord A. expressed his intention of reading the correspondence between the Duke and himself. The King laissait entrevoir that he disapproved of his doing so, but he did not prohibit him, neither did he permit him to read the letters; and he authorised the Duke to say he had not permitted it. If Lord Anglesey commences by saying he has the King's permission, the Duke is to interrupt him. If he reads the letters without saying whether he has permission or not, the Duke is only to say he has not in his reply. This was settled in Cabinet.

It was likewise settled that the Lords of the Admiralty must be re-elected.

In Cabinet we decided that we should enter into no details respecting our plan, but merely say that H. M."s Government intended, early in the session, to bring in Bills for the removal of the Catholic disabilities, with such exceptions as seemed to be required on special grounds, and with such securities as the removal of the disabilities might appear to render expedient.

We had a long talk as to our conduct with regard to Greece and to Portugal, and I think we stand well on both points.

Dinner at Lord Bathurst's to prick the sheriffs. The Duke was not there, nor Aberdeen.

The Protestant newspapers are most violent against the Duke.

February 4.

Wrote to Lord Grey enclosing a copy of that part of the speech relating to Ireland, and telling him, nearly in the words I have used above, all we mean to say as to our Bills. Wrote to Lord Eosslyn too.

Met Fitzgerald, Peel, Goulburn, and Planta at Peel's to settle the Address. Went afterwards to the Duke's to read it to him.

The Duke told me he heard Lord Anglesey meant to state that he was permitted by the King to make his defence. The Duke has well considered all Lord Anglesey's possible modes of action, and has decided upon his own line in every event.

Saw Bankes, who has had an interview with Peel. I fear we shall lose Bankes, but I advised him to continue as long as he could.

W. Ashley has copied a good many letters for me the last few days.

Dined at the Duke's. Besides the Ministers, there were at dinner the Dukes of Dorset and Manchester, Lords Sidmouth, Shaftesbury, Hill, Bexley, Wallace, Farnborough, Salisbury, Wicklow, Beresford, Chesterfield, Sydney, Maryborough. There may have been others. I think the Protestants looked a little sulky.

There can be no doubt that the speech read to-day is more important than any since the Eevolution. All feel it to be so.

February 5.

At 12 went to the Duke, and read the letters which have passed between him and Barbacena and It ab ay ana. I think our case is a good one.

Eeceived a letter from Mr. Mackinnon, thanking me for a supposed promise to support him on the next vacancy. I never gave any such promise, nor did I use any words from which it could be deduced that I did. I have written to tell him how surprised I am at the interpretation he has put upon my letter, and to say, if possibly, still more distinctly than I did before, that I will not pledge myself.

At 2 went to the House. The Duke of Clarence was there, and perhaps 30 Peers, but not so many in the House, 70 or 80 ladies, all ugly. The Chancellor was so nervous on reading the passage relating to Ireland that he did not give it its full effect.

Salisbury moved the Address. He did it very ill indeed, and was hardly audible. Lord Wicklow did well.

The Duke of Newcastle then asked the Duke of Wellington whether he meant to proceed by Committee or by Bill. The Duke gave the explanation we had agreed upon. We had then Winchelsea, Farnham, and Eldon, the latter very game and threatening. Lord Bathurst spoke pretty well. We had then Lord Anglesey, saying he put aside his private wrongs and rejoicing in the announcement made in the speech. Lord Eedesdale spoke. The Duke said a few sentences, much better than his reply to the Duke of Newcastle's question. Evidently Goderich and Lansdowne had intended to make Portugal the cheval de bataille, but the surpassing importance of the question opened by the speech cut down their orations very much. Both Goderich and Lansdowne made very unhandsome speeches, saying little of their satisfaction and nothing in praise of us. Lord Aberdeen, in reply to Lansdowne, only said he was ready to meet enquiry, and thus Lord Holland had no opportunity of making his harangue. We shall have it another day.

I would say on the whole that the Whigs were very sulky. They see the measure brought forward by those they cannot bear, and they know the carrying of it will destroy their party, by leaving it no bond of union.

Saw Castlereagh. He told me Turner was come to town, but requested two days before he answered my letter. I gave him a week. ~~VOL. i. Z~~

338
February 6.

The House of Commons seems to have been much more favourably disposed than our House; but the debate was dull, and there was no excitement.

Saw Hardinge. He said all went on very well there. So Wood told me. I saw Agar Ellis to-day. He seemed very much delighted. He observed the speech was very well written, and more correctly than it usually has been. He thought he saw in it the hand of the writer of the resolutions of the 69 Peers in 1825. That is mine. I told him no, and that Vesey Fitzgerald was more critical than I was.

Bankes told me he had written a letter of resignation to the Duke. I said he should have waited till he was obliged to vote against the Government; that he did not object to the consideration of the question; that he would approve of all the securities, and only feel called upon to vote against the Bill if, on the third reading, it should not be satisfactory to him. I said a great deal more, all to no purpose.

I saw the Duke, who was much annoyed. He said he did not know what to do with Bankes's letter. That it put him into a situation of much difficulty. That if he resigned others would that Lord Lowther, Lord G. Somerset might. That if Bankes thought it necessary to resign he should be obliged to turn out some man or other who voted against him, whose vote he might otherwise have overlooked. That it would oblige him to break with some of the first families. He wished to keep the Government

339
together. He said with great warmth, ' There is Bankes, like most other men, looking only to himself, and not caring about the public!" The Duke said Lord Eliot had written to him some six weeks ago saying he must resign if the Government did not take up the Catholic question. The Duke had a great mind to turn him out now.

The Duke seems to have thought the aspect of our House last night very bad, and that if the Opposition had moved an amendment respecting Portugal, they would have carried it by the absence of our people. I do not think this.

Lord Eldon and Lord Eedesdale begged the Duke not to mention them in his report to the King as having spoken against the Address.

Bankes is to see the Duke at 12 to-morrow. It is very inconvenient to him to resign, for on taking his office he gave up a Commissionership of Bankrupts, worth 200. or 300. a year. I went to the House of Commons to speak to him a second time; but I fear he has made his resignation known at least to his father; and that pride may induce him to adhere to it. He gave me no hopes of his yielding. I am sorry for it, for I shall hardly find a person with whom I shall go on better, and a more efficient servant of the public.

I admire the manner in which the Duke always rises in proportion to the difficulty he has to encounter.

February 8.

Eead Aberdeen's correspondence with Barbacena. At half-past two went to the Cabinet room. Eead the Duke's correspondence with Palmella, both referring to the Portuguese question, upon which we shall, I dare say, have a question this week. We have a good case. The broad principle I lay down is this that ' we are justified in preventing any act, which, if we permitted it, would give a just ground of war against us."

The facts of the case present certain capabilities, and I think a good speech may be made out of them; but our strongest ground is that of treating the Portuguese refugees at Plymouth as under Brazilian command, and Palmella as a man of straw.

I am sure we ought to take a high tone, and to carry the war into the enemy's quarters. "We should show the consequences of adopting a different line of conduct from that we pursued, and charge them with endeavouring to engage the country in the sort of war Canning rather threatened than deprecated, a war of opinions.[1]

Cabinet. The Duke said he had had a most satisfactory letter from the King, and that he thought things looked better in the Lords. It is thought the Duke of Beaufort will be with us. The Duke of Eutland and Lord Lowther usually go with him. They settle their course together. His family say that Lord Lonsdale will be stubborn. It seems Lord Lowther is quiet. Some time must be allowed to enable our people to come round. It has been a great shock to them. Most, however, begin to confess the Government could not have acted otherwise.

A memorandum, similar in substance to the Duke's [1 See his famous speech on Portugal, 1826, and on France and Spain, 1823] letter to the Duke of Eutland, will be sent to Lord Hertford.

We had the Attorney and Solicitor-General of England, and the Solicitor-General of Ireland, in the Cabinet to talk over the Bill for the suppression of the Association. I think we shall make a stronger measure and one more efficacious than the last.

The Eelief Bill has made no progress.

I told Peel I thought in case of necessity, or even of difficulty, there would be no harm in making a declaration similar to that contained in the last paragraph of the Duke's letter to the Duke of Eutland, namely that if our friends would not support us, we would go out, rather than depend upon the Eump of the Whigs and of the Canningites. Peel seemed to agree with me. He said he could not remain in. office after the line he had taken, if he did not succeed.

The Fellows of Oxford have left it to Peel to consult his own convenience as to the time of his giving up his seat. They are properly punished! They had just agreed to a silly address against the Catholics when Peel's letter was read to them. I should have liked to see the changes of countenance. God forgive me if I am wrong, but from what I saw of them at Cambridge, the persons I least respect are Fellows of Colleges, and I believe the Oxonians are even less liberal than the people of Cambridge. [1] Lord Ellenborough had unfavourable recollections of the Fellows of St. John's, Cambridge, who, when he was an undergraduate early in the century, had perhaps much of the traditional character of the eighteenth-century college Fellow. As to the Oxford

Masters of Arts at this crisis, it must be remembered that, however conscientious Sir R. Peel's change of policy, it

Cabinet. First considered the Terceira [1] question, upon which questions were expected to-day in both Houses.

Then called in the law officers and Leslie Foster, and settled with them the Bill for suppressing the Association.

I afterwards asked Leslie Foster how he got on with his 40s. Freeholders Bill. He told me they were proceeding on my suggestion of ascertaining previously to the vote being given by some scrutiny whether a man had a vote or no. They mean it should be done by a jury. I think they will find that cumbrous and not effectual. Leslie Foster told me my suggestion of the previous scrutiny was a very valuable one. I am sorry they superadd the disfranchisement. I had much rather effect that object circuitously.

House. Lord Holland very imprudently began speaking about the Catholic question. Eldon did so, too, and others.

My uncle [2] was the first bishop who declared he was unchanged. Durham followed.

The Duke has a good account of our friends. They are ready to support us generally, though they are still stubborn upon the Catholic question. However, I sup-[could hardly fail to startle and irritate them, as he had owed his seat for the University to his pronounced ' anti-Catholic' principles. Canning had always been excluded from the University representation by his opposite opinions on that question.]

[1 The question of the expedition to' the relief of Terceira, projected by Donna Maria's adherents in England, which the Government regarded as a violation of our neutrality.

2 G. Law, Bishop of Bath and Wells.]

pose in spite of the bishops we shall have a majority in the Lords, but a small one.

Eeceived a letter from Lord Grey, thanking me for the communication of the King's Speech relative to Ireland. He did not speak very warmly, but he said it would give him the truest pleasure if the measure should be accomplished by the Duke's Government. I met Eosslyn in the House. He is very friendly.

February 10.

House. The Archbishop of Canterbury and the Bishop of London, in presenting petitions, declared their opinions to be unaltered. The Duke of Eutland made a friendly and useful speech, declaring that he waited for the Bill, and should in any case support the Government.

Lord Longford made an attack on the Duke for having taken the Protestants by surprise. The Duke answered that he could not say anything before he had the King's consent.

Lord Eosslyn suggested to me that we should lose no time in looking over the lists and sending for people. I am to meet him at 2 to-morrow.

February 11.

Went to Lord Eosslyn at 2. We went over the list together. He reckons upon more than I do.

Drummond, whom I met at old Lady Salisbury's in the evening, told me the Duke now counted twenty-six transfers. Lord Bath and Lord Carteret vote with us.

We must, however, bring up every vote.

§44

I did not go to the Eecorder's report at Windsor. This is the first time I have been absent from a Council.

February 12.

Called on Lord Camden at 2 to look over the list of peers for the Catholic question. Saw Aberdeen on the same subject, and the Duke. The Duke thinks he is already sure of a majority of 12.

Office. Saw Mr. Turner. He accepts the bishopric of Calcutta, and seems quite aware of the difficulty of the duties imposed upon him, and quite resolved to do his duty. I told him to connect himself with neither party, but to rule both. He will endeavour to do so.

Lord Camden told me he heard the Archbishop of Canterbury was rather hurt at not being consulted with respect to Mr. Turner's appointment. I therefore took an opportunity of speaking to the Archbishop in the House, and of explaining to him that I only did not speak to him because I knew he would not be acquainted with Mr. Turner. The Archbishop seemed satisfied. He told me the Bishop of London thought highly of Mr. Turner, and he believed he was a very fit man.

In the House Falmouth attacked the Duke and was well answered by him.

February 13.

House of Lords. Lord Sidmouth, [1] whom the Duke reckoned upon, declared his opinions were unchanged.

[1 As Lord Sidmouth had broken with his colleagues in the ' Talents Administration' of 1806-7 on a similar question, it might seem more surprising that the Duke should have reckoned on him than that he should have been disappointed. But the crisis was one at which no man's career could be foretold.]

§45

Lord Westmoreland, in presenting a petition, made an excellent speech. The Whigs could not help laughing as old Wessy ratted, but he really spoke extremely well, and made a very useful speech. I suppose the attraction of the Privy Seal is too powerful.

Lord Winchelsea presented the petition agreed upon at Penenden Heath. He made a bold loud speech, with nothing in it. He would be a perfect Eolla at a country theatre. After some trash from Darnley and Lord Clan-ricarde, Lord Grey spoke, and at length. He answered Lord Winchelsea, which was rather like wasting great guns upon sparrows. He made a speech, very handsome indeed as regarded the Ministers, and particularly Peel; but he was rather diffuse, not very strong or pointed in any part, and I was sorry to observe that his voice was thicker than it used to be. I fear he is failing. It was, however, the first appearance I ever observed of age.

We send off a messenger to-morrow to collect proxies in Italy. I believe we shall have a majority; but I doubt whether it will be a large one. Cumberland is coming over. The Duke had written to stop him. It is feared the letter may miss him on the road. He sees the King every day. The King is afraid of him, and God knows what mischief he may do. However, there is no possibility of forming an anti-Catholic Government, and that the King must feel.

Cabinet. It was decided against voting the thanks of the House to Lord Amherst, the Government in 1827 having deliberately abstained from doing so on the ground of his not having been present. with the army.

346   I am inclined to think the Government in 1827 forgot Lord Minto's case, or wished to avoid a debate.[1]

Determined to adhere to the line we have adopted as to Greece. The French Government has not yet wavered. The Chambers do, and the Government is weak. What we hope to do is to get the French to send their Ambassador with ours to Constantinople, leaving Greece as it is for the present, if the Eussians will not send a Minister or the Turks receive one. All the real objects of the treaty are accomplished. Things are to remain as they are de facto, until we have the opportunity of making them so de jure.

Sir W. Knighton went on Monday last to meet the Duke of Cumberland and prevent his coming here. He carried a letter from the Duke. I conclude one from the King, too. It is to be feared the Duke of Cumberland may have set off sooner than he intended, and may so have been far advanced before he met Knighton, or he may have missed him. I asked, ' Suppose members holding offices should vote against us, what will you do with them?" This seems to be considered a very serious question. We are to hold very high language, but I suspect we should do little. If we do not punish those who go against us in the Commons there may be a majority against us in the Lords, and then it will be too late.

The Duke said, ' Let me take the Bill to the King, get his approval, and then I will answer for his making[1 See, however, letter in Wellington Correspondence, v. 503, where Lord Minto's case is alluded to as differing from Lord Amherst's, Lord Minto haying gone to Java]

347   the household vote; but it will not do to hold a pistol to his head now."

I fear our House does not stand as well as it should.

February 15.

Cabinet. The Duke of Cumberland arrived in town last night and went to Windsor early this morning. He must have passed or have missed Knighton on the road. Peel and the Duke are now rather glad he is come. They say his arrival will frighten the Whigs, and make them quiet about the 40s. freeholders' Disfranchisement Bill. However, I think this view of things proceeds from the Duke's disposition to see all events en beau. I wish he had not come, or was gone.

In walking down to the Cabinet I met Kosslyn, and talked to him about the numbers for and against in our House. He is much too sanguine. He expects 60 majority. Lord Grey expects 50. I shall be glad if we have 30.

The Duke said he would speak to Shaftesbury, who has been canvassing against us.

February 16.

Cabinet. Considered again the 40s. freeholder Disfranchisement Bill. The Duke, Peel, Sir J. Murray, indeed I think all but Fitzgerald, are afraid of the violent measure of open disfranchisement; although willing to adopt collateral regulations which would practically limit the franchise. I fear we should shipwreck the whole measure upon a Disfranchisement Bill, and I am anxious that in putting an end to a Catholic question 348 we might, if we carried a Disfranchisement Bill, create a new and real grievance, which would give us as much trouble as the other. The great object is to settle the question altogether. There is no settlement if we create a just ground of complaint.

Peel, Fitzgerald, Goulburn, North, Doherty, and Lord F. Gower and I are to meet to-morrow at ten upon this point at Peel's house.

The Duke's idea is that we might require the collateral security of a certain payment, 20s. a year, to the county cess. This might prove a 10. freehold. The objection to this is, that at present the assessment is unequal. Some counties pay, in proportion to their real produce, more than others. Some districts are not rated at all, having been uncultivated when this valuation was made. But, as the survey is complicated, these objections would subside. Time would rectify the inequalities. My notion is that, taking a fixed sum, say one million, as the amount of county cess, and the general valuation being made, each county should be rated in proportion to the valuation, each being supposed to bear its fair part in the payment of one million.

Then in each county the assessment would be allotted and those would have votes who would pay 20s. a year.

In addition to this security there might be the necessity on the part of the voter of producing the receipt for his last half-year's gale.

Lord Eosslyn, whom I saw in the House, told me he hoped we should not incorporate the 40s. freeholders Bill with the Eelief Bill. That in that case Grey would vote against it, and even he should doubt. That the main measure being carried he thought Lord Grey would vote for the regulation which might be proposed of the Irish franchises.

Lord Eosslyn said the same thing to the Chancellor. We are in the midst of great difficulties. I wish we were well through them.

The Duke of Cumberland arrived on Saturday night and went on Sunday morning early to Windsor. The Chancellor had fortunately been sent for. They returned together and dined with the Duke of Wellington, the Duke of Cumberland being self-invited. He spoke little during dinner.

This morning he had another conference with the Duke of Wellington of three hours. He says his opinions are unchanged, but he will not canvass or attempt to put himself at the head of a party. The Duke of Wellington wrote to the King stating the substance of the conversation, and his advice to the Duke of Cumberland.

The Duke of Cumberland was in the House to-day.

The Duke made a speech very useful, as the Duke of Cumberland heard it. Of course he gave no explanation.

Lord Holland then made a most imprudent historical speech, mooting five or six points, each of which would require five or six hours to argue. After a few words from Lord Eldon we got away.

February 17.

. At ten o'clock met Goulburn, Herries, Fitzgerald, the Chancellor, Lord F. Leveson, Mr. Forth, Leslie

Foster, Doherty, and Dawson at Peel's. We were to settle the 40s. freeholders Bill. After much conversation it was decided to fix the value of the freehold, which should give a vote, at ten pounds, and to have previous investigation as to the value before the assistant barrister and by jury. Magistrates to attend if they pleased. The existing freeholders to be entitled to vote for a time to be fixed, two or three months, leaving that interval for the formation of the new constituency. The Lord-Lieutenant to be empowered to direct at once special sessions for the purpose of registration. Hereafter registration to take place at the regular Quarter Sessions.

The idea of requiring some visible test of value, instead of the investigation by a jury, and placing that test so high as to disfranchise freeholds under Wl. (such as proof of payment of 20s. to the county cess), was rejected as not affording a real criterion of a man's solvency, as very unequal under the present valuation of Ireland, and as effecting the object of disfranchisement in a roundabout way, not so effectually, and without real concealment. It was thought better to do the thing openly, if it was to be done at all. I believe words hare sometimes more weight than things, and I fear the open disfranchisement will create the means of defeating the Bill. Doherty, North, Leslie Foster, and Fitzgerald all think the jury will work well. I cannot help thinking it will cause too much delay.

Dawson, and indeed all the Irishmen, wanted 20l. at first, but they came round to 10l, and allowed that 10l. with the previous investigation would be equal to 20l with no security but an oath.

The cities and towns are to be left as they are. The freeholders balance the freemen. There are gross abuses in the mode of creating both, but we are afraid to touch corporate rights. Yet the Corporation of Dublin lately elected as members the President, Vice-President, Treasurers, and all the officers of all the Brunswick clubs in Ireland about 1,200 persons. If the qualification for a vote from a freehold was raised to 10l. in cities and towns, it would be necessary to balance that disadvantage to the Catholic freeholder by depriving non-resident freemen of their votes. The fight would continue the same, but between smaller numbers. No one seems to be able to guess what the practical effect of the proposed measure will ultimately be upon Protestant influence; but they seem to think that the 10l. freeholder will be more free from the influence of the priest.

If the measure produces ferment, it will not be exclusively Catholic, for the intention is to make its operation general.

House at 5. Falmouth made a speech which Lord Grey answered, throwing away his shot upon a sparrow. The Duke spoke too, well, but unnecessarily. The Duke of Newcastle put some questions it was not necessary to answer, and then Lord Darnley talked again about Penenden Heath. It was all very dull; but the House of Commons must have been duller, for the space under the throne is always filled by members.

There is that degree of animosity on the cross benches that I know not when we shall all be friends again.

February 18.

Peel seems to doubt whether he can have a majority to resist the motion for a Committee on East Indian affairs. I am to tell the Chairs, they had better see him.

February 19.

Second reading Catholic Association Bill. Before the order of the day the Duke of Cumberland rose and made a violent declaration of his opinions. He said the question was whether the Parliament should be Popish or Protestant. If a Eoman Catholic was admitted it would be a Popish Parliament.

He might as well have said if a drop of wine was poured into a glass of water it became a glass of wine. Lord Grey answered the Duke of Cumberland, but not powerfully. Then Eldon came on gallantly to his defence. Lord Plunket followed, and the Chancellor concluded. There was mere assertion on both sides.

Lord Plunket made part of a speech I have heard before.

The second reading then came on.

The Duke made an opening speech which, if the old Opposition had been ill-naturedly inclined, would have exposed him to a severe attack. He insisted upon all the mischievous consequences of the divided Government of which he was so long a member, and attributed to that division the non-execution of the law in Ireland and the progress of the Catholic Association. It may be true, but it is an awkward admission. There has been no really good speech this year.

Lord Grey has been wordy and has never hit hard. There has been no elan.

Lord Darnley came up to me and asked if there was not a move in my office by Bankes' going out. I said he still did his work and we should be very unwilling to replace him.

Lord Darnley wanted his son, who declined being my private secretary, to be placed there. This would never do. The secretary must be a member of Parliament, and a good speaker as well as an able man.

February 20.

Cabinet at 1. Considered the question of obliging hereafter all Eoman Catholic bishops to give two months' notice before they exercised episcopal jurisdiction, the Crown during the two months to have the power of issuing an interdict.

It seems Parliament has never interfered except with the jurisdiction of Eoman Catholic prelates, never with their orders. After talking a long time in a very desultory and unsatisfactory manner, we separated. We are to meet again to-morrow.

In reality, securities there are none of an ecclesiastical nature. If we should find any, the Eoman Catholics would resist. If we should find none, how are we to carry a majority in the Lords? We are not through our difficulties.

The wisest course to pursue would be to act as liberally now as possible. In a few years we should then VOL. i. A A be able to connect the Eoman Catholic Church with the State. That is our best security against its wishing to injure the State. However, at the present moment men's minds are in such a state that any attempt to give a State provision to the Eoman Catholic clergy would excite resistance, both on the part of the Eoman Catholics and of the Protestants.

The Bill for the suppression of the Association went through the Committee without a word.

Lord G, who made so offensive a speech yesterday, was induced to do so by the refusal of the Duke to give his sisters the rank of earl's daughters.

F has been out of humour for a year because he was not sent to Ireland. The more I know of the interior of politics the more shabby and personal the motives of men appear.

February 21.

Cabinet at 2. I think the conclusion to which we come is that we can hardly attempt to control the Eoman Catholic Church, without in some manner recognising it. To this the Protestants of this country have strong objections, and my own opinion is, that although now the absence of such control may seem to leave us without security, yet the recognition to which such control must lead, would, fifty years hence, be more prejudicial. We must not attempt to restrain the Eoman Catholic Church in the exercise of its spiritual functions; but we must protect the Protestant Church from their aggression. I think we should do this by making it penal to do that which we force men to swear they will not do, by exacting that which we swear, and by making it penal to assert the contrary of what we exact, c.

Leslie Foster was introduced.

The Attorney-General [1] is to be asked to-morrow whether he will prepare the Bill. I hope he will not. I should be very glad to get in Scarlett [2] in his place.

I hear Lord Mansfield, who is just come up from Scotland, reports that he finds the opinions of the people much changed, that is, in favour of the measure.

February 22.

It is said the Duke of Clarence intends to make his profession of faith to-morrow in favour of the Catholic Bill, and Lord Holland to make a foolish speech defending the Association.

Cabinet at half-past 3. The Duke looked very much pulled. He has had a long conference with Wetherell, the Attorney-General, who does not so much seem to object to the Bill as to being abused for supporting it. Eldon has frightened him. He is to give his answer to-morrow. I sincerely hope he will go. The Duke of Newcastle has told Sir William Clinton he must go out. The Duke is more hostile to our Government than he was to Canning's, for he allowed Sir W. Clinton to remain in office and vote with Canning.

We had a long and not very fruitful discussion on the everlasting Bill and the securities. It was decided [1 Sir C. Wetherell.

2 Sir James Scarlett, afterwards first Lord Abinger.] that the assumption of any local title of an ecclesiastical nature, contrary to law, should be punishable.

Jesuits are not to be admitted to this country henceforward. If we can prevent the introduction of new recruits we shall gradually do away with the convents, c. They will die for want of inhabitants. There will be no objection to prohibit, in the same manner, the introduction of monks of any order, if it should be pressed upon us. The difficulty is this, that the service is in England principally performed by Eegulars.

The open display of symbols, c., will be prohibited in Ireland. It is already in England.

Peel suggested an alteration of the oath taken by members of Parliament and persons taking office, which should bind them to maintain the Union. I should prefer an oath binding them to maintain the Protestant church as established by the Act of Union.

In fact all that legislation can do has been already-done. I believe the best thing we could have done would have been to repeal all the existing laws, and to consolidate their enactments, or such of them as we wished to preserve, together with any new enactments we might think it advisable to make, in the Eelief Bill. The country would then have known the extent of our securities.

If we protect by law the existing settlement, and make men who become members of Parliament or take office swear they will maintain it, I really know not how we can throw greater securities round the Protestant church.

⌊357⌋ Aberdeen and Lord Bathurst, with whom I came home, said they expected that in twenty years the Catholic would be the established religion of Ireland. I should not care if it did become the religion of that part of Ireland which is Catholic. It is but just. ⌈1⌋

February 23.

House at five. The Duke of Clarence declared his intention of supporting the Bill for the Catholics, and denounced the opposition to it as unjust and infamous. He got into a long story about Lord St. Vincent, and I know not how many other admirals, with little episodes attached to each, and supposed them all to ' put up their heads and express their delight at seeing the Irish sailors who had fought the lower deck guns emancipated.

The Duke of Cumberland followed, and defended himself against the supposed charge of making a factious and he could not recollect the other epithet or would not, so the Duke of Clarence said aloud across the House, infamous.

The Duke of Sussex explained for the Duke of Clarence that the terms were applied generally if his noble brother took them to himself, it was a matter of taste. The Duke of Clarence said he thought his noble brother had been so long abroad that he had forgotten ⌈1 Lord Ellenborough must not be taken as having approved the disestablishment of the Protestant Church in Ireland. He was rather inclined to the idea of concurrent endowment, and so expressed himself at the opening of the Session of 1868. But he had prepared a speech against the Bill of 1869, in which he intended, as the last survivor of the Cabinet who passed the Relief Bill, to protest against the departure from the understanding on which it passed. He did not, however, speak, saying that the Bishop of Peterborough's speech had exhausted the arguments against the measure.⌋

358 the freedom of debate. I never witnessed such a scene. It was discreditable to all there, and they all seemed insane.

Eldon got up, and spoke gravely and well, but rather defended the obnoxious words used by the Duke of Cumberland the other night, ' That it was a question whether it should be a Popish or a Protestant Parliament."

Lord Grey answered him, and spoke better than he has done this year. He is very active, and fights the whole battle for us.

The Bishop of Chester laissait entrevoir, in presenting a petition that he intended to vote for the Bill. He could not have expressed himself better.

The Bishop of Calcutta is dead. So Turner will go immediately.

February 24.

Cabinet. Mentioned what Lord Eosslyn said the night before. The Duke was for doing what he thought right. So am I, but to propose with the expectation of defeat, is not to do. Fitzgerald is so acharne against the 40s. freeholders, Lord Bathurst, Herries, and Goul-burn are so determined to have what they think a security that I cannot stand the clamour.

The Duke, Peel, the Chancellor, Aberdeen, are all in reality against disfranchise-ment that is, they fear it, as I do, for I think the measure would be most beneficial to Ireland.

[359 After much talk it seemed to be decided that we could not call upon the Catholics to swear they would maintain the Protestant establishment, though they will willingly swear they will not injure or weaken it. I had sketched two drafts of oaths, one embodying the Coronation oath, the other the 5th Article of Union.

House. 3rd reading of the Catholic Association Bill. Lord Anglesey made an injudicious speech, in which he attributed the Relief Bill to the Catholic Association, and said the Eelief Bill alone would have extinguished them. Take away the cause, and you take away the effect. Goderich used the same language as to cause and effect, and said he was not enamoured of the principle and details of the Bill. I said, ' Neither were we. The object of all our measures was to establish such a state of things in Ireland as might enable us to govern that country by the ordinary course of law. We would not have proposed the Bill had we not thought it absolutely necessary, and we should be most happy when we could dispense with the power it gave us. But not only was it essential to the character of Parliament that the Association should not be allowed to beard it, that Parliament should not go cap in hand to those who had acted in contempt of its declared intentions, but no statesman could have thought of proposing the Eelief Bill without preceding it by this of coercion. This Bill was necessary for the satisfaction of the Protestant mind.

' I had heard with regret some expressions which fell from Lord Anglesey. He represented the Eelief Bill as one of grace. This as one of coercion. Yet he said the Bill of grace was forced upon us by the Catholic Association. Thus taking from that Bill altogether the character of grace which he before attributed to it.

360 In reality His Majesty's Ministers, in advising His Majesty to make that rec- ommendation from the throne for the consideration of the laws affecting the Eoman Catholics, in which the great body of the people of England had acquiesced, looked to the whole condition of Ireland, to existing dangers, and to those which would grow up, and increase under existing laws. The Bill on the table would put down the Catholic Association. The Eelief Bill would keep it down. Each was necessary to the other. The noble lords on the cross bench must feel that without the Eelief Bill this could not have been proposed. The King's Ministers felt that without both Bills they could not keep the peace of Ireland.

' Both Lord Anglesey and Lord Goderich had been in error when they said the effect would cease when the cause ceased. That was not true in politics. Men who, by the means of a real grievance, had obtained power, would make efforts to retain it when the cause which enabled them to obtain it was removed."

I had not spoken for so long a time, and the discussion was so little animated, that I did not speak to my own satisfaction. However, the Chancellor told me I had spoken well, and that my speech was so well timed. It is true it was the first occasion I had seen on which I could speak with advantage.

Lord Mansfield spoke very spitefully. Lord Melbourne not hostilely. I thought his manner had been better.

February 25.

I did not go to the Council at Windsor. The King never asks me to dinner, yet I 361 think he has asked all the others, unless, perhaps, Fitzgerald, and I think my colleagues imagine it must annoy me. I really do not care about it. I daresay all those who went there to-day will dine there.

Office. Turner wishes to have Australasia excepted from his diocese, as he can never go there.

Foreign Office. The French Ministry is so weak and so hard pushed by the Opposition that it begins to diverge a little from us, and to talk of making further conquests in Greece.

Lord Stuart has been desired, I think prudently, to be quiet; not to press them; and to wait the turn which will take place probably, for the King and the Ministers are really with us.

Peel's election begins to-morrow. It is expected to last three days. I believe he is sure, but his majority will not be large.

February 26.

Cabinet at 2. The Duke said his conversation with the King had been very disagreeable. The King begged he would not speak to the household, and seemed to intimate that they were to vote against the Government. The King's conversation before mixed companies and his servants has been most imprudent. The Duke of Cumberland has had a great effect upon him.

The Duke of Wellington consequently wrote to the King last night, telling him that he would communicate the heads of the Bill to him to-morrow, instead of Monday, and at the same time that the Government could not go on unless the Bill had His Majesty's support.

362 I do not think these were the words; but the meaning was, that the Government were committed to the measure, and must resign, if the King did not go with them.

The King seems to have been very nervous at dinner, and absent. He seems to have intended to say more to the Duke than he did; but being interrupted by the Duke, he perhaps regretted he had already said so much.

An Oxford voter, who had promised to vote for Peel, wrote to him to say that, as he understood the King was hostile, he must retract his promise. This letter the Duke to-day sent to the King, to show him the evil effects of unguarded conversation.

The Duke at the same time wrote to Knighton to say that if the Duke of Cumberland thought he could make a Government, he had better give that advice to the King at once, and so end matters.

The Duke goes to Windsor with the heads of the Bill to-morrow, and will bring the question to a point.

In the meantime it is beginning to be known that the King is shaken. The Manners [1] are off. The King is supposed to have said more to Sir John Beckett than he did to the Ministers. Lord Lowther talks very violently.

A good deal depends upon the interview the King will have had with the Duke of Cumberland to-day. If the Duke of Cumberland has told the King he can make a Government, the King may be firm. Lords Mansfield, [1 See correspondence between the Duke of Wellington and the Duke of Rutland, Wellington Correspondence, vol. v. 489-493.]

363 Winchelsea, and Colchester, probably Lord Eldon, certainly the Duke of Newcastle, would have nerve enough to form a Government. [1] They would do well enough for

our House, where little is required, but what could be done in the House of Commons? There is George Bankes, who would succeed me, Lord Lowther, and really I do not know who else there would be.

If the King should yield, and it should be known with what difficulty he has been brought to do so, the Whigs must, if they mean fairly by the Belief Bill, support the securities.

Planta calculates 289. I think with Government 120 against concession, and 180 against securities.

The difficulty is in our House; but if the Whigs joined the anti-Catholics they would beat us on the Franchise Bill.

The Association Suppression Bill came up from the Commons to-day. We have determined that we will not advise the putting of the Great Seal to it till the King has acceded to the Bill of Eelief. To do otherwise would be a fraud upon Parliament.

The King yesterday suggested the bringing in of the Franchise Bill before the Eelief Bill, that is, Eldon has moved Cumberland to suggest that we should be exposed to all the unpopularity of the two coercive measures, and then be turned out for the purpose of defeating the Bill of Eelief.

[1 Almost the same words are used by Lord Palmerston (Ashley's Life of Lord Palmerston, p. 193): ' In the Lords they might get on with Eldon, Colchester, Mansfield, Sidmouth, and some others, but in our House it would be absolutely impossible. The Speaker (Manners Sutton) is the only man in the whole House who is not pledged the other way."]

They want, too, to get our plan out of us, to have that to expose, to make the King break upon that. All this will be defeated by the Duke of Wellington's straightforward conduct, and if we go out I hope we shall go out before our plan is proposed.

We had some discussion as to parts of the plan today; but it was languid, as the idea of our being turned out before we could introduce it made us naturally a little inattentive.

In the House Lord Londonderry made a foolish attack on Lord Anglesey for a speech he did not hear. Lord Anglesey made a gentlemanlike reply, and reserved his defence of his conduct till the Bill should have passed.

Lord Plunket then defended himself against an attack made upon him and upon the Government under which he had acted, for not enforcing and executing the Bill of 1825. In the course of his speech Lord Plunket spoke in favour of the Bill for disfranchising the 40s. freeholders. His support will be of great value should we live to bring that Bill in. He gave it to be understood that he would not have brought in the Association Bill of 1825, unless he had expected that it would have been accompanied by a Bill of Belief that Bill to be proposed by the Government. After a few words from the Duke of Wellington Lord Plunket acknowledged it was only his private opinion, that there was no pledge on the part of the Government.

Lord Longford answered Lord Plunket and really well. In point of fact the Bill of 1825 was never executed, because Lord Plunket used in the House of Commons expressions stronger than those used by Sheil and others in the Association.

Lord Plunket's was a good and useful speech to us. The House was not full. It rained so hard that people were not much inclined to go down.

February 27.

Eeceived a summons to a Cabinet at 4. We sat till 5 doing nothing. The Duke did not arrive. Went to, the House. Lord Longford made a prepared speech of 2 hours, not so good by any means as his speech of 2 minutes yesterday. Lord Plunket answered him, and went too far, representing the Brunswick Clubs as worse than the Association.

Eeturned to the Cabinet room. The Duke had not returned at 7 when I came away.

Both Peel's friends and Sir E. Inglis's are sanguine.

In the House of Commons Goulburn said a member of the Government would bring forward the Catholic Eelief Bill on Thursday. Much cheering. This was in reply to a question from Lord John Eussell.

Our House adjourned as usual over Saturday that the circumstance of there being no commission to pass the Association Suppression Bill might be less observed.

Fitzgerald had been making a Protestant Government this morning.

Sir R. Inglis, India Board.

Exmouth, Admiralty.

G. Bankes, Chancellor of the Exchequer.

Mansfield, Foreign Office.

Knatchbull, Home.

Eldon, President.

366 The difficulty they would find would be in the House of Commons. In our House they would make a fair show.

At 11 heard from Lord Bathurst that at 4 Sir E. Inglis was 119 a head; at 12, that the Duke had had entire success at Windsor.

February 28.

At the close of the poll Peel was 126 below Inglis. It is now much to be regretted that Peel ever stood. The violence of the parsons was beyond belief, and far beyond decency; they made faces at and abused each other; but the Protestants were the boldest and the most violent. Now 700 parsons, flushed with triumph, will return to their parishes like firebrands, and excite the whole country. Peel is himself perfectly indifferent, and really I must confess that he has shown himself a great man by his equanimity in all that has taken place.

Cabinet at 4. The Duke said he had an interview of 5 hours with the King. The King ultimately yielded all points, even to the extent of desiring the Duke of Cumberland to leave England. The King declared himself more satisfied with the Bill than with anything he had seen. He had great unwillingness to write himself to the household, desiring their attendance in the House of Lords during the Catholic measures, but he had no 'objection to the Duke of Wellington writing to them in his name. That is, he acquiesced in this, but he did not much like it.

367 Accordingly the Duke read to the Cabinet a letter which he proposed to submit to the King before he sent it, in which, referring to his general request that they would attend the House, made to them at the beginning of the session, he informed them, that it being the intention of His Majesty's Ministers to introduce measures in

conformity with the gracious recommendation in His Majesty's Speech, he had His Majesty's commands to desire their attendance in their places during the progress of those measures.

The Duke of Cumberland was to have seen the Duke of Wellington at 12 to-day. He managed to arrive in town at one, and then wrote to the Duke to say that, as he came up to town, he had thought that under present circumstances he could not see the Duke, or the Duke call on him, without exciting public attention. He therefore wished, before he saw the Duke, to know whether he had any objection to his communicating the substance of their conversation to Lord Eldon and others of his friends. The Duke wrote in reply that he did not care who knew what passed between them. He was going to ride out, and should be home at such an hour. [1] The Duke of Cumberland called and they talked of the badness of the roads, c.

The Duke had intended to recommend the Duke of Cumberland's retiring to Hanover.

Copies of these letters will be sent to the King.

I suggested that, although the King could not force the Duke of Cumberland out of the country, he might prevent his going so often to Windsor. The Duke of [1 These letters are to be found in Wellington Correspondence, vol. v. 513.] Cumberland's remaining makes the Duke of Wellington's letter to the household the more necessary.

Wetherell's letter was read. He stated that he could not support the measure. I hope the Duke will replace him immediately. It is quite essential to give some unequivocal proof that the Government has life in, it.

The Duke represents his interview with the King to have been very painful indeed. The King was in a very agitated state, and even spoke of abdicating. The Duke said it was the more painful in consequence of the very peremptory language he was obliged to hold to him. However, the King was very kind, and kissed him when he left him.

The Duke, before he left the Castle, wrote a note to the King expressing his gratitude for His Majesty's kindness during the painful interview he had had with him, assuring His Majesty that nothing but a deep sense of the importance of the objects at stake would have led him to insist as he did upon the several points he had submitted to His Majesty, and declaring that His Majesty's kindness would induce him to guard with increased anxiety the interests His Majesty had justly so much at heart.

It seems, I suppose by communication from Knighton, that the King was much pleased by this letter.

The Duke spoke with much feeling of the painful-ness of this interview.

After having received this communication we proceeded to the consideration of the Bill, and went through a large part of it.

I heard from the Ashleys that Peel's Oxford committee had been very weak, apologising for asking votes on the ground of securities promised! The other side sent a chaise and four for a man with a letter conjuring him to come forward in defence of his religion.

March 1.

Cabinet at 4. The Duke absent. He went to Strath-fieldsaye to receive the Judges. The Chancellor received at the Cabinet a letter from the King which arrived in town at one but which he did not get till past four, desiring him to go to Windsor immediately.

It's unlucky he did not get it sooner. He would arrive just as the King was going to dress for dinner. This looks ill, and as if the result of the Oxford election had made the King waver. We have not heard what answer the King gave to the Duke's letter, nor whether he approved of the intended letter to the Household.

The great object is to remove the Duke of Cumberland from Windsor. This might be done.

Lord Plunket having complained that we kept the secret of our intentions rather too well, it was considered right to remove the interdict from Lord F. Gower, and he may now tell Lord Plunket confidentially what our intentions are with regard to the 40.5. franchise.

I shall tell Lord Eosslyn to-morrow, and at the same time put him au fait of our position at Windsor, and show him the necessity of adhering to it.

The Oxford election and the sensation produced in the country makes it necessary for us to have stronger ~~VOL. i. B B~~
securities, and at the same time enables us to carry them.

In the meantime the reports are that the King is ill, if not mad. In fact the excitement in which he is may lead to insanity, and nothing but the removal of the Duke of Cumberland from his presence will restore him to peace. The Duke of Cumberland takes to him Lord Eldon's suggestions.

In Cabinet we went over the Bill till we came to the clause respecting the Regulars of the Church of Eome, whom the Solicitor-General mistook for Regulars of the Army, and so solvuntur risu tabula?.

Lord F. Gower was present. He said nothing. We have no new Attorney-General yet. This is a great error.

The only proof we can give of having Windsor with us, and of an expectation of surviving, is that which is afforded by cashiering a recreant servant. It would besides be such a good thing to get rid of the man.

If I had to write a Catholic Eelief Bill it would be very short. In the first clause I should repeal the Acts or parts of Acts requiring the oath of supremacy, and the declaration against Transubstantiation. In the second I should specify the excepted offices. In the third I should write the fifth Article of the Irish Union, and then insert that, in lieu of the oaths and declarations repealed, an oath should be taken to maintain the United Church of England and Ireland, according to that Article.

March 2.

Eode down at 12 to the House of Lords to see the Chancellor. He told me he had arrived at Windsor just as the King was going to dinner. The King desired him to sit down as he was. At dinner the King was in excellent spirits. The only people there were Strathearn, Keppel, two other men of the household, and the three women.

After dinner the King was alone with the Chancellor; only Knighton was sent for and was present a part of the time. The King began quietly, but at last he was very vehement. He wanted the Chancellor to take a letter to the Duke of Cumberland which he showed to him. This letter requested the Duke to leave England referred to the expression of a similar wish before conveyed to him by Knighton but at the same time declared that his mind was not made up that he waited to hear the opinions of the bishops and law officers, that he might at a subsequent period require the Duke of Cumberland's assistance and support.

The letter was full of the most tender expressions of regard for the Duke of Cumberland, spoke of the relation in which the Duke had stood to the late King, and of their opinions being blended upon this question.

The Chancellor declined taking the letter. The King said there was a copy made of it, which was in Watson's [l] handwriting, which he might show to Lord Eldon! The Chancellor begged he might communicate with the Duke of Wellington, The King did not like [l Sir F. Watson, Master of the Household) B/B this, but at last consented. The Chancellor did not reach Strathfieldsaye till 3 in the morning. He saw the Duke, who of course took exactly the same view of the matter that he had done. The Chancellor went to bed for two hours, and then set off at twenty minutes after six and arrived in four hours at the House of Lords, to sit on the trial of causes.

Srathfieldsaye was full of people who had been invited to meet the Judges amongst others, Palmerston and Sturges Bourne were there. Of course the Chancellor's nocturnal visit must have been known.

The Duke called at Windsor on his return to town. The King could not be brought to consent to the Duke's writing the letter he proposed to the household. He became quite violent. He declared he was better satisfied with his present Ministers than with any he had ever had; that he could not go to Lord Lansdowne. He would pass the Belief Bill with out that for putting down the Association.

He asked the Duke if he thought he could trust old Eldon! The Duke shook his head and laughed, and said he would not advise His Majesty to do so.

The King confessed he had looked round, and could find no Minister but himself. He then spoke of abdicating, and said he should retire to Hanover with his present income. He had thought of desiring Lord Bexley to take a message to that effect to the House of Lords. The Duke told him any person bearing such a message must advise it, and he would find no one willing to make himself responsible.

The King then desired the Duke to take the opinion of the Cabinet upon the affixing the Great Seal to the Commission for giving the Eoyal Assent to the Association Suppression Act.

We had met at a quarter to 2, and having heard the Chancellor's report, and determined that we could not go on with the Bill without communicating the heads of it to the King, and having his approval in writing, we set to work with the Elective Franchise Bill.

The Duke arrived about 4. He reported what I have already mentioned. We then considered the terms in which the Cabinet should signify its opinion.

I made a draft, which was superseded by Peel's. The substance of both was, that there had been an understanding that the Suppression Bill was only the first of a series of measures of which the measure of Eelief must be one, that in consequence of that understanding the Bill had passed without opposition; that we could not advise His Majesty to give the Eoyal Assent to that measure, without having the assurance of his Eoyal approval, or that he continued to approve, of the course of measures of which the consideration had been recommended by His Majesty's Speech, and that in the progress of those measures His Majesty's Government would have the whole influence of the Crown with them.

This is only the substance.

In the Lords made a very mischievous speech, though a very bad one. The Duke answered him admirably. I never heard him speak so well or so effectively.

The Duke is, however, much exhausted. He was three hours with the King this morning. The King was in bed, and throughout was very kind to him. He kissed him when he went away.

The Duke has a very kind heart, and I really believe the King works upon it and takes advantage of it. The Duke cannot bear to see the King in distress. He told me the other day the King was, he believed, attached to him, and would be very sorry to hurt him, but he did not fear him. This seems to be the case. One would have expected that the Duke would have drawn the Popilian [1] circle round the King, and would not have left him without an assurance in writing of his determination to support the Bill.

It is dreadful to think what the result of a change of Ministers may be. In Ireland, I fear, general disorganisation, and a system of rapine and murderous outrage. In Europe our influence will be lost, and the weak Government of France may plunge the nations in war. The Church of England may be safe; but the Church of Ireland will fall.

March 3.

Office. Cabinet at 2. While we were there at four arrived a letter from the King to the Duke, acknowledging the receipt of his letter, and saying he must take some time to collect his thoughts, before he could answer it.

We had Leslie Foster, Doherty, the Solicitor-General, and North at the Cabinet, and considered the Bill. North objected strongly to the clause relative to titles [1 Alluding to the story of the Kornan general Popilius and Antiochus Epiphanes.] assumed by Popish Archbishops, c. He thought the assumption of such titles essential to the performance of their functions.

House. The Duke's speech of last night has done much good. In the first place it overset the Bishop altogether. Besides it showed a conciliatory spirit, and the Duke of Eichmond told me he was glad to hear it, as he saw we should all shake hands and be friends again when the Bill was passed. We had nothing but petitions. Lord Lansdowne went out of his way to rejoice in the existence of a united Government, and to declare the impossibility of ever returning to a system of neutrality. He seemed to apprehend we might give way and unite with Eldon. Eldon dexterously introduced an allusion to the India Bill, and the dissolution of Parliament consequent upon it.

In the Commons Brougham and Huskisson held the same language as to a neutral Government, which had been held by Lord Lansdowne.

Cabinet at half-past 9. We went on with the Bill, and determined to adhere to the clause preventing the Assumption of titles, but to abandon that preventing the giving of them. Peel, Sir G. Murray, and Fitzgerald were for giving up both; but we resolved to maintain the first on the King's account, as well as for effect.

At 10 came a letter from the King to say he was much embarrassed by the letter the Duke had written, and wished to see him, the Chancellor, and Peel together at 12 to-morrow.

They think the King sent a copy of the Duke's letter to the Duke of Cumberland, and that he and

Eldon were not ready to tell the King they could form a Government.

The Archbishop of York presented a petition, and said he waited to see the securities, and should be sorry not to be able to vote for the Bill.

I do not think much of our Solicitor-General Tindal. He is evidently not fit to be made Attorney.

March 4.

Office. Saw Aberdeen. The Austrians wish to be placed on the footing of the most favoured nation in India. I must desire some one at the office to make a memorandum on the subject of the intercourse of European nations, not having settlements in India, with the territories of the East India Company.

Cabinet dinner at Lord Bathurst's. The Duke having gone down to Windsor with the Chancellor and Peel, they joined us at a quarter before 10.

The Duke told iis that the result of the interview was that Peel would to-morrow declare in the House of Commons that he could not bring on the Eelief Bill because he was no longer Minister.

The King talked for six hours.

The Duke says he never witnessed a more painful scene. He was so evidently insane. He had taken some brandy-and-water before he joined them, and sent for some more, which he continued to drink during the Conference. During six hours they did not speak 15 minutes. The King objected to every part of the Bill. He would not hear it. The Duke most earnestly entreated him to avoid all reference to his Coronation oath. The King at one moment talked of postponing the consideration of the Bill till he had seen the Archbishop of Canterbury and the Bishop of London but he gave up that idea of himself. It seems that he really does not know what his Coronation oath is. He has confused it with the oath of Supremacy.

The Duke saw Knighton after he had left the King. Knighton said the King was in a deplorable state, and declared he had not a friend left in the world, Knighton wanted the Duke to see Lady Conyngham, but he was afraid of meeting the King there, as he usually goes there after a scene.

The Duke's idea is that he may be sent for on Tuesday, on their finding they cannot make a Government, and he thinks that is the King's expectation; but that he wishes to obtain popularity, and to seem to be forced.

It is impossible not to feel the most perfect contempt for the King's conduct. We should be justified in declaring we will have no further intercourse with one who has not treated us like a gentleman.

I dread the effect of this overthrow of the Government. We may possibly come in again in ten days, but under what different circumstances the King having declared his dissent, and having made an appeal to the people. The measure, if carried by us, would have a very different effect from what it would have had, had we carried it at once as Ministers.

There are two money bills now waiting for a third reading in our House, and likewise the Catholic Association Bill. The last we will not pass: but it came up first, and my belief is that the precedent would be most dangerous and unconstitutional of putting aside a Bill coming up in order, without taking any notice of it. I hold the King to be obliged to say either that he assents or that he will consider of, which is held to be a dissent to, a Bill brought up from Parliament. The question will be looked into before to-morrow, when we have a Cabinet, if indeed the meeting of 11 gentlemen no longer His Majesty's Ministers can bear that appellation.

I think Aberdeen was much annoyed at our discomfiture. It is a serious inconvenience to Goulburn and Sir George Murray, should it continue.

It is not convenient to me. However I like Opposition so much better than office that I shall console myself.

There seems to have been a curious scene when the lawyers went away at 2 o'clock this morning. The Solicitor-General then first heard the Chancellor, the Duke, and Peel were to go to Windsor to-day, and that there was a hitch. He was quite astonished and shocked, and cried out, ' 0 Lord, I am committed, I am pledged. We shall all fall together!" Doherty enjoyed the joke, and said, 'Well, I shall have the consolation of thinking that I was engaged with Tindal and Leslie Foster in drawing a Catholic Eelief Bill!" Certainly the two last men we should have expected to have been associated with on such a business.

March 5.

At a quarter past 12 received a message from the Duke to go to him immediately. I went, thinking he had to announce the King's insanity. He, however, had to announce a complete victory. A quarter of an hour after he got home last night he received a letter from the King declaring that to avoid the mischief of having no Administration he consented to the Bill proceeding as a measure of Government, but with infinite pain. The Duke immediately wrote an answer, in which he stated clearly and strongly his understanding of the King's letter. The King replied that his understanding of it was correct.

So the Commission was immediately sent down to Windsor for signature, and the Association Bill will be passed to-day, if we get the Commission in time.

I went to the office and saw Bankes. I told him our victory was complete, and had some conversation with him upon the general subject. I showed him all the dangers which would have attended a change of Government, or even a temporary suspension of our functions. He has behaved very well, and has abstained from going to any meeting of the enemies of the Bill on the ground that, as a member of the Government, he knew more than he otherwise should have done. His conduct has been very honourable.

Sat on the Commission at half-past 4. Peel and Planta had begun to be very anxious about the arrival of the Commission.

House very dull. Lord Winchelsea put off his motion because everybody went to the House of Commons.

Lord Eosslyn seems to be in some alarm about the Franchise Bill.

Salisbury appeared not to like our securities. I did not tell him all; but he wished to have some control over the priests. I told him that we had considered the several securities proposed for many days; that several which at first sight seemed most plausible, appeared, on further consideration, to be really injurious; that I was convinced, even had it been possible to carry it now, that a State provision for the clergy of the Catholic Church would ultimately have proved most fatal to the security of the Protestant Establishment.

The man I like best, and who seems to have more the talent of speaking in him than any other great person, is the Duke of Richmond. [1] I should be very glad if he were made Privy Seal when the Bill is passed. It is an office which should be given to a man of high rank.

March 6.

Peel spoke for 4 hours. He spoke very well indeed better than he ever did before. The House was with him, and cheered him enthusiastically. The Whigs are quite satisfied, and had a meeting to-day at which they determined to give full support to the whole measure.

O'Connell is satisfied with it, and so are the priests.

Lord Grey is rather sulky about the Franchise. It is said the Canningites are too.

The Duke of Cumberland is most venomous. He has hitherto been in good spirits, thinking he should beat us, but the event of last night has made him mad.

[1 His opposition to the ' Catholic Relief Act' was so great as to make him temporarily coalesce with the Whigs and take part in carrying- the Reform Bill of 1832.]

I fear Salisbury will vote against us.

Lord Bathurst said to-day he believed the King to be quite capable of pretending to be mad in order to carry his point. His yielding only two hours after he had dismissed the Duke looks a little like it.

I received to-day, signed by the King, the confirmation of Lord Dalhousie's appointment and the nomination of Mr. Turner as Bishop of Calcutta. I wrote to Mr. Turner announcing it, and directed my letter to him as Bishop appointed of Calcutta.

Lord Mountcharles went to the Chancellerie at Esterhazy's yesterday, and related all the King's conversations at table, respecting the Bill and the votes of the household. He even said, ' yesterday the King was mad' I never saw the world in better humour than it was to-night in the House. Even the Protestants did not seem very ill-humoured. Such is the effect of a good speech.

Sir G. Murray spoke admirably. Sir E. Inglis, the new bigot elected at Oxford, most particularly ill.

March 7.

At half-past 3 I received a note from Mr. Fergusson to tell me the House had divided on the Speaker's leaving the Chair. Ayes, 348. Noes, 160. Majority, 188. I had expected more. Mr. Fergusson says the minority had 20 or 30 more than was expected. The House was not so full by 50 members as I thought it would have been. As the Protestants intended, or said they intended, to have a five nights' debate, I think there must have been some trick in coming to a division. I am very glad they did divide. A majority of 188 will settle the feeling of the country.

I told Belfast they would not be able to hear a five nights' debate. They would be bored to death by the dulness of their own speeches.

Cabinet at 2. Leslie Foster, North, the Advocate of Scotland, and the Solicitor-Generals of England and Ireland were there. We went through the Elective Franchise Bill.

Afterwards we had some conversation respecting Wetherell and the others who voted against us last night. The Duke is for doing nothing yet. He thinks we are strong enough in the Lords, and may risk one chance of recovering our friends if we adopt any measure of severity. Lord Lowther voted against us, and has resigned. Lord O'Neil has intimated that he intends to vote against us, which is an intimation that he resigns. The two Corrys voted against, and Sir Alexander Grant. Planta miscalculated twenty or thirty.

Had at dinner the new Bishop of Calcutta, the Chairs, Hardinge, the Bishop of Bath, and Fitzgerald. We talked of nothing but the Catholic question. The Bishop of Calcutta gave me his list of the Bishops. London and Chester have been won by the repudiation of the Catholic Church. On the whole he makes 11 certainly against, 3 to stay away, 9 certainly for, 2 with the King, 2 with the Duke of Northumberland, 2 doubtful.

383 March 8.

The Duke of Wellington read his list of voters in the lords.

He makes 13 certain transfers, 22 more probable, 11 uncertain, besides 15 new votes; as 44 are to be worked down in the first event, we should have a minority of 3; in the 2nd, a majority of 41; in the 3rd, of 63. This is without counting any English Bishops; but it is on the supposition that all who voted in 1828 for the resolution will be brought to the vote now. Under these circumstances, relying upon a majority, he thinks it better not to have any question with the King about displacing any of the men who have voted against us, till the Bill is passed. It is a difficult point. The fear is that many Peers not holding offices may think they may as well please the King if they can do it without displeasing the Government. The Whigs are indignant at Wetherell's being suffered to continue in office. They wish to convert the 160 Tories into an Opposition and to join the Government. They will come over as soon as the Bill is passed, and take their seats on our side; but if they see an indisposition to break with the Tories they will, I dare say, be more hostile than ever. Our policy, however, is to get back the Tories. We never could get on with the Whigs.

Salisbury votes against us. He says the majority will be 30 less from the want of securities. I believe he is altogether wrong,

W. Bankes gives a majority of 6. He thinks we shall have 5 bishops. I think we shall have ten certainly.

384 At the Cabinet we went through the Belief Bill. It was very dull. The feeling against excluding O'Connell is universal. I was always against it.

33 members of the House of Commons voted against Peel who were expected to vote for us. Belfast told me at dinner that they expected to divide 200. That would leave us 458. Still the same proportional majority. We have clearly 2 to 1.

March 9.

Cabinet at 1. The Duke said he had had a good account from Windsor, that is, from Sir W. Knighton. It seems the palace was in rebellion after the three Ministers had left the King on Wednesday. Knighton, finding they were gone, went into the room and found, the King lying on the sofa. The King began to tell what had passed. Knighton accompanied him to his room, and, guessing the purport of the communication, thought he had better get what had passed from the Ministers than from the King. Accordingly he went to them as the Duke mentioned on Wednesday. He returned to the King. The Conynghams went to him too. They all told him he could not make another Government; that he was left alone; that if he put his breaking off upon his oath, as he had intended to do, he would be unable to retract, and would be ruined. He hesitated some time, but at half-past 9 wrote the letter he sent to the Duke, and which he dated 8 o'clock. The Duke's answer he received in bed on Thursday morning, and replied to it without any communication with any one, and without keeping a copy.

After all the excitement of the interview, and of the family insurrection which followed, he eat a good dinner, not sitting down to it till 10 o'clock, and was as gay as ever.

The Duke of Cumberland went down to Windsor early on Saturday morning with an account of the division and debate. He stayed there all Saturday and Sunday. When the King took leave of him he said, 4 My dear Ernest, don't talk to me any more about it; I am committed, and I must go through with it."

The Duke of Wellington did not seem at all well today. He looked very pale, and was languid and silent. We sat in Cabinet, making little progress with the Bill, from a little after one till five. The Bill will not be brought in till to-morrow, and I fear it will be very ill-drawn. Lord F. Gower, North, Tindal, and Doherty were present.

Lord F. Gower tears the Franchise Bill may lose all the support which has been promised to it, if the writs'-are to be suspended till the new registry is completed. It is a matter of little real importance, for probably no-election will take place.

The universal feeling is against excluding O'Connell from the benefit of the Act, and forcing him to take the: present oaths; but I fear the Bill will stand so.

In the House I found Lord Harrowby, Camden, and Eosslyn shocked and alarmed at the non-acceptance of the resignations offered. Last night Sir J. Beckett resigned. Lord Lowther on Saturday. Wetherell is to make a violent speech against us to-night. The Chancellor agrees with me, and thinks that execution should ~~VOL. i. C C~~ be done, or at least the resignations accepted. He intended to go after the House to speak to the Duke about it.

Lord Grey told me he disapproved of the elective Franchise Bill, and of the two oaths, one for the Protestant and one for the Catholic. Of the latter I disapprove; but it was necessary for the King's satisfaction.

At the Cabinet we did not know the Duke had been blooded, but Lord Jersey, Lord Grey, and others knew it in the House.

Lord Winchelsea offered to postpone his motion, which stands for to-morrow; but Lord Bathurst told him the Duke would not like to have it postponed on his account. I rather doubt, however, whether he will be able to be there.

March 10.

Cabinet at 12. At last finished the two Bills. We had a long discussion relative to the question whether the issuing of writs for Irish counties should be suspended until the registration of the new freeholders was complete, or whether, until it should be complete, the 40s. freeholders should vote. I was from the first against legislating for an individual case. I wished to keep things quiet, and to allow O'Connell quietly to take his seat on taking the new oath. That having been overruled this new difficulty occurs.

I doubt our carrying the suspension of the writ, although no doubt it is better that the writ should be suspended than that the election should be confined to the 20. and $50l$. freeholders, until the registration of the new $10l$. freeholders is completed. But the House of Commons cannot endure what seems to be the persecution of an individual.

In the Morning Journal is an account, wrong as to dates, but still substantially correct, of what took place at Windsor relative to the Belief Bill. The Duke says the account, although inaccurate, is as accurate as any account could be that proceeded from the King, or the Duke of Cumberland, and that he has no doubt they think it accurate.

House. Lord Winchelsea made his motion for a return of Catholic priests, c., and a very foolish speech, in which he declared his opinion that a Government could be easily formed, that a dissolution should take place, and that there should be a reform of Parliament! The Duke in answering him took occasion to say that in introducing the Catholic Bills he had the sanction and support of His Maj esty, and that he had no doubt the perseverance, the honest perseverance of the Government, would lead to a satisfactory conclusion. In saying he had the sanction and support of His Majesty the Duke looked at the Duke of Cumberland, who sat down at the end of our bench. We all cheered, so did the Whigs, so did the doubtfuls, and I think since 1819 I have not heard so good a cheer in the Lords. The Duke's declaration has gained us ten votes. Downshire, Darnley, Eosslyn, and others, all came to express their satisfaction. I asked Falmouth and the Duke of Bich-mond if Eeform in Parliament was a measure of their new Cabinet. They said no, and afterwards both got up and declared they only agreed with Lord Winchelsea in thinking the Bill a bad Bill. Old Eldon seemed bothered by the Duke's speech, and made a formal declaration of opposition to the Bill, to be conducted however in a very Parliamentary manner. The Duke of Eichmond spoke in a very gentlemanlike and good style.

A number of persons, perhaps 100, collects every day at the door of the House. The word is given to cheer or hiss. It is a Cumberland trick, but others in the opposite faction are sent down, and he got some hisses to-day. The Duke of Wellington got more cheers than hisses.

Eldon is to make a motion for a return of Catholic priests who have taken the oath since 1813, on Friday.

March 11.

Occupied all the morning in looking through Acts of Parliament relative to Lord Eldon's motion.

The Cabinet dined with me. Goulburn was absent. He has a bad cold.

The Seraskier, who lately through Consul Meyer made some pacific overtures, has been created Grand Vizier.

The gallant defender of Yarna has been displaced.

After dinner I asked the Duke who he wished to go out as Governor to Bombay. He said Courtney. He thought he would do very well, and he wanted a Privy Councillor's place.

V. Fitzgerald said the Whigs were very much annoyed at the vacant places not being filled up. The Chancellor wants to make Scarlett Attorney-General.

The Duke of Athol announced his adhesion, and that of Lord Strathallan to-day. This is a consequence of the Duke's Speech of last night.

March 12.

Occupied all the morning in looking into Acts of Parliament. House. Only petitions. The Duke of Newcastle went to Windsor yesterday. It is not yet known whether he saw the King. In presenting a petition the Duke of Newcastle complained of the Opposition continuing to occupy their seats when they were the only supporters of Government. This is throwing away the scabbard; but I apprehend few feel as he does.

March 13.

The Duke of Newcastle presented his petition and said his say to the King; but got no answer. The King was made so angry by him. two years ago, that he was the worst man they could have employed.

I was occupied all the morning in looking over the several English and Irish Acts of Parliament relative to the taking of oaths by the Eoman Catholics to relieve them from the Penal Code.

Called upon the Duke as I went down to the House, to tell him the substance of what I had gleaned.

Lord Lansdowne made a speech of an hour in presenting a petition. Very useless, and partly mischievous, that is, as regarded the Franchise Bill, to which he seemed to say, jpm No che SI, on account of the principle as applicable to England.

Lord Eldon moved for returns of the Eoman Catholics who had taken the oaths required by the Act of '91. In the course of his speech he read paragraphs from the King's, and said, the King was pledged to nothing the King's own words, which he has got from the Duke of Cumberland. He seemed to say that the King must, in giving his assent to the Bill, act for himself, without his Ministers, a notion Aberdeen has too, and which appears to me to be most unconstitutional. The King can do nothing without an adviser. It is on that ground that he can do no wrong. His adviser does it for him. Lord Eldon alluded to the half-declaration the present Archbishop of Canterbury made of His Majesty's opinions in 1827, and said the King should refuse his assent if he thought the Bill contrary to the Constitution.

No notice was taken of this. The Duke could not say more than he did the other day. Lord Gort, who was once for the Bill, is now against it, because it does not disfranchise freeholders in towns, and give him a borough.

The Lord Chancellor accused Lord Eldon of insinuating, which made Lord E. very angry. Lord Plunket made a very good attack upon Eldon and Eedesdale. The Duke got Eldon and Plunket to withdraw their motions, and we are to have a Bill of Indemnity.

March 14.

Chairs at 11. Proposed to them Courtney as Governor of Bombay. They received the proposition very unfavourably, and said they thought the Court would not be brought to consent to it. He had made himself very unpopular during the time he was

Secretary of the Board, and he was a man of undignified manners and appearance. I said what I could for him. He knows Indian affairs well, and is certainly a clever man.

They think he does not fill a sufficient station in this country, having been but lately made a Privy Councillor, and they consider his unfortunate declaration, that the minds of himself and his colleague were sheets of wastepaper, has let him down. They would like to have a good general officer or a peer.

Cabinet at half-past 3.

We heard a paper of Aberdeen's which is to be placed on the protocol at a conference to-morrow.

Lieven will place his paper, in which he consents to charge the French and English Ambassadors with the negotiations relative to the Greek treaty at Constantinople, provided we all agree first as to what propositions shall be made to the Turks. The Eussians require the extended frontier from Volo to Arta, and the establishment of an hereditary government.

The French, having once acceded to our proposition for confining the limits of the new State to the Morea, have gone over to the Eussians in consequence of the weakness of their Government, and the strength of the party in the Chambers. Polignac will place on the protocol a paper declaring their adhesion to the Eussian proposition.

Aberdeen's paper repeated our unanswerable reasoning against the extended frontier, and then suddenly fell into a conditional acquiescence in making a first proposition on that basis to the Turkish Government. The condition annexed being that the Turkish answer should be fairly considered.

Aberdeen has been led to believe by Polignac that France will accept the conditions annexed by us to our acquiescence.

The paper contained several expressions of ill-temper reflecting upon the conduct of all the allies in the execution of the treaty, which others observed. I put my finger at once upon the acquiescence in the Eussian proposition as to the extended frontier. If we once made such a proposition we should never get out of the treaty. France was much more likely to come round to our opinion, which has once been her own, if we showed ourselves determined to adhere to it, and gave good reasons for doing so, than if we evinced a vacillation of purpose, and a disposition to go with the majority.

The Turkish Government had reason to suppose we should ask no more than the Morea, and would probably give such an answer to our first proposition as would put an end to all negotiation.

The Duke and all disapproved of the sudden dip to acquiescence, and it will be made less sudden and more reasoned; but the mischief will be done.

Lord Heytesbury, in one of his recent dispatches, said Eussia was more anxious about establishing an hereditary Government in Greece than about the line of frontier. I said the plan of our paper should have been this. We should have placed in the foreground all the unanswerable arguments in favour of our own proposition. We should then have shown the objections to the enlarged frontier, and pressed very strongly indeed upon the hereditary Government being hardly reconcilable with the terms of the treaty; just leaving an opening in our argument upon that point sufficient to enable us to conclude by expressing a most reluctant acquiescence in the making of a proposition to that effect to Turkey. We should then have said that the objections

Turkey might reasonably make to that proposition were such that it would be idle to hope to overcome them, unless we adhered to what she had some right to expect on other points, and even showed a conciliatory disposition, leading to adjustment.

The object of the allies was not to throw insuperable difficulties in the way of the execution of the treaty; but to get out of it, and therefore propositions must be made which Turkey might accept.

This would have led to a return to the line of the Morea, which should have been our condition for acceding to the hereditary Government. Thus we might have brought round Russia.

Aberdeen said Matusckewitz did not seem to care so much about the hereditary Government. Of course he would not press that point and appear anxious for it when he saw Aberdeen showed facility upon it.

I am quite out of heart about our diplomacy. I see Matusckewitz has succeeded entirely. The Greek question will be kept open as long as it suits the interests of Russia; her armies will pour down irresistibly upon the diminished forces of the Turks, for I fear the Turks have latterly suffered more than the Russians from cold and want, and Constantinople will be occupied after a carnage from which human nature shrinks shuddering. We shall have done nothing to avert this dreadful catastrophe.

Aberdeen seemed to have shown his papers to the Duke, but not to have written it from his suggestion. 77 commence a s'emanciper, and everything will only go on worse.

The Duke of Newcastle had an interview of two hours with the King. He read a long paper which bored the King very much, and the King finished by advising him if he had any further communications to make, to make them to the Duke of Wellington. This is Lord Mountcharles's account. The Duke of Wellington, however, says a great deal more passed. That the King discussed Lords Eldon, Manners, Bexley, and Colchester[1] as Ministers, and rejected them all, and concluded by asking the Duke of Newcastle if he could even make a Government in the Lords, how would he even conduct the ordinary business of Government in the House of Commons?

The Duke of Cumberland is gone down to Windsor, and of this we shall feel the effects on Monday.

Peel is very angry with old Eldon, and says all he stated the other night respecting his conduct in the Cabinet as to the Catholic Association was false.

Our accounts from Ireland are good. The Catholics have shown no indecent or intemperate exultation.

[1] These were the principal peers who could have been included in a Cabinet opposed to the ' Catholic Belief Bill." Lord Colchester's health would, in any case, have precluded his taking office, as it prevented his attending the subsequent debates. He died in May following.

The Protestants have overcome the first shock, and are in good humour. All begin to look forward with satisfaction to the end of a state of things which has disorganised society.

Money has been already remitted to a large amount for investment on mortgage.
March 15.

Met Lord Beresford, who told me he heard, that is, from the Primate of Ireland, that all the English Bishops were to have a meeting to-morrow. I doubt it; but I told him he had better ascertain the fact, and let the Duke know immediately if it was so. Wrote to tell the Duke.

March 16.

At the House of Lords met the Bishop of London, who wishes the Mauritius and the Cape to be annexed to the See of Calcutta, and Australasia to that of London.

House. A speech from Lord Kenyon about the Coronation Oath. It seems to be the line the Brims-wickers 1 take now. Old Eldon made a very disgraceful speech, holding out that he might be driven to take that line himself, never having yet expressed an opinion on the subject.

Lord Winchelsea has published a letter to the Secretary of King's College, in which he announces his intention of withdrawing his name as a subscriber. He says 1 This was a name given to the determined opponents of ' Catholic Emancipation," who had formed what were called ' Brunswick Clubs' in allusion to the Protestant succession to the Crown in the House of Brunswick.

he never felt very sanguine as to the good effect of establishing such a College, when he saw the Duke of Wellington come forward in a new character ', as the Advocate of Morality and Religion. He says this was done insidiously, to make a show of a zeal for Protestantism, in order to introduce Popery.

I do not know how the Duke will bear this. It seems to me to be an attack unjustifiable, and not within the limits of political hostility as it refers to his private character.

Lord Eosslyn says he cannot make a less majority in the Lords than 60. Drummond says 51. I shall be satisfied with 30.

The Bishops meet to-morrow. It seems they have always hitherto had a meeting on the Oath oh'c Bill, and some of the violent ones desired they might have one now. The Archbishop, not adverting to the mischief which might result from it, acceded. The Duke had some conversation with him about it in the House. I know not with what effect.

The Archbishop of Canterbury is a weak man.

March 17.

Office. Found a letter from Ashley complaining of my not having shown him enough official confidence. He thought the Writers' Bill had been introduced into the House of Commons by Astell, and that there was to be something in the House of Commons respecting the Bencoolen case, he not having been consulted. I set him right as to the facts.

In the House we heard the Bishop of Meath had ratted to-day at the meeting of Bishops; but we know no more.

Chester and Llandaff presented petitions, and gave us to understand their opinions were in favour of the Bill. I asked the Duke as to the Bencoolen case. He considers it, as I do, closed. I am to let Courtney drop for a time.

Went to the House of Commons. Second reading of the Belief Bill. Heard G. Bankes, Castlereagh, Sir E. Knatchbull, Sadler, the Duke of Newcastle's new man for Newark, and Goulburn.

Goulburn mouthed. Castlereagh was prepared in bad taste. G. Bankes would speak better if he adopted the conversation style. Sir E. Knatchbull was about as good as I expected, the best of them. As for Sadler, he made some good hits, but he will never have power, nor have any of them. They all speak abroad of the point, and are unimpressive.

I met Hardinge in the House, and had a long conversation with him and A. Stewart. March 18.

I did not go to Windsor. The others did, to the Eecorder's Eeport. The King seemed not well. He has recurred to doses of laudanum. He leaves his bed at 5 and returns to it at half-past 10. He had a short interview with the Duke. The Duke told him that if he was attacked by the Duke of Cumberland to-morrow he must defend himself as well as he could. To this the King made no objection.

The Duke spoke to the King of the intended visit of the Irish Bishops. The King said he should hear them as he did the Duke of Newcastle, and say nothing. The Duke told him he should receive them surrounded by his household. To this the King neither assented nor objected, and therefore it is expected that he will receive them alone, and make them a speech, telling them he would turn out the Government if he could find another.

The King complained of being very unwell, and seemed to be so.

Knighton finds Windsor so uncomfortable a residence that he has quitted it, and remains in London; but he will be told he really must go back. The King's health requires it, as well as his policy.

The King evidently receives the most exaggerated and absurd statements of what passes in the House. The Duke told him he heard from Goulburn that there was no violence. The King said, 6 Why, there was a violent altercation between Sir E. Inglis and that damned fellow Lord Howick!" damned because he is the son of Lord Grey. It was just nothing at all.

The Duke said he was convinced we ought to keep the vote of Supply in our hands, and he would speak to Goulburn about it to-morrow.

I am glad he has come to this opinion. I have always thought that Herries was pushing on the votes very unnecessarily. I distrust him, and have ever done so.

I am sure we must keep the King and the Bruns-wickers in our power.

The Duke has received the proxy of the Duke of Cambridge. It is sent to Lord Shaftesbury to be entered to the Duke; and the Duke has received a letter from the Duke of Cambridge to tell him so; but perhaps Shaftesbury may make a demur; in which case a messenger will be sent to Hanover immediately. If Lord Shaftesbury makes no objection the proxy will be entered to the Duke's name to-morrow.

All this I heard at Aberdeen's, where we dined after their return from Windsor. March 19.

The Duke of Cambridge's proxy was entered to the Duke of Wellington.

Jhe Duke has desired Goulburn not to proceed so rapidly with the Supply.

Wetherell last night attacked the Chancellor in the most violent and vulgar manner. I am glad of it. He has justified us in making a distinction between him and every one else. He was a discredit to the Government, and I am delighted at our prospect of getting rid of him.

In the House to-day the Chancellor had not yet read his speech. Palmerston spoke admirably. E. Grant very well. The numbers were 353 and 173. They have gained 13, we 5.

Colonel Wood met Sir E. Knatchbull in the lobby. Sir E. said he was glad to see him there. Wood said he was there reluctantly, in obedience to his constituents. Sir E. said that was in reality his case; and yet he made a violent speech against the Bill!

We had expected in our House a skrimmage, to be begun by the Duke of Cumberland; but he made a quiet speech, that of a beaten man. Eldon said nothing violent. Winchelsea was not in the House, nor the Duke of Newcastle. They seem to give it up.

We had a speech from Lord Grey on the Newcastle petition, unnecessarily long, but bothering to Eldon, to whom it first communicated the fact that the Newcastle petitions said nothing of ' Protestant Establishment in Church and State," because the Wesleyan Methodists, by whose assistance alone the parsons could carry their petition at all, would not consent to insert these words.

I have got some votes for Fergusson, but I fear he will not succeed. To-morrow is the day of election. W. Ashley told me he had given my letter to-his brother, who was satisfied with it. He did not come today when Mr. Prince came by appointment on the Ben-coolen case, nor has he, which he should have done, written to me to say he had before written under a misconception.

I cannot help thinking the Duke of Cumberland had had a hint from the King that ' those who play at bowls must expect rubbers." Certainly between the giving of his notice and to-day something must have occurred to quiet him.

March 20.

Cabinet. Discussed the expediency of removing' Wetherell. He betrayed official confidence by mentioning the time at which Peel first made a communication to him of the intentions of Government. He certainly kept us in ignorance of what he intended to do till the 23rd of February, and I know I feared he meant to support it. His dismissal is to be placed, not distinctly upon the Catholic question, but upon his conduct in abusing the Chancellor, betraying confidence, c. I expect that the King will make no objection to displacing Wetherell, but he will wish to fill his place (with Scarlett) immediately. However, it is thought we had better defer that till the Bill is passed. If the King should resist we are not to go out upon it now, but sacrifice everything to the carrying of the Bill, and deal with Wetherell afterwards. It is thought that should the King refuse to turn out Wetherell we shall hardly stand worse than we should if we did not notice his conduct. The Duke, and indeed many, seem to think that the King will now go through the measure with us, and take his revenge by turning us out afterwards. I care very little about what happens afterwards. We must do all we can to carry the Bill, happen what may.

In the House we had nothing but petitions.

The Duke of Cumberland said to the Chancellor, c The Duke is a bold man, but I do not think he will dare to turn out Wetherell. It will create such a feeling in the country

The Duke of Cumberland dined at Prince Ester-hazy's yesterday, and was quite flat, contrary to his usual habits, for generally he is quite buoyant there. I cannot help thinking he begins to feel he shall be beaten.

The accounts we 1 have from the country are very good. All the intelligent part of the people seem to be in favour of the Bill. People begin to accustom them-
VOL. i. D D selves to the contemplation of it, and to rejoice in the prospect of general union.

In the House of Commons we divided, 223 to 19 on the Franchise Bill. Palmerston, Bankes, and Herries, each with his little band of people, voted in the minority.

The ' Times' very well calls the minority on the Eelief Bill' the forty shillingers' of the House of Commons.

March 21.

Chairs at 11. Astell said I was not to consider the opinion expressed on the subject of Courtney as more than the opinion of himself and the Deputy; but they thought the Court would never consent to appoint him.

I was in hopes Fergusson would have come in; but he is beaten by a majority of more than 400 Astell having been the leader of Sir W. Young's people.

Wrote to Planta suggesting the immediate adoption of measures for securing Fergusson's return on the next vacancy.

We must break through the phalanx of Directors and Indian agents, who now make the Court a self-elected body.

While I was expecting the Bencoolen claimants, I received a note from Hardinge, desiring me to call immediately at the War Office to hear the account of the meeting with Lord Winchelsea.

I concluded the Duke had had a meeting with Lord Winchelsea. I went immediately. By Hardinge's manner I saw nothing had happened. He was the Duke's second. The correspondence had been going on ever since Tuesday. Falmouth was second to Lord Winchel-sea.

He thought Lord Winchelsea's letter to Coleridge unjustifiable, but still went out as Lord Winchelsea's friend, which he should not have done. He should have forced Lord Winchelsea to apologise.

The first feeling of every one is that the Duke should not have gone out; but when they read the letters they think he was right, as somehow or other he always is.

Throughout he gave every opening to Lord Win-chelsea to get out of the scrape. Lord Winchelsea behaved like a gentleman and a man of courage on the field. The Duke said no one could have behaved better.

Falmouth wanted to have 18 paces, but Hardinge insisted on 12.

Lord Winchelsea was placed so near a ditch that the Duke said he was on the point of crying out, ' Damn it, if you place him there, he will fall into the ditch." The Duke said he considered all the morning whether he should fire at him or no. He thought if he killed him he should be tried, and confined until he was tried, which he did not like, so he determined to fire at his legs. He did hit his coat. Lord Winchelsea fired in the air, and then presented a paper already prepared, expressing regret at what he had unadvisedly written. Hardinge insisted on the insertion of the words in apology, which, after discussion, were adopted and inserted.

I found Hardinge with Sir H. Taylor. Sir W. Gordon came in. I went to the Treasury to read the papers, where I found Arbuthnot, Drummond, and Greville copying. The copies were not ready, so I went to the office to receive the Bencoolenites. I then returned to the Treasury, and followed the papers to Peel's, where we arranged them for publication in the Courier.

The Duke went to Windsor. The King seemed colpito at first by the proposal respecting Sir Charles Wetherell, but acquiesced. The Duke then said, c I have another subject to mention to your Majesty, personal to myself. I have been fighting a duel this morning." The King said he was glad of it.

He afterwards said he had heard of Lord Winchel-sea's letter but had not read it. The Duke showed it to him; then the King said it was atrocious, and if he had seen it he should have recommended it to the Duke's notice. It is lucky the Duke saw the King before Eldon, or that rascal the Duke of Cumberland had an opportunity of infusing poison into his mind. The Duke read to the King all the letters.

The King is in better health, and everything was couleur de rose.

I heard all this from the Duke, whom I met at Arbuthnot's at dinner.

March 22. Sunday.

Cabinet. The King has sent for the memorandum which was written by the Chancellor, and sent to him on the 24th of January. The memorandum was in Knighton's possession. The King at the same time desired to have the letter he had intended to send to the Duke of Cumberland on the 2nd of March. This letter the Duke advised the King not to send. It is thought the King now intends to show the memorandum to the Duke of Cumberland, and to give him the letter as a set-off against the dismissal of Wetherell.

The Chancellor has no copy of the memorandum. Knighton came for it in a hurry on the 26th of January and carried it off before a copy was made. The Chancellor was to have made one that night.

The Chancellor told me this when I met him at Sir J. Beckett's at dinner, but he said he would that evening get a copy from Knighton.

Various alterations have been made in the Eelief Bill.

The Duke writes to-day to Wetherell, and directs his letter to Sir Charles, acquainting him that his recent conduct having been inconsistent with his duty as an official servant of the Crown in a situation which he had not intimated his intention of resigning, he had thought it his duty to represent it to His Majesty, and had received the King's commands to inform him that His Majesty had no further occasion for his services.

Peel intends to be very severe upon Wetherell should any notice be taken of his removal.

We rest it principally upon his betrayal of official confidence in mentioning in the House of Commons the day on which he first had the intentions of Government communicated to him. I thought Peel should not enter the lists with him as an equal, but treat him with scorn.

This Wetherell unbuttoned his braces when he began to speak, and put his hands into the waistband of his breeches. He almost swept the ground with his head, and stood in the middle of the House. His repetitions were more numerous than ever. Horace

Twiss said he was very mad, and had but one lucid interval, which was between his breeches and waistcoat.

Much doubt arose as to dates at the Cabinet. I promised to make for the Duke an extract from my memoranda, which I have done.

Saw Fergusson to-day. He had 1,100 or 1,200 promises, and polled not 700 votes. He says the Chairman has the votes of the tradesmen, c., about 70. The Jews under Eothschild, 70. The Alexanders 30 of their own, and in all about 70. The total number of votes about 2,500.

March 23.

Occupied all the morning in writing out extracts[1] from my memoranda to put before the Duke the history of all that has taken place since the 15th of January.

The Duke has found a copy of the Memorandum of the 24th of January, upon which the King- had put the date.

House. Peel sent to the Chancellor for the Attorney-General's oath. The Chancellor sent to the Crown office for it, and it seems that Wetherell had sent for the same thing five minutes before.

Nothing but petitions.

Dined at home, and went to the House of Commons at a quarter to 11. The House was in Committee on the Eelief Bill. Before I had been there 10 minutes they divided on the silliest of points, and I went away.

[1 These extracts are to be found in Wellington Correspondence, vol. v. 548-553.]

Aberdeen told me he wanted to have a Cabinet respecting the removal of Stratford Canning.

March 24.

In riding down to the office received a note from Peel telling me it was to be proposed to insert the Governors of Indian Presidencies among the excepted offices. He intended to oppose it, and asked for reasons. I sent him facts. They now may be Catholic. They take no oath excluding them. They translate, but they do not appoint chaplains, and they only translate with the advice of the bishop.

The majorities increase.

Lord Londonderry asked some questions about the coal trade. The Duke promised a committee, which will be moved for on Thursday. It will be a bore.

March 25.

Dined with the East India Company. Lord Camden, Bishop of Bath, Lord Melville, Graham, Ashley, Bankes, Sir T. Acland were there. Was introduced to Major Barnewall, who has brought over the dispatches from Sir John Malcolm. I told him I would see him whenever I had received the Solicitor-General's opinion.

The new Bishop of Calcutta made a good speech. His manner was excellent and impressive. Astell said he did one credit. I think he did.

March 26.

The Chancellor wrote to Wetherell to know whether he would resign his patent or have it revoked. He answered sulkily he would do nothing in the matter. This is the man who pretended he had resigned! This patent must be revoked.

Lord Kosslyn told me Lord Chandos said they meant to divide on the first reading in the Lords, and take us by surprise. They will divide on fixing the day for the second reading. However, we shall be prepared.

Lord Morley told me Lord Chatham's vote might be got by a little civility. I told the Duke, who is going to call upon him.

The Chancellor told me the Bishop of Winchester's speech was excellent.

An advertisement has been circulated, calling a meeting in Hyde Park on the 7th of April to reassure the timid, c. This will not answer. They think Tuesday will be the day of the division on the second reading.

March 27.

Cabinet. We met in consequence of news having arrived that the Eussians had seized two Turkish vessels, or rather Egyptian, off Candia, and that they had established a blockade of Alexandria. They had recently raised the blockade of Candia as parties to the Treaty of London. My position is that we cannot act in concert with them under the Treaty of London, if they so use their belligerent rights as to lead to results different from those which they propose to themselves as parties to the Treaty of London. We cannot allow them as belligerents against Turkey to adopt measures subversive of the engagements they enter into as our allies.

[409] Shall we carry France with us in resistance to this measure? Aberdeen says Polignac seems to think we cannot submit to it; but Polignac does not know what orders he may receive.

It seems to me that we ask France to go with us, but do nothing to lead her to take our views. Here we have every advantage. France deprecates the blockade of Alexandria as injurious to her commerce. Every French statesman must be jealous of the encroachments of Eussia, and Eussia, having agreed to exclude Candia from the proposed limits of new Greece, having on that account agreed to raise the blockade of Candia, as a party to the treaty of London, now establishes a blockade of Alexandria and Candia, with the double object of serving her own cause immediately, by preventing the throwing of supplies into Constantinople, and indirectly by separating Candia from Turkey. The French should dread, much more than we have any reason to do, the annexation of Candia to Eussia. It is impossible that we should not be able to work upon their national feelings so as to induce them to view the conduct of Eussia with jealousy. But nothing of this will or can Aberdeen do. I declare I think we are unjustifiable before God and man for having done nothing, and permitted, what we might have prevented, the horrors of the campaign which is now about to commence.

The idea seems to be that the French Chambers are in such a state that the King could not form a Government which would have a certain majority.

Sir G. Murray thinks the wounds of the Eevolution are not yet closed, and that France will yet suffer convulsion.

[410] Aberdeen thinks their prevalent feeling is hatred of us.

I believe that if we carry the Catholic Bill and remain a Government, we shall feel our power doubled. France and America will no longer see a vulnerable point. All the world will know that we are a united people. The Foreign Ministers form, what Aberdeen calls, vain and exaggerated ideas of the value to us of the settlement of this question. I do not believe their ideas are exaggerated. I believe that in ten years the influx of capital into Ireland will make that country resemble England. As we have not yet received official intelligence of the blockade, nothing was decided upon. In the meantime Polignac is to be approached quietly.

I am quite indignant at seeing the entire success of Matusckewitz. The object of Eussia was to prevent the return of our Ambassadors to Constantinople. Their return has been delayed till it will be no longer useful, and they go to make demands to which Turkey cannot accede, and which will only make her desperate.

The King saw Lord Mansfield yesterday for two hours. The King says Lord Mansfield told him the Bill would only be carried by five in the Lords, in which case he said he would-not give his consent.

There has been a meeting of Peers at Lord Kenyon's the Duke of Cumberland in the chair. Lord Chandos secretary. Violent resolutions were agreed to, and a petition to the King.

Old Eldon was not in the House to-night. Perhaps he may be gone to Windsor with the petition.

411

We are to vote as little money as we can. They think one safeguard against dissolution is the circumstance of the Franchise Bill not coming into operation, in the event of a general election, until the new registry is completed. This would require three months. It is imagined they would fear to dissolve, Ireland remaining as it is. I do not believe they would. They are too stupid to have the fears of rational men. [1] I heard somewhere a day or two ago that the Duke of Montrose had gone back.

The Duke says if that be so, the King has spoken to him, as he has been given to understand what the King's wishes are.

Lord Eosslyn expects a majority of 70. I shall be quite satisfied with 50.

March 29.

Met Lord Hill at dinner.

Sir J. Oswald has declined the command at Bombay; so I have succeeded in getting him to offer it to Sir Sidney Beckwith. This will please the Duke. Lord Hill has heard nothing more of the supposed mutiny, but what he had heard referred to a regiment at Madras. The mutiny now reported was at Cawnpore the 11th Dragoons. Lord Hill's story was about. the 13th Foot.

March 30.

I see Lord Eldon went to Windsor on Saturday and was four hours with the King. Eeally the King's con- [1 In fairness to this party, it may he supposed that they felt resistance to he less dangerous than concession avowedly made from fear of civil war. But the conduct of those who coalesced with their old opponents from a feeling of revenge on the Ministry might justly be called irrational.)

412

duct is most dishonourable towards the Government. [1] Provided we all go out together, and upon this question, I care little about the loss of office; but it is awful to think what might be the consequences to the country of a change of Government, and of disappointment on this question.

The Duke is gone to Windsor. A handbill has been circulated intimating that many persons having expressed a wish to meet or accompany the Duke of Newcastle in their carriages when he goes with a petition to Windsor on Wednesday, the King has permitted they should do so. Lord Bathurst told me the substance of it. It is said to be cautiously worded.

House. Nothing done. Lord Grey asked me whether it was true Stratford Canning had been recalled and Gordon appointed. Not knowing whether the King's pleasure had been taken, I made as good an answer as I could. I afterwards asked Aberdeen, and found it was so. Stratford Canning had sent a conditional resignation, which was accepted the condition being, I believe, that his instructions should be in tenor and spirit precisely the same as those of his colleagues. Whether Gordon has ability I do not know, but he will at any rate be faithful. Canning had had views directly contrary to those of the Government.

March 31.

The division on the 3rd reading of the Eelief Bill was 320 to 142 majority, 178. So the foolish Protes-⌐1 The Ministers believed him to be secretly encouraging opposition to the Relief Bill, in the introduction of which he had, though reluctantly, acquiesced.⌐

413

tants must have paired off to the number of 40 or 50. The most unwise thing a minority can do. However, our majority should have been greater.,

Saw the Duke, who was at Windsor yesterday. The handbill invited persons to go to Windsor on Wednesday, there to deliver the petition of the inhabitants of London, c., to the Duke of Newcastle, who was to present it to the King. It stated that this intention had been communicated to His Majesty.

The King told the Duke it had not been. The Duke impressed upon the King the danger of the precedent; and showed the object was to collect a mob to overawe Lady Conyngham and persons residing under his protection. He showed the King the Act of Charles II. limiting the number of persons who might present a petition.

He obtained from the King authority to write to the Duke of Newcastle and inform him that the meeting announced in the handbill had not been communicated to the King; that the King desired the petition might be sent through the Secretary of State, and that the King would receive the Duke if he desired an audience as a peer.

The Duke of Newcastle replied that the handbill had only been shown to him last night, the 30th; that he did not entirely approve of it; that he was not going to present the petition; that he understood the idea of presenting it had been abandoned, as it had been ascertained it w ould not be agreeable to the King, which would account for the King being ignorant of it. An odd conclusion.

414

The Duke of Wellington wrote to the King, and sent his Majesty his letter to the Duke of Newcastle, and his answer. Again impressed upon the King the danger of the precedent of allowing peers to present petitions at audiences. That if they gave answers in the King's name they became responsible for those answers, and in fact usurped the functions of the Secretary of State. The Duke told the King the petition in question was, he heard, to be presented by four peers, and he repeated his advice that it should only be received through the Secretary of State.

The Duke of Wellington says the five minutes Lord Camden thought would be sufficient for him to obtain Lord Chatham's vote would be jive hours, and he could as little afford five hours as five days.

House. 173 members present. Bills brought up. Peel, followed by Government members. On the motion for printing, question asked as to mode of proceeding. On the Duke's saying he should propose the second reading on Thursday, there was much dissatisfaction and some talk, which ended, however, without any division. I spoke, and just said what I wished. I gave Lord Eldon a slight touch, but was very temperate.

Lord Eldon threatens to produce all his petitions on Thursday to create delay.

The Duke is indifferent whether Sir Sidney Beckwith or Sir James Lyon goes to Bombay. If Sir James Lyon goes Sir Sidney Beckwith will succeed him at Bar-badoes.

We had a long discussion about having the galleries put up in the House of Lords, We decided against having them, because it would have been necessary to have an address to the King.

The heat will be intolerable. The largest number of peers who ever divided in the House was 206. We expect 260.

Benches have been placed before the fireplace, which is blocked up. This gives us twenty more seats, and makes the House look handsomer. It is much more convenient, too, as we keep more of our friends near us, and avoid the collecting of little mobs near the table.

THE END OF THE FIRST VOLUME,

LONDON: PRINTED BY
SPOTTISWOODE AND CO., NEW-STREET SQUABE ASD PAELIAMENT STREET

Lightning Source UK Ltd.
Milton Keynes UK
15 December 2010

164417UK00001B/151/P